# The Art of Acquiring

## A Portrait of Etta and Claribel Cone

MARY GABRIEL

bancroft
press

⇔

Published by Bancroft Press
"books that enlighten."
PO Box 65360, Baltimore, MD 21209
800.637.7377
www.bancroftpress.com

ISBN 1-890862-06-1
Library of Congress Card Number: 2002109262
Printed in the United States of America

First Edition

Cover design, insert design, and author photo:
Steven Parke, What?design (parke@imagecarnival.com)
Interior design: Theresa Williams (theresa@visuallee.com)

For the most famous sisters in MY life:
Ursuline, Grace, and Rosemary

# Table of Contents

# Preface

$\backsim$

$A$s an undergraduate at the Maryland Institute College of Art, I first encountered the Cone collection in its natural habitat— the stark white walls of the Baltimore Museum of Art. Absorbed by the art in brilliant display—the Matisses, Picassos, and magnificent Gauguin, *Vahine no te Vi* (Woman With Mango)—I wouldn't have given even a moment's thought to the collectors, Etta and Claribel Cone, if the museum had not recreated, albeit behind glass, a small sliver of one of the rooms in one of the private Baltimore apartments where the Cone sisters had originally housed all their illustrious holdings.

This BMA recreation was no bigger than a large closet, but it glowed with warmth, and it beckoned with a sensuality precisely mirroring the Matisse paintings that I, the aspiring student of painting, had just been examining and dissecting. At that moment, I was struck by the fact that the Cone sisters not only bought paintings to live with, but had stepped through the canvases to live in the paintings they bought.

I was both amazed and curious. For me, the essential question was: why did two seemingly severe, upright women, both born around the time of the U.S. Civil War, both clinging to the cloak of Victorianism in their dress and attitude, surround themselves with such avant-garde and erotic art? Etta and Claribel Cone were paying tens of thousands of dollars for art pieces that were as scandalous in their day as Robert Mapplethorpe's or Damien Hirst's are in ours.

In my search for an answer, I found only more questions, so I began to read. The ample literature narrating the events of 1905 Paris, when Leo Stein discovered Picasso and Matisse, frequently mentions the two Cone sisters, I discovered. But Etta and Claribel Cone are most often referred to peripherally as Baltimore acquaintances of Leo Stein and his sister, Gertrude, who had decided to be a writer. Sometimes Etta and Claribel are described as the Steins' distant relations. And just as often, they are dismissed as wealthy spinsters convinced by Gertrude Stein to spend some of their fortune on artists they neither understood nor appreciated. They are depicted as decidedly lesser lights in the luminous Paris of the early twentieth century.

In those rare instances where the two sisters gain even a modicum of credit for courageously collecting works by artists the world ridiculed, Dr. Claribel Cone is identified as the more important and visionary of the two sisters.

From this early research, I reached one preliminary conclusion that I believe still to be correct. Had they been men, annually purchasing works by Cézanne, Matisse, and Picasso, the two sisters would have immediately been accorded the status and stature of accomplished art collectors. Because they were women, however, and women from Baltimore, no less, they were dismissed as indiscriminating "shoppers"— and not just for art, but for many other collectibles as well.

History, I later concluded, was content to ignore or misrepresent the Cones. I came increasingly to blame their plight on Gertrude Stein. In her famous book, *The Autobiography of Alice B. Toklas*, Gertrude dismissed the sisters as mere figures from her past, and Etta as a provincial simpleton. No matter that much of the Stein autobiography was discredited, then and later, by those living during the times and in the places she described. The book she wrote in just six weeks somehow became "history," and Gertrude's interpretation of events and personalities was incongruously accepted as historical fact. As a result, it is primarily Gertrude's version of the Cone sisters that has survived—which is to say they have been acknowledged but largely ignored and almost completely marginalized.

I found, too, that the Cone sisters themselves deserved some of the blame for their own obscurity. As one of their close friends wrote, the sisters were content to remain in the background while their collection, parts of which they often lent out, won plaudits as one of the world's best. Anything less, they believed, would be undignified. While they had well-stated reasons for each of their artistic purchases, their notes and diary entries suggest a general, nearly Victorian, desire to avoid the spotlight. Unwilling to tell their own story, the sisters recede into the obscurity of history, two barely recognized links between Europe's famous, groundbreaking artists and the public.

In studying the Cones, however, I came to realize, more fundamentally, that collectors are the invisible, indispensible, and underappreciated hand that first provides artists with the money needed to create their work, and then provides the public the opportunity to see their creations. All collectors but a few are left out of the folklore of art history, as if the people who pay for the art are somehow less important than the other personages orbiting the artist—the dealer, for example, or even the critic.

But the collectors' passion for art, not to mention their discerning eye for up-and-coming artists, have allowed some of the world's greatest artists to survive and thrive—and contemporary audiences to appreciate them first-hand. But for the collectors, art history might well have taken an entirely different shape and direction.

During their lifetimes, the Cone sisters allowed selected visitors to view their collection, and lent pieces to specific exhibitions, but the entire Cone Collection was not available for public view until after Etta's death in 1949, when it was bequeathed to the Baltimore Museum of Art. In January 1957, the BMA opened the Cone Wing, and the works went on permanent exhibition, finally allowing the public to see exactly what those two "crazy" sisters had been hiding in their Baltimore apartments—what exactly had kept them so busy for so many decades.

They roamed the galleries of Europe like addicts, for 45 years that spanned two world wars, and built and donated one of the most important art collections in the world. Yet the story of Etta and Claribel Cone has been the subject of only a handful of publications. In her latter years, Etta Cone herself worked furiously on, and spared no expense for, a catalogue setting forth all the elements of the collection. But when the catalogue became popular, she decided not to reprint it or to widen its distribution.

The Baltimore Museum of Art, which houses the collection, has published several Cone catalogues linked to exhibitions or anniversaries, the most recent being Jack Flam's *Matisse in the Cone Collection: The Poetics of Vision* (its 2001 publication coincided with the April 2001 opening of the renovated Cone Wing); and Brenda Richardson's *Dr. Claribel & Miss Etta* —first published in 1985, and reprinted in 1992, it apparently went out of print in 2000.

In addition, Barbara Pollock, for Bobbs-Merrill, authored a biography of the sisters in 1962, *The Collectors: Dr. Claribel and*

*Miss Etta Cone*, which is out-of-print as I write this prologue, and has been for some time.

Finally, various members of the Cone family have added their writings on the sisters over the years.

But in the general literature of 20th century art history, the full and accurate story of the two Cone sisters has been omitted. In this book, I have attempted to do what is long overdue: resurrect and bring to life two of the world's greatest art collectors, and to depict their undying passion for art that so many others initially despised, and that now is almost universally revered.

*Mary Gabriel*
*Baltimore*
*July 5, 2002*

# Prologue

# Baltimore, 1930

*... My two Baltimore ladies ... are sisters—one of them ... a*
*great beauty, noble and glorious, lovely hair with ample waves in*
*the old style—satisfied and dominating—the other with a majesty*
*of a Queen of Israel ... but with a depth of expression which is*
*touching —always submissive to her glorious sister but attentive to*
*everything ...*

—Henri Matisse to Simon Bussy, May 24, 1934

*O*n December 17, 1930, Etta Cone waited anxiously in her
Baltimore apartment for Henri Matisse to arrive. Eight stories
above a once grand street, now the site of scattered gambling
dens and prostitutes, Etta and her sister Claribel had built a
virtual shrine to the French master. Like his paintings, their
rooms off the dark halls of the Marlborough Apartments were
vibrant with exotic patterns and bursting with color: Eastern
rugs on the floor, needlework pillows on overstuffed chairs,
and Indian shawls and Italian textiles that luxuriously draped
every available surface.

And, as in so many Matisse paintings, there was a woman
in the scene. But instead of the artist's willowy model, lounging in Moroccan pantaloons, the figure in this tableau was a
sixty-year-old spinster sitting bolt upright.

The liberating styles of the Jazz Age left Etta unmoved. Heavy black fabric hung from her waist in layers and under-layers that hid every hint of the body beneath. Etta's handsome face was framed by thick dark eyebrows and a crown of silver hair drawn back in a knot—the same style she had worn for more than 30 years. Like a bird, with eyes trained to compre-hend, she quietly watched the world.

Etta Cone was considered a bit deranged by at least some of her fellow citizens. At the very least, hers was a world apart. Outside her expensive apartment, America was suffer-ing from the excesses of the previous frenetic decade. Wall Street had crashed with a mighty thud, ushering in the Great Depression, but Etta's world had not changed, nor had her annual income, which was about $60,000 at the time. She lived in her perch high above the city—a sentinel guarding a time capsule. Her home preserved the art from turn-of-the-century Paris—art that had given her young life meaning and purpose. Now, in her later years, she was sustained by that art and the memories that each piece evoked.

Etta, and for a shorter time her sister Claribel, made a career out of collecting. They spent the bulk of their fortunes on works by artists who, at the time, were dismissed as char-latans, or denounced as pornographers, and sometimes both. The Cones were oblivious to the criticism, selecting art with-out regard to fashion (at the time, Barbizon was all the rage), and also largely without expert advice, unless that advice came in the early years from Leo Stein and in later ones from Matisse himself.

In 1930, Matisse, for the first time, would see his works in the sisters' home. Etta's only regret was that sister Claribel was not alive for his visit.

Etta first met Matisse in Paris in 1906, when the artist was so poor and in such disrepute that he vowed to stop painting because, he said, it was driving him mad. So dire was his situation that while carrying his paintings home from an exhibition where he received nothing but ridicule, he considered burning his works for the insurance money. Etta was not an art collector at the time, but she came to the rescue and bought two of Matisse's works on paper out of a sense of "romantic charity," which was the same reason she purchased a few drawings some months earlier from a young Spanish painter named Pablo Picasso.

In those days, the prim Miss Etta Cone was an "angel," helping to support the artists seeking to launch an aesthetic revolution. In Paris, she could shed her strict Victorian standards, ignore the filth, the opium, the absinthe, the illegitimate children, and the ever-changing mistresses, and see only the men who needed her help to survive and paint. While Etta, at the beginning, didn't understand their art, it eventually consumed her as much as it consumed the artists who produced it. In fact, Etta and Matisse would argue years later over whether she had "made" him or he had "made" her. Their relationship was symbiotic. The artist could not exist without his collector, and the collector had no life without his art. Together, the two thrived.

By 1930, the Matisse collection Etta had assembled, with sister Claribel's help, was considered by some to be the most important in the United States. Fortune by then had also smiled on the artist. The once penniless Matisse had become the highest paid living artist of his time.

∽

Matisse finally arrived in Baltimore just before lunch. The day began as cold and rainy, and by afternoon, snow had begun to fall. But inside the Cone apartments, warmth radiated from the walls and from a woman thrilled to be escorting her favorite artist through her family's suite of apartments. Normally, it could take Etta up to two hours to guide a visitor through the family collection because she would explain each work's rich history and recall anecdotes about that heady time in Paris when the art world revolved less around the official salons than it did the shabby Bâteau Lavoir in Montmartre, and a studio on the rue de Fleurus in Montparnasse. But Matisse had lived those stories, so she did not repeat them.

Claribel had once told Matisse "art and its appreciation are a God-given gift," to which Matisse replied, "Yes, but sometimes the artist has to descend to hell to get it." Yet there was no evidence of that hell on the Cone walls—only the stunning fruit of the artist's travail.

Matisse surveyed the Picassos hanging alongside Renoirs, Van Goghs, and Cézannes, but everywhere were his own paintings and sculptures. The Cone home was a harem of Matisse's women. His painted nudes beckoned from every room. Nearly every surface was dotted with his lustrous figures in bronze. After weeks in America, performing official duties as a judge at the Carnegie International Exhibition and meeting admiring crowds, Matisse must have finally felt at home. Later, in an interview, Matisse paid Etta the ultimate compliment. The Cone apartments, he said, were the perfect setting for his work.

Claribel and Etta were so different from America's other great collectors—Albert C. Barnes or Mrs. Isabella Stewart Gardner, for example. The latter two created temples to themselves and their treasures. The Cone collection, however, was a private affair gathered by two bachelorette sisters who lovingly kept their masterpieces in cramped apartments among bric-a-brac from around the world. Every wall was covered in layers of paintings, drawings, and prints. Even the bathtubs were employed as repositories for works of art. A friend of the artist once said Matisse liked to be so close to a model that he could touch her with one hand while painting with the other. The Cone collection afforded the sisters that same intimacy. The paintings that hung on their walls were their noisy companions—companions who were given the complete run of the place.

Matisse and Etta attended the symphony together that night, causing a stir in Baltimore, which was, despite its aspirations, a sleepy southern town. The artist's work had been the target of barbs by the *Sun's* most famous newspaper columnist, H.L. Mencken. But Etta braved convention to display her foreign friend. If Baltimore was looking for a bohemian, however, it came away from the encounter disappointed. The bespectacled artist in spats, with eyes as steady as a marksman's, looked much more like a well-fed German professor than the painter whose stabs of gloriously hideous color once earned him the title "wild beast."

The artist spent the night in the apartment adjoining Etta's and departed for New York the next day. Among Baltimore's Jewish community, there had long been rumors that Matisse and Etta were lovers. Why else, went the speculation, would she spend so much money on his crazy pictures? And for many, his overnight visit only confirmed their suspicions.

But in fact no such relationship existed. Etta worshiped Matisse as an artist, perhaps because he committed to canvas the sensuous life she didn't dare live. She also venerated him because he was strong and bold and brilliant—a lion, in her eyes. Etta lived her life in the shadow of lions—her brother Moses, Gertrude and Leo Stein, and, of course, sister Claribel. Despite her revolutionary collection, Etta was nothing more than the perfect Victorian woman.

# Two Sisters

# *Baltimore, 1872*

*I have none of the usual inducements of women to marry. Were I to fall in love, indeed, it would be a different thing! But I never have been in love; it is not my way, or my nature; and I do not think I ever shall. And without love, I am sure I should be a fool to change such a situation as mine. Fortune I do not want; employment I do not want: consequence I do not want.*

—Jane Austen, *Emma*, 1816

*C*laribel and Etta Cone were among thirteen children born to Herman Kahn of Bavaria, and his sweetheart Helen Guggenheimer, whom he married in Richmond, Virginia, in 1856. The young couple, now bearing the anglicized last name of Cone, did not stay long in Richmond, however.

The established Jewish community there scorned him as a new immigrant, the family history indicates, and his "friends" so wanted him out of town that they gave him a stock of goods and a horse and wagon to set himself up elsewhere as a salesman.

Cone moved his growing family to Jonesborough, Tennessee, where Etta and Claribel were born, but life was not easy there, either. The Civil War forced the closure of the store Herman Cone started with a cousin. Cone and his part-

3

ner were Conferederate sympathetizers. Many of their East Tennessee neighbors were Unionists. That, coupled with the order by General Ulysses S. Grant to expel "the Jews as a class" from Tennessee, compelled Cone to move his family to a farm to wait out the war.

After the fighting ended, Cone's reputation as a Confederate sympathizer lingered, and he and his partner found it necessary to add a Union man to their partnership in order to attract customers. But by 1870, it was evident that one of the three partners had to leave the business because it wasn't big enough to support the families of three men. Once again Herman Cone moved on, this time taking his brood north to Baltimore.

The move was not without its reasons. Southerners— black and white—hoping to escape the turmoil of the war years or the financial ruin of its aftermath, settled in the busy town of Baltimore, where shipping and rail businesses were thriving on Reconstruction era trade. Baltimore was home to a large German Jewish population among whom the Cone children could find suitable mates. The city was also about to enter its Golden Era.

But the place in which the Cones found themselves was by no means an example of civilization at its finest. In the second half of the 19th century, Baltimore was a border town. It straddled North and South, offering the best and worst of both.

In 1870, only about thirty percent of Baltimore's school-age children attended classes. Sweatshops were rampant, with a steady stream of European immigrant workers flowing in from the port's Hamburg American line. Southwest Baltimore, not far from where Herman Cone opened a wholesale grocery store, was described as "foul streets, foul people, in foul tenements filled with foul air." In the center of town, opium dens run by Chinese immigrants contributed to the general decadence of the place.

In addition, horse-drawn cars were the main means of transportation between the downtown and the city's outlying areas. But an epidemic wiped out many of the horses in 1872. Rather than stop the flow of cars entirely, car owners hitched black men to the vehicles. That cruel spectacle, of men pulling wagons full of other people or goods, passed directly in front of the new Cone store.

Herman Cone and his two oldest sons, Moses and Ceasar, worked in the midst of the chaos not far from the city's waterfront. But the family resided well out of its reach—on Eutaw Place, an elegant boulevard northwest of the city's center that was styled after the Champs-Elysées in Paris and the Unter den Linden in Berlin.

Eutaw Place, the widest of Baltimore's streets, was divided in the center by a narrow park and dotted with fountains, benches, and flowering trees. From May to September, a canopy of leaves and flowers offered relief from the hot sun and intense humidity. Children played in the park under the watchful eyes of nurses and nannies. Along the street, massive homes were constructed by the families who dominated the city's retail and apparel industries. The Cone family home sat on the 1600 block of Eutaw Place, surrounded by a who's who of Baltimore gentry.

A photograph of Claribel in the 1880s shows a young woman with thick, dark hair wound into a bun and plaited in the back. Second oldest of three Cone daughters, she had the romantic look of the period. Dressed in flowing fabric and lace, she carried a single rose in her gloved hand. But the picture of nineteen-year-old Claribel was not that of a pretty girl; it was of a handsome one. Her back was straight and strong, her feet large, and her demeanor challenging. Her voice, though melodious, boomed. She fired questions at her brothers' friends and laughed raucously—women of the time were viewed most favorably when they emitted polite giggles, or when only the gentle swoosh of their skirts was heard.

The role of the proper Victorian woman was to protect and preserve the hearth, but Claribel hated women's work. She refused to assume charge of the family household after the marriage of her older sister, Carrie, and was a general nuisance unless busy reading. The summer after her high school graduation, when Claribel made it clear that those in her immediate circle didn't suit her, her parents sent her to a hotel in Atlantic City so she could meet a nice young man. But she mailed strange messages home that must have sent her parents' hopes for marriage sinking.

"Today, for the first time, I succeeded in rising early and taking a stroll, which was enjoyable because I was entirely alone with my book and the ocean. . . ."

Claribel Cone was well-enough educated to realize that a woman aspiring to independence would encounter more than ample pitfalls during the courtship process, not to mention during marriage. The 19th-century woman was expected to subjugate herself to her husband—to become "less" than the man. She was supposed to strive for a "bee-stung" mouth, and if the shape didn't come naturally, to pepper her speech with words like "prunes and prisms" in order to force her lips into the proper configuration. She was to pretend she had no appetite (it was unladylike to enjoy food), and to dress in clothes that were, in effect, torture chambers.

Photographs show Claribel did not rebel against the clothing deemed appropriate for a woman of her age. Her waist was bound tight and her skirts hung heavy. But she would challenge the other part of the equation defining ideal womanhood—that a woman was not to develop intellectually, because to do so would destroy her feminine nature.

In 1874, Dr. Edward Clark wrote that a great many American girls became ill because they were forcing their brains, through study, to use up the blood that was needed for menstruation. He called excessive education for women a "crime before God and humanity that physiology protests and that experience weeps over."

In a speech to the Maryland Chirurgical Society in 1881, Professor William Goodell of Philadelphia issued a dire warning: there were grave dangers threatening the American home life, he said, because of a trend among women not to become mothers, an increasing number of divorces, and abortion. He advocated "redeeming women from the bondage of her education."

Claribel did not heed the warnings. She would have none of the courtship, marital, or intellectual submission that her parents, and society, expected of her.

While most of the Cone family was irritated by the head-strong middle daughter, one family member seemed to enjoy Claribel's rebellion—her younger sister Etta. Etta delighted in Claribel's strength and was only too happy, while still in high school, to take on more household chores so her sister could continue at-home studies in botany and German.

Etta was physically similar to Claribel, with the same dark eyebrows and dark hair pulled back in a knot at the nape of her neck. She, too, was large boned, and slightly taller than Claribel. But while Claribel's physical size carried over to her personality, Etta simply seemed awkward. Where Claribel was fierce, Etta was shrinking. Where Claribel was direct, Etta was tentative. Where Claribel was noticeably brilliant, Etta barely displayed her intellect at all. Claribel was what Etta could not be, and Etta grew to adore her.

In 1884, Cone brothers Moses and Ceasar retired their father on a guaranteed annual income and took over the Cone family business with the help of two younger brothers, Monroe and Solomon. That left Herman Cone time to worry about his daughter Claribel's future and, with that in mind, he took her to Germany in 1886.

He and his twenty-one-year-old problem-child spent the fall and winter with relatives in Munich. Whether Herman was seeking a European spouse for his daughter is unclear. What is clear is that Claribel returned to the United States with a commitment—she announced she would study medicine.

In the second half of the nineteenth century, a batch of popular novels told stories of conflicts between a young woman's "mistaken desire for medical education and her true vocation as a wife and mother." The formulaic books had similar endings—the young woman abandons her studies and finds true fulfillment not in becoming a doctor, but in marrying one.

In Germany, a number of articles were written at the time on why women should not be allowed to practice medicine. One reason offered was that women were inferior because of lower brain weight.

The novels and articles were a backlash against reality. During the late-nineteenth century, U.S women in significant numbers were becoming doctors.

In the mid-1800s, a Boston city directory listing "women physicians" included clairvoyants, Indian doctresses, and midwives. Thirty years later, the field had not only grown, but also became more regulated. The U.S. boasted more than 2,000 women doctors and four medical schools specifically for women—one each in Philadelphia and Chicago, and two in New York.

In February 1882, Baltimore joined those cities, opening the Women's Medical College with twenty-eight students. It was founded on the premise that "women were 'particularly fitted' to treat diseases of women and children." Its goal was to provide a medical education for ladies of the South and the adjacent Midwest and Western states. In 1886, Claribel enrolled at the Women's Medical College of Baltimore, graduating first in her class in 1890.

Women doctors at the time usually indicated their professional attainment by placing the letters "M.D." after their names. But when Claribel printed her calling cards, she declared herself to be "Dr. Claribel Cone," demonstrating to others that she considered herself a doctor first, and a woman second.

# Baltimore, 1892

*Then we went to Baltimore and there everybody knew us and it did*
*not make any difference about our knowing them since they all*
*knew us ... So Baltimore was full of everything which was natural*
*enough and soon it was natural enough that there were so many*
*and we knew them. Not now but then.*

—Gertrude Stein, *Everybody's Autobiography*, 1937

*C*laribel continued her medical studies until 1893, first at the
Women's Medical College of Philadelphia, Pennsylvania, then
at the University of Pennsylvania, and finally at the
Philadelphia Hospital for the Insane, known as Blockley.

Though granted two of Blockley's five medical residen-
cies, she and a female colleague did not receive the same
treatment as their male counterparts, they discovered. The
women were put in charge of arranging teas for the male
members of the medical staff. Claribel returned home.

Much had changed while she was away. Her brother
Monroe had died of a syphilis-related illness. Her brother
Moses had married and built a country estate near Blowing
Rock, North Carolina. In 1890, the family dissolved H. Cone
and Sons. The following year, Moses and Ceasar established
the Cone Export and Commission Company in New York as

a selling and financing agent for forty-seven southern cotton mills. While Etta managed the family household, a brother and sister duo from San Francisco arrived to breathe new life into the Eutaw Place social scene.

In 1892, Gertrude and Leo Stein, accompanied by their older sister Bertha, moved to Baltimore to live with a maternal aunt, Fannie Bachrach. Gertrude was eighteen and Leo twenty. Their family was financially insecure—their father habitually made speculative investments and lost, often requiring them to relocate. The two youngest Stein children were so accustomed to physical upheaval that they stocked up on books during the good times in anticipation of their father's subsequent and not-too-distant ruin.

When Gertrude was fourteen, her mother died, leaving her and Leo with almost no parental guidance. They began raising themselves and each other. Three years later, their father died, and they went to live with their oldest brother, Michael.

Michael Stein was a bit of stability in an otherwise tetherless existence. An assistant superintendent at a cable company, he scored a financial coup by selling his father's railroad franchise to Collis P. Huntington of the Central Pacific Railroad. From the proceeds of the sale, he was able to give each Stein child a modest income for life. Leo and Gertrude took the money and headed east to Baltimore.

To the Cone circle of wealthy children and settled families, Leo and Gertrude Stein must have appeared like two unbridled horses. Fiction often depicted women from the West as independent. Now the genteel Baltimore society of gloved men and mute women saw that independence first-hand.

Gertrude was a dark, attractive, buxom young woman with flashing eyes. Her cousin, Helen Bachrach, said she was "quick thinking and speaking . . . you found yourself laughing

at everything she found extremely amusing, even yourself . . . ."
Everyone, according to Bachrach, found themselves drawn to
Gertrude—even casual acquaintances.

Leo, a tall, slender, serious young man, had strong ideas
on just about everything. It was Leo who first attracted the
attention of the women in the Cone circle. He was something of a dandy compared with the industrious Baltimore
men Etta and her friends knew, and he flirted with women.
Rather than discuss money and business—perhaps the only
two things he knew nothing about—he spoke of art and
music and travel.

Claribel, having by now moved back to her family's
home on Eutaw Place, hosted Saturday evening salons where
people from the worlds of art and science would meet. The
Baltimore *Sun* said Claribel's "weekly gathering together of
friends more nearly approaches the old idea of the salon than
any other drawing-room coterie in the city."

The Steins attended, but knew no rules and had no regard
for appearance. While other women, shored up with corsets
of bone and wire, sat politely—if uncomfortably—on the
edge of their chairs, Gertrude put her sandaled feet up on the
furniture and let her chubby, corset-less body breathe freely.

The eighteen-year-old Gertrude was among the youngest
of the Cone entourage, but she was most like Claribel, ten
years her senior. In fact, Dr. Claribel would serve as a role
model for Gertrude. Her friendship was to be the first important relationship Gertrude had outside her own family.

It is easy to imagine the younger Stein roaring out her
reaction to Claribel, who held forth during evening salons, or
see her cheeks flushed or her eyes streaming with laughter,
while others less appreciative of the bold doctor's wit sat quietly
aghast. Etta, a mere shadow participant, no doubt delighted in
the proceedings just the same.

As Gertrude looked up to Claribel, Etta would look up to Leo. At twenty-two, Etta was two years older than Leo, but his grasp of a world much wider than her own must have made him seem more mature. It may have been his influence that brought Etta out into Baltimore's cultural life—to recitals and lectures. It was clearly Leo who awakened in Etta an interest in visual art.

Leo's stay in Baltimore, however, was brief. He left for Harvard in the fall of 1892—the first time he and Gertrude had ever been apart. During their separation, Gertrude wrote that she became more "humanized and less adolescent." But by the next fall, though she hadn't graduated from high school, she enrolled in the Harvard annex for women, later called Radcliffe, and rejoined her older brother.

&#10058;

That fall, everyone was busy except Etta. Claribel was doing research, and Gertrude and Leo were attending college, but Etta had no activity to call her own. With no immediate prospect of marriage or a career, Etta fell into managing the growing Cone household and caring for her elderly parents. Her world revolved around the many gas-lit corridors of Eutaw Place, and especially her brother Moses, who had assumed the role of patriarch as their father grew more frail.

Moses was a large, handsome, square man with arresting brown eyes under dark brows. Inside the family, he was warm, passionate, but stern. Despite his marriage, he was, Etta felt, especially fond of and dependent upon her.

Hands crossed neatly on her lap, Etta became the nurturer, the manager, the helpmate. She was the epitome of "a redundant woman"—without a home and family of her own. And though she liked and took part in music, she had no truly consuming interest. Hers was not a world of William

James' philosophy, as it was for Gertrude, or scientific research, as it was for Claribel, or history and art, as it was for Leo.

But, thanks to brother Moses, art would soon become Etta's world, and her passion.

～

In the 1890s, artists began to attract the attention of Americans who might not have thought of them a decade before. Popular magazines featured stories on the artists' bohemian lifestyles, and etiquette books described the proper ways for women to visit artists in their studios. In 1894, George Du Maurier added to the craze with his racy novel *Trilby*, about an artist's model in Paris. The book became a huge hit in the United States.

Interest in artists grew at about the same time home decorating began to focus on culture rather than simply comfort, and the trend became one of filling a home full of stuff. Against that background, Etta made her first grab at independence.

A year after their father's death, Moses gave Etta $300 to buy something to freshen up the family home. It would have been reasonable to expect her to buy new curtains or rugs, or furniture for the parlor. But Etta had been introduced by Leo Stein to the world of art, and it was to art that she turned with her brother's money. After seeing paintings by American Impressionist Theodore Robinson, she authorized a bidder to get "as many for the money as possible" during an estate sale in New York on March 24, 1898. Her money purchased five Robinson paintings.

When the purchases arrived in Baltimore, most of the family was shocked, though Moses' wife Bertha admired the pictures. Not only were they of the ultra-modern Impressionist school, but they were astronomically expensive.

Most families that hung art in their homes then showcased reproductions of Italian Renaissance Madonnas whose prices started at 15 cents. Louis Prang and Company of Boston offered popular facsimiles of paintings touted as equal to the original, and cost from 10 cents for landscapes and floral paintings, to $15 for a large Madonna based on an original by Murillo. But few families paid $300 for original art.

For Etta, these purchases did not represent decoration but personal rebellion. She had taken one of the few liberties afforded a woman in Victorian society—the opportunity to buy something—and she had made a bold statement.

⌒

In the fall of 1897, after concluding her studies at Radcliffe, Gertrude Stein chose not only to remain in Baltimore, but, following in Claribel's footsteps, enrolled in medical school. Johns Hopkins Medical School had opened its doors in 1893, with fundraising assistance provided by a group of women on the condition that the school accept women students. Hopkins became the first major U.S. medical school to do so. The place had the excitement of an experiment.

Apparently having nothing more pressing to do, Leo decided he, too, would return to Baltimore and to take up research at Hopkins in biology.

Claribel at the time was one of forty-six people at Hopkins taking special courses for doctors with the renowned Dr. William Welch. Her interest in science was based on a love of abstract principle—the mysteries of life under a microscope. Gertrude was interested in the meat of life—blood, birth, and death. For her, medical school was a way to continue studying human behavior.

Until 1900, Gertrude and Leo lived together in a house on Biddle Street, not far from Etta and Claribel's Eutaw Place residence. The four were good friends, mingling socially and taking part together in the city's meager cultural offerings. Leo, declaring he could "do nothing in a laboratory," disrupted the relationship and routine, declaring that he would go to Florence (Italy) to study art history and to find his "great idea." With that proclamation he was gone.

Gertrude, however, remained in Baltimore to continue her medical studies. Claribel and Gertrude would ride the trolley together and then stroll leisurely toward the school and hospital—two black, mountainous, hat-topped shapes, their skirts swaying as they walked.

It was during one of these walks that Claribel asked Gertrude to address a Baltimore women's group. Gertrude philosophized often on the role of women in society, based partly on her scrutiny of classmates at Harvard, and partly on the women she saw at a Hopkins clinic for poor patients, where she put in time. Seeing the socio-economic gap between the two groups, Gertrude came up with a theory that Claribel asked her to lecture on. The result was the first public piece by Gertrude Stein: "The Value of a College Education for Women."

Anyone who knew Gertrude wouldn't have expected her to mince her words. Her years in school hadn't tamed her. In fact, she had recently begun sparring with a welter-weight boxer to improve her health. But those at Claribel's lectures unacquainted with Miss Stein were in for a surprise. Women's rights were a favorite subject among the enlightened group assembled before her. What was not common ground was an open discussion of sexuality.

Gertrude's thesis was that women used sex to pay for their keep. She explained that as women spent less time with household duties—such as making clothes, growing vegetables, caring for children—in the maintenance of their homes and households, they would become more like sex objects than their husbands' equal partners. If women did not use their freedom from household responsibilities to go to college, Gertrude concluded, they would become mere "peacocks," spending useless years "learning the mysteries of self-adornment."

Claribel must have seen something of herself in her young friend—a disinterest in the approval of her peers and an unshakable self-confidence. And intellectually, Claribel's and Gertrude's time had come. The "new woman" or "bachelor girl" debunked Victorian myths of womanhood. She was mentally assertive and physically vigorous. Exercise was the rage and the tall, thin, and athletic Gibson girl was the image of the age.

Even Lillian Russell, the former standard bearer of beauty, got in on the craze. In the second half of the 1890s, the American press ran columns of copy on Russell's struggle to drop pounds from the voluptuous figure that had made her famous.

Etta, however, was not a new woman, intellectually or physically. Her immediate fate was to live retiringly among her family in the home where she was raised, caring for her nearest relations while their lives changed and expanded. In fact, by age 30, the only real mark she had made were the five Robinson paintings she purchased and hung on the parlor walls.

But those paintings did not just represent the past for Etta—they represented the future. They were evidence of a world beyond her family—windows into a world of light made from swift brush strokes and rich earth oozing from ochre. They represented a world where a child's delicate movement was forever frozen in a mesh of thinly applied blues and yellows and pinks—where a mother's love was conveyed by a barely discernible thread of paint.

The Robinson artwork transformed the dark, formal rooms of the Cone home in the same way a brilliant newcomer enlivens a dull family gathering. For Etta, the five paintings would turn out to be the first of hundreds of new and welcome friends.

# Florence, 1901

*There was an open door in her prison wall! If she chose to slip through it, who could follow? The voice of scandal was loud and bitter, but it would be lost in the great breadth of the Atlantic.*
—Sidney Nyburg, *The Buried Rose: Legends of Old Baltimore*, 1942

*D*uring the years Gertrude attended medical school at Hopkins, she summered with Leo in Europe and brought back to Baltimore numerous stories of their wild escapades abroad, including nude bathing and drunken revelries. But, thanks to Leo, summer vacations also involved an immersion in art. Etta's fantasy of life on the other side of the ocean must have been fueled by the Steins' tales, but it was not until 1901 that she finally embarked on a similar excursion.

After their father's death, she and Claribel began receiving an annual stipend of $2,400—their brothers gave them their share of the inheritance because, by then, they assumed that neither sister would ever marry. Celebrating her new financial independence, Etta boarded a ship that May with her cousin Hortense Guggenheimer and a friend, Harriet Clark, to make a summer tour of Europe.

In addition to trunks, hat boxes, travel guides, and numerous books, Etta took with her a leather bound diary, its cover engraved *"Etta Cone, Baltimore, Maryland,"* in gold lettering. That diary detailed a transformation in Etta that has been described in other women as a "holiday from Victorianism."

On the very first day of her Atlantic crossing, Etta threw overboard the woman her family knew—the retiring, eager-to-please, sexless helpmate—to become an adventurer. By the second day's diary entry, she was drinking champagne.

On May 23, the ship reached Naples. "Awoke at 4:30 am to find the steamer had anchored and on looking out of the port hole the most wonderful spectacle I have ever seen greeted me," she recorded. "There in the dim dawn was Vesuvius just in front and the densest, blackest smoke I have ever seen issuing from the crater. As the sun gradually arose from behind one of the peaks of the mountains that completely surround Naples on the three sides, the smoke of Vesuvius became lighter until with the sun's full rays it was almost white by reflection.

"Leo Stein surprised us by being at the docks and we almost hugged him with delight."

A travel book, published in 1900, offered suggestions for women venturing abroad alone. ... "As a general rule, if the woman will dress quietly, walk quickly, and look ahead of her, she will not be molested." But when the three women docked in Naples, the travel guide was jettisoned. Shedding the constraints of family and society, Etta and company had only one goal—to enjoy themselves with the inimitable Leo.

The Etta who visited Italy that May was not a beautiful woman. Her mouth was thin and straight, her jaw protruding and large, and her body, though curvaceous, was not sensuous. "Isn't it odd," she once remarked, "that someone who loves beauty as much as I do should look the way I do?" But as in so many people with a vivid inner life, her eyes betrayed a keen eagerness for beautiful things.

Etta's diary entries from her first excursion to Italy contain the usual tourist outbursts on native charms. After visiting the Colosseum in Rome by moonlight on May 29, 1901, she wrote: "It was glorious. The quiet with only the crickets in the ruins and exquisite shadows was delightful. We walked backwards down a street so as to get last glimpses of the magnificent spectacle."

But the diaries also contain page after page on the world of art according to Leo. It is quite clear from Etta's private writing that she loved even the sound of his name—it dots every page like a punctuation mark. With the help of his friend, Bernard Berenson, Leo would introduce Etta to the art he had been studying in Italy for more than a year.

Whether it was Leo himself who inflamed Etta, or the world he was unveiling before her, is unclear. But whatever the source, her writings in Italy contain a passion and intensity it would be difficult to ascribe to the woman who left Baltimore less than a month before.

While in Naples, the group stayed at the Grand Hotel, a luxurious five-story building on the bay whose shuttered windows looked out on Mount Vesuvius, the Castel dell'Ovo, and the bustling city that smelled of the sea. From their rooms, they could see the huge white rocks that littered the shore as if they had been spit up and deposited there by the hovering volcano.

Fishing boats bobbed off the coast, and the morning air was filled with the shouts of fishermen as they pulled up their nets and brought in the day's catch. The cobble-stone streets clattered with horse-drawn carriages. The intense heat of the place made everything shimmer.

Etta and company used Naples as a base for side-trips to

Pompeii, Amalfi, Sorrento, and Capri. Day after day, they dragged themselves and their long dark skirts along the dirt roads of southern Italy, beneath a scorching sun that rose early and set late. Leo, it appears, accompanied them on these journeys. Etta appreciatively acknowledged his contributions in her diary.

En route to Rome on May 27, 1901, she wrote: "Saw women ploughing and working the fields side by side with the men. Also saw the women washing in the streams, using rocks as wash boards. (Leo tells us this is a common practice) ... the beautiful red poppy fields are a delight to our eyes. Had veal sandwiches and wine on the train."

While in Europe, Leo added a long beard to the mustache he sported in Baltimore, and now looked even more the intellectual that he aspired to be. He still did not have an occupation, but continued to immerse himself in art history, and considered writing a book about the Italian Renaissance painter Mantegna.

In Florence, he visited often with Berenson at his villa, I Tatti, to discuss art and to use his library. Berenson, thirty-six, was also a Harvard graduate, and had been living in Florence for sixteen years. Mary, Berenson's companion and soon-to-be wife, observed that all Leo appeared to want in life was "an ear."

That is precisely what he had in Etta. She had been trained to do nothing so well as listen. Soon, she would also learn to see.

↦

Leo's pet maxim when looking at paintings at that time was simple: "Keep your eye on the object and let your ideas play about it." But Etta rarely had "ideas" that were not someone else's, or if she did, she didn't express them. That deference to others, rooted in a lack of self-confidence, began to change as she became more acquainted with art.

On May 28, during a visit to the Vatican, Etta saw her

first original Michelangelos and Botticellis. Her comments are full of a neophyte's exclamations, but also include the bold observation that the *Last Judgment* is "too much covered in drapery to still belong to 'Angelo.'" The phrase may in fact have been Leo's and only copied into the diary as Etta's own, but in either case it is the first time in writing she criticized an object of art.

On June 1, the touring party arrived in Florence, where Etta would spend nearly a month—mostly at the Uffizi— immersing herself in the Italian masters. It was expected that a traveler, on her first visit to Florence, would pay an obligatory visit or two to the great museum. Then her attention would likely turn toward the city's other charms—especially its many shops and restaurants. For Etta, Florence held one main attraction—art. On June 3, she made her first trip to the Uffizi and returned there nearly every day during her stay.

"Made our third visit to the Uffizi and as usual had Leo in his own leisurely way flitting (I should say creeping) from one to the other of us, each one of us delighted to welcome this wonderful brain."

Based on her journal entries, Etta's initial interest in art appears to have been literal. Fascinated by the stories behind the paintings, she wrote of being "keenly" interested in Filippo Lippi's *Madonna with Child and Angels* because the madonna was actually a nun the artist married.

On June 13, 1901, she wrote: "Finally reached Uffizi by 11 am, had a delightful time wandering around among my pets, reading up stories of saints, gods and bible characters. I had a long sit before Botticelli's 'Birth of Venus' and then had a good time going from picture to picture becoming better acquainted with my St. Jean the Baptists, St. Sebastians, and the other saints and saintesses."

Etta had not yet developed to the point where she could

look at a painting and appreciate it as a painting. She still looked at it as a picture of something. In fact, her taste in art was largely limited to the Renaissance. Late in June, she went to the Galleria dell'Accademia to see modern paintings, but wrote, rather matter-of-factly, that those works did not appeal to her.

On June 18, Leo left the group. For the first time since arriving in Europe, not only were they without male escort, but the driving force behind their little group was gone. Etta described their "lonely march" without him down the arched, marble tile walkway to dinner at Gambrinus on the Piazza della Republica. As their footsteps echoed in the dark shadows of the city's many monuments, Florence must have seemed more melancholy than usual.

Two weeks later, the band of traveling Victorian ladies left Florence, first for Venice, then for Germany.

An independent woman for more than two months, Etta first encountered her distant German relatives on the Munich leg of their trip. In her diary entry for July 21, 1901, she barely disguised her resentment, writing that she found their "hospitality touching but I am glad I do not live among them."

Etta's diary in Italy was sun-drenched, light-hearted, and bursting with enthusiasm. It was the journal of a woman doing what she wanted, when she wanted to do it, without thinking for a moment how her actions might be viewed.

The woman in Germany was suddenly shuttled from place to place by a hovering family whom she did not really know, and whose tastes were unlike her own. Irritated by the place and the people, she found herself annoyed even by the art. During a visit to Dresden, she saw a Rembrandt and proclaimed it "vulgar but beautiful." By the time the group left to head south to France, Etta was weary of traveling, more thrilled to receive letters from home than intrigued by her exotic environment.

When Etta and company arrived to the heat and haze of Paris in August, they had been touring Europe for three months. "I was not in the mood to enjoy the prospect of living in one of the narrow obscure Paris streets," she wrote. "However, we ended up at the Quai de Voltaire and found to our amazement that Leo and Gertrude had arrived an hour before us. Of course we talked a lot and had dinner at the Boeuf a la Mode and it was fine. Coffee at the Café American on the Italian Boulevard and Paris with a vengeance." In less than one day, Etta had revived.

The Hotel Quai de Voltaire was a small, intimate, woody place on the left bank of the Seine. An occupant of one of the hotel's front rooms had a commanding view of the Louvre directly across the river—to the left the Tuileries, and to the right, Notre Dame. It was a picture postcard world that evidently captivated Etta.

"Went to the Louvre and had a perfectly delicious time. In fact the whole place is so redolent of glorious warm color and form that I actually felt enthused once more and forgot any fatigue I had."

If Leo had been the commanding presence in Naples and Florence, Gertrude became the driving force in Paris. Etta had not seen Gertrude for several months, and even when together in Baltimore before Etta's trip, Gertrude had been closer to Claribel because of their work at Hopkins. But Gertrude dropped out of school two weeks before graduating, saying that her medical education was a farce and that she had no interest in pursuing medicine as a career.

In fact, the decision to stay or leave Hopkins was really not hers to make—she had flunked four senior-year courses.

And she had drawn the ire of the chief of obstetrics, Dr. J. Whitridge Williams, who, according to H.L. Mencken, "detested women doctors and, in addition, had a violent prejudice against all women who were fat."

During those tumultuous Baltimore days, Etta lost track of Gertrude. Now that they were reunited in Europe, both women found the other changed.

⤳

The air of experimentation at the Johns Hopkins Medical School extended into the social life around it, and some of the students engaged in same-sex relationships. Gertrude, now twenty-seven, had been involved in a romantic triangle with two women—May Bookstaver and Mabel Haynes—during her last years in medical school. The affair is generally believed to be documented in Gertrude's book *Q.E.D.*, which was not published until after her death.

In it, she described the summer of 1901 as the time when the character Adele began to understand the meaning of her relationship with the character Helen. Did the passage indicate that Gertrude discovered her sexuality during her summer in Europe—the same summer she met up with Etta in Paris? The answer is unclear. But scholars are in general agreement that the Bookstaver-Haynes affair was Gertrude's first foray into lesbianism.

The entire issue of a woman's sexuality at the turn of the century is difficult to gauge. Delicacy dictated that the nature of relationships—heterosexual or homosexual—not be spelled out clearly. And in some cases, relationships that would today be described as lesbian were regarded then as mere friendships.

As early as the eighteenth century, women were engaging in relationships with other women that were referred to and accepted as "romantic friendships," and contained all the elements of great passions, including physical intimacies.

Even mainstream publications like *Ladies Home Journal* and *Harper's* carried romantic tales of relationships between women. The unions were not believed to be sexual, because women themselves were thought not to be interested in sex except to please their husbands, or to procreate, and so society had no objection to the attachments.

But by the late nineteenth century, as the movement toward women's general independence grew, research into the nature of women's relationships emerged, and an alarm bell sounded from Europe. Women who were attracted to women were found to be abnormal and neurotic by German psychologist Carl von Westphal, who said the condition "explained why some women had such a grave craving for independence from men."

In 1897, Havelock Ellis, a noted American expert on sexuality, declared that love between women was a form of insanity that led to murder and suicide. A sensational 1892 case, where a Tennessee woman, Alice Mitchell, slit the throat of her female lover, Freda Ward, supposedly reinforced Havelock's view.

It is not clear whether Gertrude's first affair in 1901 progressed beyond the intensity of a "romantic friendship" and into a sexual relationship. But, from her writing in *Q.E.D.*, it can be assumed that she was in the thrall of a grand passion when she arrived in Paris that summer.

Etta, for her part, was a new woman, too. Out from the shadow of her dominant older sister Claribel, she was broadening herself with travel, and was in the grip of a passion of her own. In the museums of Europe, she had discovered an occupation—the study and appreciation of art.

In Paris, Etta traveled across the Pont des Arts to the Louvre, where she would wander alone for hours, eagerly hunting out clues to the treasures housed in the famous French museum. Her visits there were almost obsessive, as her diaries attest. It was as if she had set herself a task of making art and its history her own by constantly roaming among the Louvre's artistic masterpieces.

Etta spent her days expanding her intellectual horizons, but devoted her nights to reviving her spirits. Her diaries were full of dinners and cafés and the theater, which sometimes resulted in her remaining in bed until 1:30 the next afternoon. And at the center of each activity was Gertrude.

During the first portion of her trip, it was Leo whose name appeared most frequently in Etta's diary. But after the reunion in Paris, it was Gertrude who consumed the younger Cone. "Arose late & Gertrude came in most inopportunely to my room ..."

"... Got up at 1 p.m. when Gertrude came in with her enthusiasm over French literature ..."

"... talked with Gertrude on her pet subject of Human intercourse of the sexes. She is surely interesting."

Etta describes a dinner with Gertrude at the Gare de l'Orient as "the greatest meal for me in Paris." Gertrude left her at 2 a.m. that night. Etta retired for the evening at 3:30. Etta, once the picture of Victorian womanhood, found her way to the bawdy Follies Bergère, noting in her diary, "I never saw more charming athletics."

Gertrude and Leo were interested in Japanese art and sought it out in Paris galleries. Etta accompanied them on their visits and, on September 17, according to her diary, she purchased 41 francs' worth of Japanese prints.

It was her first art purchase since the Robinsons in 1898, and foretold her future as a collector, not so much because of what she bought, but how she bought it. In her diary of that day, she stated her initial intention of spending no more than 15 francs, but, she confessed, "I've got the fever bad and could not help it."

During that visit, none of the Stein-Cone circle appears to have visited the galleries displaying the work of artists living and working in Paris. The only diary entry that hints they might have seen work by modern artists was on September 13, when Etta wrote that she visited the Luxembourg and saw works by Rodin and the "so-called impressionist painters, Monet, Manet and others."

She also noted that she "went with Gertrude to Rue Lafitte & saw art stores." But it is certain she knew nothing of the painter working less than a mile from her hotel who would dominate her life.

While Etta and her group ate and drank with abandon, Henri Matisse and his family, living along the Seine in a studio on the Quai St. Michel, subsisted on rice brought back to Paris from the artist's father's store.

The Baltimore group's brief sojourn in Paris ended on September 24, when Etta and Hortense Guggenheimer left for London. The bleak grayness viewed from her room at the Victoria Hotel perfectly reflected Etta's mood—she was sullen and tired. Even when Etta and Hortense met up with Gertrude, who would travel with them to America from Southampton, Etta continued to be blue.

Her diary entry on October 3 declared the day "uneventful in every sense of the word." On October 7, in slow and sloppy handwriting, she noted, "... I fear I am not in a sociable mood. I want awfully to get home."

But on October 8, Etta had a change of heart, writing in a brisk hand, "Clear beautiful day which I spent mostly below in a most beautiful state of mind but one which brought out the most exquisite qualities of Gertrude. My vanity ..." The underlined phrase is the only such emphasis in Etta's 1901 journal, and is all the more curious because the unfinished entry is the last in an otherwise well-documented trip.

Neither Etta nor Gertrude indicated which event—if any —put Etta in a "beautiful state of mind." But a hint might be found once again in Gertrude's book. *Q.E.D.* begins in 1901 with a boat trip which the character Adele takes with two women—the same configuration as Gertrude's 1901 crossing from Southampton with Etta and Hortense Guggenheimer. In *Q.E.D.*, Adele describes a growing closeness to the character Helen, and several incidents during the journey involve "pressing fluttering fingers" to lips or "warm kisses."

But even if Etta and Gertrude ended up comforting each other physically, as described in *Q.E.D.*, it was not outside the bounds of what was considered "decent" behavior for two women of their time and culture.

Still, the intimacy, whatever its intensity, made it harder for Etta to return to her role on Eutaw Place as housekeeper and youngest sister. Her eyes had been opened to a world that not even her beloved brother Moses had seen.

When Etta returned to Baltimore, its monotonous skyline, endless brick row houses, and marble stoops must have seemed to her a kind of prison compared with the grandeur she had left behind in Paris. Immediately, she began plotting her escape. But Etta did not shed her domestic responsibilities for another two years, until after her mother's death in 1903.

With the last Cone parent gone, there was no reason for her to stay in Baltimore—and no reason to keep up a large household. Etta spent the first months of the year relocating the Cone family possessions to the home of her brother Sydney, farther north on Eutaw Place, and preparing the Cone house for sale. That done, Etta was technically homeless, which was the best excuse of all to return to Europe.

The timing of Etta's next European trip also fit neatly into Claribel's schedule. On the faculty of the Women's Medical

College of Baltimore, she became the school's president in 1902. But Claribel, while considering a leave of absence from the college to do research at the Senckenberg Institute in Frankfurt-am-Main, decided she would go along on a European tour with Etta, and cousin Aimee Guggenheimer, and visit the Senckenberg while in Germany.

～

In May 1903, Etta was once again on a ship taking her to Italy. But this time, she was the experienced traveler, guiding her older sister along the course she had traveled two years before. This time, when their ship docked in Naples, there was no Leo at the quai to escort them on their adventures.

And this time, Etta's travel diary showed she had assumed the role of tour manager. She was now more concerned with the price of things than their glory. While the trip might not turn out to be the lark her first tour had been, Etta could take comfort in the fact that she was in Europe, and she would be surrounded by art.

After a brief stay in Naples, the party moved on to Florence and registered at the Helvetia, a villa hotel in the heart of the city near Etta's favorite restaurant, Gambrinus, and a short walk from the Uffizi. Just after their arrival, Gertrude wrote Etta, asking her to meet her in Rome in July, where she was to be with Mabel Haynes and May Bookstaver.

The request indicated that Gertrude's relationship with Etta was more than just friendship because, by bringing Etta to Rome, she would be forming a couple with Etta in front of the women with whom she had had a turbulent entanglement. But Etta declined the invitation, partly to take care of Claribel and partly to continue what she now referred to as her "work" at the Uffizi.

Etta was now a much more sophisticated observer than

two years earlier. No longer interested in the stories behind the paintings, she focused instead on what made each artist unique.

"We went to the Uffizi. Here I wandered off alone learning to be familiar with the portraits of such men as Ingres, David . . . I began to feel more and more how merely superficial is one's first knowledge of great paintings."

The next day, Etta wrote of the "enormous difference in tactile values" between different paintings. And she began "working out the influence one old master had on the other." But her serious studies were cut short that day by Gertrude's arrival.

Though 10 years older than when she first arrived in Baltimore, Gertrude was still a hellion who could turn even pious Florence, with its ever-tolling church bells, into the setting for a lively romp. If Leo, and by extension Etta, looked to Florence for edification, Gertrude roamed the city and its galleries looking for fun.

"Went to the Academy with Aimee. Gertrude came along and found us in the Botticelli room and then we had a good time finding charm and humor in the various paintings . . . Gertrude was in fine humor and we had a good talk on me and my future life."

"Started off after breakfast with Gertrude and had a beautiful time with the Michael Angelo's room in the San Lorenzo. Gertrude found a strong likeness between Michael's 'Night' & me & we had a good time."

"Walked to the Fiesole with Aimee, Gertrude and Sis C and heard nightingales for the first time. It was superb. Had a table d'hôte dinner at Fiesole and all got drunk. Took a cab from Fiesole back to the hotel and sat up as usual talking over the situation."

Etta did not describe what that situation might be. But

within four days, she wrote in her diary, "Gertrude and I had a fine walk and she almost worked me up to the pitch of going to Rome with her but I was able to resist." It appears Gertrude was still trying to convince Etta to accompany her to meet Bookstaver and Haynes.

Unfortunately, there is no way of knowing how much of her private life Gertrude detailed for Etta, and why Etta continued to decide against making the trip to Rome. Etta may have simply felt obligated to remain with Claribel. Throughout her life, when given the choice, Etta would choose her family and their needs over her friends'. Whatever the reason, Gertrude and Etta would soon part.

On July 2, Etta wrote, "The woods were gorgeous and the scenery all about most ideal. Gertrude was at her best and we were all happy. We went into the woods overlooking a wonderful valley ... had our lunch and afterwards Gertrude and I lay there and smoked while Sis C and Aimee went through the buildings with the little director ...

"Were sad when we had to wend our way to the depot for it meant leaving Gertrude. Gertrude went on to Rome and we back to Florence."

Shortly after, Claribel and Etta left Florence for Germany. Claribel had made arrangements to join the Senckenberg Institute in Frankfurt and work with the institute's director, Eugen Albrecht.

For Etta, being in Frankfurt with Claribel must have been like being back in Baltimore. Architecturally, the area around the Senckenberg was similar to the Eutaw Place corridor, only more massive. Its houses were built of the same brown stone, with rows upon rows of windows—some rounded, some shuttered—but all closed and silent, offering no hint of the life inside.

Claribel shunned physical closeness, feeling comfortable in the quiet of the residential neighborhood, but Etta had traveled to Europe to escape just that.

Etta endured a summer of isolation in Frankfurt before returning with Claribel to Paris, where Leo and Gertrude had taken up residence at what was to become a famous address—27 rue de Fleurus. When she first arrived in Paris in 1901, Etta had referred disparagingly to the street as narrow and obscure. It extended in bends between the Boulevard Raspail and the Luxembourg Gardens, not far from the cafés of the Boulevard Montparnasse.

Leo had settled on a studio rather than an apartment because, he declared, he would be an artist. Gertrude announced that she would be a writer. For the brother and sister duo, it was as if saying it made it so.

The Steins' studio, accessible through the building's courtyard, looked like a strange afterthought—a kind of two-story pagoda growing from the inside of the building. On the walls, Gertrude and Leo hung Japanese prints, and Leo displayed his first "modern" painting, which he had picked up the previous year in Britain.

It was by the post-Impressionist artist William Steer and, though hardly daring, Leo said it made him feel "like a desperado" and "proved that one could own paintings even if one were not a millionaire." In fact, the brother and sister were living on about $150 a month.

The visit was a short one for the Cone sisters. Claribel went back to Germany to begin her work in Frankfurt. Leo remained in Europe, establishing his home on the left bank of Paris.

Gertrude said she would live with him there, but only on the condition that she be allowed to take a trip back to

America once a year. Within several months, she set out on that visit.

In the fall of 1903, Etta returned promptly to Baltimore, more to take care of herself than her family. She may have needed the grounding of a family in order to be the free-spirited bohemian she fancied herself becoming in Europe. But her family was changing and growing, and her role in it was becoming less clear.

The city, too, was about to change. In February 1904, the Baltimore laid out in 1730 was destroyed in a fire that lasted three days and consumed 70 blocks and more than 1,500 buildings. The eastern portion of the city was left a charred rubble, and those areas that hadn't been licked by flame were left smelling of it. It would be a turning point for the city.

It was also a turning point for Etta. She left that spring for Europe, and saw Baltimore for the first time again three full years later. On her return, it was as if a new, more modern city had grown up where the old had previously stood. Among other things, it installed a sewer system, which it had always lacked.

Etta herself was no less changed. In her pursuit of art, she left behind the safety of the museum to enter the sordid, subterranean world of the artist's studio.

# Etta

# Paris, 1905

*The art of the time is paradoxically that which only a tiny minority at the moment consider as such, and which even they can't be sure ... will be considered so in retrospect ... What counts vitally is one's experience, to use superior people as stimulants to one's attention, but not as authorities, which they aren't. They are just a little herd who have their own herd leaders...*

       —Leo Stein, Appreciation: Painting, Poetry and Prose, 1947

In June 1904, Etta and Gertrude left New York together for Europe. Etta did not return to the United States until 1907, and Gertrude not until 1934.

As they embarked from New York harbor, the two found, to their surprise, fresh grapefruit in the cabin they were sharing. Claribel, then in Germany, had asked brother Bernard to send the fruit. "I told him not to have it dressed up fancy, just to have it sent plain so you can have your dressing done from day to day," wrote Claribel. "I sincerely trust your ocean trip may be a comfortable one—that the captain and passengers will be 'nice' and that you may enjoy it to the utmost.—Also Gertrude (this may be taken in both ways.)"

Their European itinerary was familiar. First came Italy, where Etta split from Gertrude. Then traveling to Germany,

Etta stayed with Claribel until March of 1905. Finally, in September 1905, after a summer of travel, Etta and Claribel returned to Paris together.

Gertrude and Etta exchanged numerous letters during their months of separation. But though they were full of gossip, they apparently didn't discuss Leo's latest endeavors. While the Cone sisters were away, Leo had come upon a new generation of artists and, as Etta wrote earlier, "had the fever bad."

In 1903, Bernard Berenson had told Leo about Cézanne after Leo complained that the salon art he was seeing in Paris was "not art with a big A" and that he was in search of a larger adventure. What he found in Cézanne was more foreign than even his precious Japanese prints. And with this discovery, out went any notion of writing a biography of Mantegna. His interest in art, he said, was aesthetic, not historical, and he "didn't really want to write it anyway."

Like a detective, Leo followed Berenson's trail to Cézanne, which led him to Vollard's gallery on the rue Lafitte. But to call Vollard's a gallery was a slight exaggeration—the place looked more like a junk shop. With pictures piled on the floor and against the walls, there was no readily apparent exhibition. There was nothing to even indicate a visitor would be welcome, said Leo, but he went in anyway and soon bought a Cézanne painting, *La Maison du Printemps* (The Spring House).

The purchase was not his first in Paris, but it was the most important, in part because it introduced him to the right-bank street, and enabled him to find works by artists later known as the most important of their time.

The rue Lafitte was a narrow, short, dusty stretch between the prosperous Boulevard des Italiens and the rue de Chateaudun. The street was easily missed, nestled as it was between two larger boulevards. But in its unassuming storefronts—at Vollard's, Bernheim-Jeune, Durand Ruel, Berthe Weill, and Clovis Sagot—an adventurer like Leo found a treasure of contemporary art.

Soon Gertrude was accompanying him on his visits to the rue Lafitte galleries. Vollard, said Leo, liked to sell them pictures because "we were the only customers who bought pictures, not because we were rich, but despite the fact that we weren't." Leo stretched out on an armchair in Vollard's, his feet up to relieve digestive troubles, and Gertrude squatted on a chair as his partner, contemplating their next joint purchase.

During his frequent musings on art, Leo developed then one of his many theories. The art being produced in Paris, he asserted, was built on a foundation of artists he called "The Big Four"—Manet, Renoir, Degas, and Cézanne. Soon the Japanese prints on the walls of his rue de Fleurus studio were overwhelmed by the works of these four artists and their more obscure offspring. And Leo himself found an occupation—collector.

The Leo who haunted Paris' galleries was rail thin, and his long rabbinical beard made him look drawn, the very picture of an aesthete. But his emaciation seemed even more extreme next to his younger sister. Gertrude was a short, round woman of 30, who, taking a cue from her brother, covered herself in brown corduroy. She wore a top knot in her hair, and sandals on her feet, and everything in between jiggled with life and energy.

While Leo immersed himself in visual art, Gertrude began to write. Set up at a huge table with a tiny typewriter she could not master, Gertrude finished one manuscript, about a love triangle involving three women, but put it aside in a cupboard. Now she moved on to another project called *Three Lives*.

૮ૐ

It had been two years since the Cone sisters had seen Gertrude and Leo's place in Paris, and though they surely came to expect anything from their unpredictable friends, they could not have been prepared for what they found. On the walls of the rue de Fleurus studio were images the likes of which they had never seen. The Impressionism of a Theodore Robinson, as revolutionary as it had seemed in 1898 in the Cone family parlor, was nothing next to the shattered image of a Cézanne or the savage color of a Gauguin.

Etta must have felt especially disturbed by the scene because she was the more fluent of the two sisters in matters artistic, but what she found at the Steins was a new language in art that she did not speak.

Years later, Leo wrote, "'What you don't know, won't hurt you,' says the proverb. But it often makes you talk nonsense and what one man sees and another does not, makes intercourse difficult when it has to do with the kinds of things that are not really capable of explanation. The qualities of art are perceived, as it were, by a multitude of senses, and he who hasn't them operative, is not in communication with him who has."

Etta suffered from that very communication problem when she and Claribel first arrived in Paris that fall. But with her usual attentiveness, she listened to Leo, as she had years before in Florence, and became as absorbed in the new art as he.

She could not have been more fortunate in her choice of art teacher. From 1905 to 1907, wrote Matisse biographer Alfred Barr Jr., Leo "was possibly the most discerning connoisseur and collector of 20th-century painting in the world."

In addition to "The Big Four," Leo had stumbled upon a new painter along the rue Lafitte at a drugstore-turned-art gallery. Clovis Sagot's establishment was even more bizarre than Vollard's. To the public, he sold art. To the artists, he dispensed medicine a former chemist had left in the store.

With a pointed beard, bright eyes, and a hat tipped on the back of his head, Sagot was about as far from the official salon crowd in Paris as one could get. This ex-clown, said Leo, "twinkled with enthusiasm" when the subject was either the Zan licorice he always chewed or contemporary painting. More important, he told Leo of a promising young Spanish painter who lived in Montmartre. Sagot, as the owner of some of this artist's work, assured Leo he was the "real thing." His name was Pablo Picasso.

To look at the twenty-three-year-old Picasso, it would have been difficult to see anything more than the leader of a band of derelicts with artistic pretensions who did their drinking on the butte of Montmartre. A photograph from 1904 shows a handsome, if disheveled, young man with thick dark hair split by a crooked part and combed back from a broad forehead. His mouth is full and sensual, his almond-shaped eyes black as coal, and penetrating. When Picasso looked at a drawing or a print, said Leo, little was left on the paper because his gaze was so absorbing.

But while Picasso's face was bold and arresting, his dress was shabby. His short canvas jacket, because of frequent washing, was a bleached, powdery blue. He favored a spotted, red-and-white shirt and a crêpe de chine tie that was torn and dirty.

And to top off his costume, Picasso wore an old felt hat, which he had brought from Spain to Paris. But he reserved that bit of adornment for what he called "occasions"—an infrequent dinner with an art buyer or dealer. Picasso's mistress Fernande Olivier described life with the struggling artist as hard: "There weren't many collectors, and the dealers were still suspicious and kept away."

Montmartre was rural when Picasso joined a colony of art students and writers on the peak overlooking Paris. It had none of the sophistication of Montparnasse. In fact, it might as well have been another city—its denizens knew nothing of their counterparts across the Seine. One ramshackle building on the Place Emil Goudeau at 13 rue Ravignan attracted Picasso. It had been home to painters, sculptors, writers, washerwomen, dressmakers, political anarchists, and other Catalan artists. Picasso moved there in 1904.

Opposite the building later known as the Bâteau Lavoir was the Hôtel du Poirier, which was filled with poets and painters. And on tangled and steep streets emanating from the square were cafés and bars whose prices were cheap and whose owners often allowed the artists to eat and drink on credit. It was not necessarily a good idea. The Picasso gang would come home drunk and shouting, and wake up any still-sleeping neighbors by firing shots from the Browning revolver Picasso always carried. Then they returned to their warren of studios for work that no one recognized and no one bought.

The Bâteau Lavoir (so called because it looked like a washboat) stood one story above ground and two below street level. On the bottom floor, Picasso occupied two studios—one for his work and the other in which to live.

On arriving at the rue Ravignan, the young artist was still in his "blue period," painting images of despair in a monochrome palate. Considering his living situation, it is not surprising that he continued that style for some time. Picasso painted at night, but André Salmon, who also lived in the building, said the Bâteau Lavoir lacked electricity or gas. If he really wanted to see the canvas, Picasso was reduced to painting by the illumination of an oil lamp and using a candle as an auxiliary source of light.

Shortly after purchasing the Picasso painting at Sagot's, Leo and Gertrude visited the artist at his studio. Pierre Roché, whom Leo described as a natural-born liason, made the formal introductions. The pair made as much of an impression on Picasso as he did on them.

Fernande Olivier wrote: "I remember how surprised Picasso was one day when two Americans, a brother and sister, visited him. What an odd couple they were! He looked like a professor, bald and wearing gold rimmed spectacles. He had a long beard with reddish streaks in it and clever eyes. His large stiff body fell into curious attitudes, his gestures were concise and neat. He was a typical American German Jew.

"She was fat, short and massive, with a broad, beautiful, noble head, over accentuated, regular features, and intelligent eyes, which reflected her clear-sightedness and wit. Her mind was lucid and organized and her voice and her appearance was masculine."

Leo described Picasso as saying little and being "neither remote nor intimate—just completely there." On that first visit, the Steins purchased a number of Picasso's rose period works and gave the artist the vast sum of 800 francs. At some point during the fall of 1905, Picasso also agreed to paint Gertrude's portrait.

～

The Cone sisters began to accompany the Steins on similar artistic outings. One such event, the Autumn Salon of 1905, took place in October. In addition to Leo and Gertrude, the Steins' older brother Michael and his wife Sarah (whom the family called Sally) joined the party. The Michael Steins had moved to Paris and were living with their young son Allan, not far from the rue de Fleurus.

The fall salon exhibition was a favorite among the Parisian art world because new artists showed their work there. The sisters entered at the Grand Palais, through plush chambers—its walls covered in purple fabric and its floors in dark green carpet. Paintings were visible from between the ladies' plumed hats—the public came dressed in high fashion befitting an important gathering.

The Cone-Stein group made its way through salons containing paintings from the recognized schools toward a room called the "central cage," which contained works by painters roundly condemned by those in attendance. The art critic Louis Vauxcelles had reviewed the exhibition the day before it opened and declared the artists in the "central cage"— Matisse, Manguin, Marquet, Jean Puy, and Rouault—*Les Fauves (Wild Beasts)*.

That commentary set the tone for the works' reception. Hushed, respectful murmurings from the outer chambers gave way to raucous sarcasm in the "Wild Beast" room. Etta and Claribel watched in horror as the normally cordial Parisian crowd turned savage, trying to scratch the offending paint off the canvases.

Claribel wrote: "The walls were covered with canvases . . . presenting what seemed to me then a riot of color—sharp and startling, drawing crude and uneven, distortions and exaggerations—composition primitive and simple as though done by a child. We stood in front of a portrait—it was that of a man bearded, brooding, tense, fiercely elemental in color with green eyes (if I remember correctly), blue beard, pink and yellow complexion. It seemed to me grotesque. We asked ourselves, are these things to be taken seriously.

"As we looked across the room, we found our friends the Steins all earnestly contemplating a canvas—the canvas of a woman with a hat tilted jauntily at an angle on the top of her head—the drawing crude, the color bizarre. This was *La Femme au Chapeau*."

The Steins were among the few visitors to the salon to

appreciate Matisse's painting. Leo found *La Femme au Chapeau* (Woman in a Hat) brilliant and powerful, "but the nastiest smear of paint I had ever seen." He declared it to be exactly what he was looking for.

The other critics generally followed Vauxcelle's lead and denounced the new works. In the *Journal de Rouen*, the critic Marcel Nicolle wrote, "What is presented to us here—apart from the materials employed—has nothing whatever to do with painting." But to Leo, it was "art with a capital A," and on the last day of the salon he purchased the painting of Matisse's wife in a plumed hat for 450 francs, about the equivalent of $100.

The purchase was a significant one for the thirty-three-year-old collector. He had just $150 a month to pay his living expenses, and it is unlikely Leo had managed to set aside much if any money for discretionary purchases. He told Matisse, through the secretary of the salon, that he could offer 400 francs for the painting, but Matisse, despite being broke, would not accept it. The price, said the artist, was not excessive, and he would take no less than 450 francs. Leo apparently wanted the painting badly enough, accepting the artist's price.

The sale of *La Femme au Chapeau*, as much as the painting itself, caused a stir in the Paris art world. Leo and the Steins gained instant notoriety. The artist who painted the portrait became notorious too, but not necessarily in the way he would have liked.

Henri Matisse, considered the leader of the "Wild Beasts," was accused of perpetrating a hoax on the Parisian art world. Horrified at the reception his paintings received at the salon, he ordered his wife to boycott the show, in part out of fear for her safety. The money from the sale to Leo Stein was welcome, but it was only a temporary salve to Matisse's floundering career.

Matisse had not set out to be a painter. In fact, he had studied law, but very early in that career, his interest in visual arts became overwhelming. After much persuasion, his father allowed him to enroll in the Ecôle des Beaux Arts in Paris, where he studied and lived on an allowance from home.

Matisse followed the traditional course for an art student, studying with respected masters. In 1896, at the age of 26, he even received some official recognition in the Salon de la Nationale for work done under the guidance of Gustave Moreau. But soon Matisse's personal and professional life plunged into turmoil.

Caroline Joblaud, the woman with whom he was living but had not married, gave birth to their child, Marguerite Emilienne. The child, however, could not keep the couple together, and they split. In 1897, Matisse met Amelie Payrayre and, a year later, married her, just as he fell into disrepute as a painter because of his early experiments with color.

By 1900, Matisse and Amelie had two sons, and his daughter Marguerite had come to live with them. Though his wife worked in a millinery shop around the corner from the rue Lafitte, the family was destitute. Matisse took a job painting theatrical scenery, but it soon became clear this was not his métier. He was so different from his fellow artisans that they called him "the professor."

His poverty notwithstanding, Matisse's outward appearance was dignified. A large solid man, with a full blonde beard, small, thick glasses, and worn-thin but respectable clothes, he carried himself with a stiff, straight back—as if his shattered life were not getting the better of him. But it was.

In the spring of 1901, Matisse and his fellow artist Marquet used a wheelbarrow to transport ten paintings to the Salon des Indépendants. Matisse's father was so shocked at the work that he cut off his son's meager allowance.

In order to collect the insurance money, Matisse and Marquet considered staging an accident that would destroy the works at the end of the exhibition. They didn't follow through on that scheme, however, and no money issued from the exhibit, so Matisse was forced to divide up his family, keeping Marguerite with him in Paris and temporarily sending his sons to their grandparents' homes.

In August 1904, Matisse wrote to the artist Manguin, "I think painting will drive me crazy. So I'm going to try to drop it as soon as I can." But the next fall, he was still at work, and entered his paintings in the Salon d'Automne, where Leo made his initial Matisse purchase.

Early in his struggles, Matisse tried to establish a syndicate of twelve art collectors who, in return for paintings, would guarantee him an income, but the plan collapsed when only his cousin expressed an interest. Matisse did not know that Leo Stein's purchase would start a similar, informal syndicate. He did not know that his money problems had ended with the sale of just one painting to just the right collector.

For his part, Leo could not have understood the importance of the purchase. Unbeknownst to him, he had now stumbled upon the "Big Two." Leo's previous theory had been about the four primary artistic forces who would influence, and provide a foundation for, the new crop of painters. What Leo didn't know was that Picasso and Matisse, his latest and least heralded discoveries, would leap past Cézanne, Manet, Degas, and Renoir to become the most influential European artists of the twentieth century.

Soon after the exhibit closed, Gertrude and Leo met the 35-year-old Matisse. Leo found him intelligent, witty, and capable of discussing his art, which Leo said was "a rare thing with painters." Matisse and his family were living in a studio on the Quai St. Michel, which looked out on Notre Dame from the left bank of the Seine.

The household was not particularly bohemian. Amelie Matisse was a traditionalist, but the Matisse family life revolved around the artist's work. Even during their worst poverty, Matisse used the few coins he had to buy a Gauguin and a Cézanne for inspiration, and did not eat the luscious fruit he used in his still lives.

Leo continued to buy Matisse's works, but his brother Michael and sister-in-law Sally bought even more. Sally considered herself an artist, and it was under her direction that she and Michael began filling their apartment on the rue Madame with Matisse paintings. In fact, years later, Matisse would say that Sally was the "really intelligently sensitive member of the family."

Etta must have taken part in conversations about Matisse, and seen and heard the Stein family's interest in his work, but there is no indication she was inclined to follow suit. In fact, the only recorded Cone comment about Matisse at that time was when Claribel, at the salon opening, wondered if his work was to be taken seriously. Perhaps Etta was still not sure she spoke the language well enough to buy something as bold as a Matisse.

The artist's subjects were recognizable as a woman or a landscape or a vase, but beyond that they were almost frightening in their intensity. The color, departing harshly from reality, appeared to be randomly applied, with alternately violent and sensuous brush strokes. But if the excitement of the Steins' discovery did not embolden Etta to buy a Matisse, it did whet her appetite to buy something.

Ten days after the fall salon opened, she purchased a painting by a Russian artist living in Paris named Nicolas A. Tarkhoff. It was timid stuff compared with Matisse's work, but the purchase was, for her, a tiny, additional step into the collecting pool. Three days later, Etta truly plunged in.

On November 2, 1905, Etta wrote in her account book that she had purchased "1 picture 1 etching Picasso 120." That brief mention was all Etta recorded—she eventually owned 113 of Picasso's works.

~

Etta must have known Gertrude was having her portrait painted by an artist in Montmartre. Gertrude made frequent trips to the artist's studio—as many as ninety of them in less than a year. Gertrude most often walked to the Bâteau Lavoir from the rue de Fleurus—a one-way, two-hour journey, with a good deal of it uphill. In early November, Gertrude invited Etta along.

No doubt Etta imagined a sun-drenched studio and an uplifting afternoon of tea and chatter on her favorite topic, "the arts." She had met many artists at Gertrude's and Leo's Saturday night gatherings, and the events were always lively and stimulating. But when they arrived at 13 rue Ravignan, Etta entered a squat building, closed up with shuttered windows, that was nothing if not derelict.

Once inside, she must have wondered if her friend had gone a bit mad. The building smelled of fetid water and cat urine. A smiling though harried concièrge, Madame Coudray, tried unsuccessfully to bring order to the chaos. Coudray knew Picasso worked at night and slept during the day, so she woke him only when the visitors were "serious" about purchasing. Etta and Gertrude qualified, and were escorted into a dim entryway.

Gertrude led the way down a wooden staircase that opened onto a labyrinth of intersecting corridors. The doors were scarred by doodles and inscriptions from the tenants. The walls seeped.

One can imagine Etta, her long skirt folded over her arm to keep it from dragging along the dirty floor, walking on tiptoe to avoid the damp conditions, yet trustingly following her determined friend into the depths of the squalid den. Etta must have been surprised that anyone could live in a building that relied upon the dripping faucet of a communal sink, rather than a hall clock, to keep time.

Gertrude finally found her way to Picasso's studio. At the end of the row in the building's bottom floor, Etta, relieved about reaching their destination, probably looked forward to the friendly comforts inside. But the room she found herself in was even worse than the corridor that led to it.

The studio was filthy. Cinder was piled beside a round cast-iron stove held together by wire. Broken furniture was scattered about the floor. A rusty frying pan, politely called a "chamber pot," was also on the floor, and a tin bucket overflowed with dirty water.

The curtainless windows let in tremendous amounts of heat in the summer, so that Picasso and his friends were forced to wander around naked, or with a scarf tied at the waist if they had visitors. In the winter, a bitter cold came in through those same windows, which caused tea left in cups at night to freeze by morning.

Etta was introduced to the artist and his companion Fernande, whom Etta, remembering her upbringing, referred to as Madame Picasso. With Gertrude seated, Etta too found a place to rest in the cold and dismal room, and the painter got to work.

Picasso painted standing up or sitting on a low stool, with his colors, brushes, and rags spread out around him on the floor. He could afford paint, but oil was a luxury, so he used the same oil for his paintings and for his lamp. His palette was dirty, as were his brushes. And, in fact, after the Steins bought a canvas, Picasso would go to the rue de Fleurus with a paint brush to "clean" it up.

Whether Gertrude had suggested in advance that Etta buy something, or Etta was moved to make a purchase by the artist's obvious poverty, is not known. But she spent her time in his studio sifting through the drawings that littered the floor. She found not the radical deviation from convention that she had seen at the fall salon in the work of Matisse and his group. Picasso was a masterful draftsman, and his drawings showed it.

There is no documentation indicating exactly what Etta purchased on that first visit, but her choices would have been from among "rose period" paintings of animals and acrobats, or sketches Picasso made while on a trip to Holland in 1904.

In any case, before she left, Etta gave the artist 120 francs for two works on paper. The money must have been a tremendous help. At the time, Fernande said, the Picassos were living off 50 francs a month, and Etta had just handed them more than twice that amount. Later, Gertrude teased Etta, saying she had indulged in "romantic charity."

Sometime during the fall of 1905, Claribel returned to Frankfurt, while Etta remained in Paris. Now thirty-five, she set up house for herself for the first time in her life. Not entirely prepared to be independent, Etta chose an apartment in the building at 58 rue Madame, where Sally and Michael Stein lived, which was also just a few minutes away from Gertrude and Leo's studio.

Etta justified the choice by saying the concièrge was a piano instructor, so she would be able to continue her music lessons. But, most likely, there were many other reasons for the selection, ranging from a fear of being alone to wanting to be part of the flurry of activity surrounding the two Stein households.

In the sedate district not far from the Luxembourg gardens, it is difficult to imagine what the Parisian neighbors thought of all the comings and goings between the rue Madame and the rue de Fleurus. Both residences attracted a mixed crowd of rag-tag artists and writers, and foreigners of every breed. The Michael Steins were known to have quieter, more reserved, Saturday evening gatherings than Leo and Gertrude. They lived in an apartment once part of a Protestant church, with a huge living room that had been an assembly and Sunday school room. The various Saturday evening visitors warmed up here until the crowd of merry-makers spilled onto the street and moved around the corner to Leo and Gertrude's, where they stayed until two or three in the morning. "They all had a sense," said one writer, "that these were their heroic days."

Pierre Roché, the "natural born liaison officer," brought many international types to the soirées. His circle included Brits, Germans, Austrians, Hungarians, and Russians. Picasso contributed his ever-growing Montmartre gang—Apollinaire, André Salmon, André Derain, Marie Laurencin, Max Jacob.

The resulting combination, which also included a smattering of Americans, proved electric. In their early Paris days, before Matisse and Picasso, the Steins drew their crowd with Japanese prints and plentiful food.

But after the walls at both the Michael Steins and Gertrude and Leo's became filled with the new art, it was that new art which drew their visitors. "From 1905 to the beginning of World War One," as one writer put it, "27 rue de Fleurus was the most vital and exciting center of modern art in the world."

# Paris, 1906

*The most clear-sighted view M. Matisse as nothing but a mediocre, ordinary figure tortured by the desire to be original. He is taken seriously only by two or three Jews from San Francisco and by a few dealers who think that works of art . . . need have no more real value than stocks do.*

—Louis Rouart, writing in the art review magazine *L'Occident*, November 1907

Etta soon abandoned her daily museum pursuits in favor of meeting the living artists of Paris. In January 1906, she had her most important encounter. Sally took Etta to meet Matisse.

Judging from the work of his that she'd seen, Etta could have expected a bohemian who would put even Picasso to shame—someone as personally offensive to the bourgeoisie as his paintings. Picasso's work was tame and sometimes even sweet. But that was never the case with Matisse.

There may thus have been some trepidation when Etta set out to meet the artist who so consumed the Stein clan. Was she in for something much worse than the Bâteau Lavoir and its crew?

But if a picture existed of Etta's first encounter with the artist who dominated her later life, it would have shown a visibly relieved face. This leader of the "wild beasts" was a charming gentleman.

Henri Matisse was Etta's age, he was warm, he spoke easily, and he had an engaging manner. His studio was neat and tidy, as was his appearance. Judging from his looks, he could have been a scientist more easily than an artist. And certainly he would never be mistaken for the man who painted his wife with a green stripe down the middle of her face. At this initial meeting, Etta purchased two Matisse drawings. After listening to the artist ably describe his work, she wondered why she had ever thought it unusual.

Etta Cone of Baltimore, the quiet little sister whose mission in life was to make her large family happy and comfortable, was now firmly entrenched in the heart of Paris. To the artists who needed her support for their survival, she became an angel, using the money left her after her parents' deaths to buy art whose creators were despised, and whose work was ridiculed.

Monsieur Matisse was particularly vilified by critics who sought to preserve the safety of the salon tradition. He had even ordered his wife to hide the press clippings about him because, it was said, "The dirtiness of some of the art critics drove him to desperation."

Etta had entered another world, one in which the artist's daily struggle revolved around creating. She was one of a small but indispensable group of people who ensured that the artist was able to do just that. It could have been that Etta was developing an eye for the new art, but it was more likely that, at the beginning, when she purchased works by living artists, she was less interested in the images produced than the artists who produced them.

Whatever the reason, she continued to buy. Two weeks after she purchased her first two Matisse drawings, Etta bought a Cézanne lithograph. Two weeks later, she revisited Matisse, purchasing a lovely watercolor, *Port de Collioure* (The Harbor of Collioure), and a drawing. On February 28, she purchased a Renoir lithograph, and on March 17, two Manet etchings. Etta was clearly following Leo's lead in her budding collection—she purchased works by only those artists who had his stamp of approval.

When not visiting studios and galleries, Etta was busy with a new occupation. Gertrude needed someone to type the manuscript of her book *Three Lives*, and Etta volunteered. Gertrude said she was inspired to write the book by Cézanne's portrait of his wife, which Leo had purchased and hung in the room where she worked.

She began writing under the pseudonym Jane Sands, but eventually claimed *Three Lives* as her own, boldly declaring it to be by Gertrude Stein. By the time she was finished, she was satisfied that the book represented a "noble combination of Swift and Matisse."

*Three Lives* marked the start of a new phase in Etta and Gertrude's relationship. Prior to the typing, they had been on equal footing, in that both were under the influence and at the mercy of a dominant older sibling. Now Etta and Gertrude entered into an arrangement in which Gertrude became the dominant one, and Etta continued her role as the helper. It would be the first time Gertrude had been administered to and she, consciously or not, modeled the relationship on what she had seen of Claribel and Etta's.

Describing the sisters, Gertrude wrote that Claribel was the "more" of the two—she was older, better educated, more articulate, and more forceful. Claribel belonged to that rare breed that did not consider life's little necessities to be her concern. She sought an elevated existence of the intellect, but in order to remain at that lofty peak, she needed someone to take care of business.

Etta, who was that person, fell into the role of caretaker to her older sister. Now that Claribel was in Germany, Etta accepted a similar role in her relationship with Gertrude.

Gertrude benefited from the relationship in several ways. In addition to having her written scrawl turned into legible type, she had an adoring companion who would support her in her literary pursuits—much as Alice Toklas would for the duration of their relationship.

Etta's assistance in 1906 was critical to Gertrude because she and Leo suffered a major disagreement at that point. Leo would not say he liked Gertrude's writing, and Gertrude in turn refused to say she liked Leo's painting. Etta, on the other hand, would be sure to support Gertrude's work and consider her friend remarkable for the undertaking.

Years later, when Gertrude and Etta were no longer close, Gertrude described what led up to Etta's typing of *Three Lives*. Etta, she wrote, was lonesome and interested in helping, so she agreed to type the book. But Gertrude did not give Etta explicit permission to read the manuscript, so Etta typed the book letter by letter so as not to connect words into sentences and sentences into meaning. After realizing the laborious impact her unstated rule was producing, Gertrude gave Etta permission to read the manuscript, and the typing proceeded more quickly.

Most likely, that whole narrative was revisionist history, written by Gertrude for the benefit of Alice B. Toklas. When Gertrude wrote of Etta's typing episode, she was well into her "marriage" with Toklas, who made no secret of her dislike for any woman who might have been intimate with Gertrude prior to her arrival on the scene.

The more likely truth concerning the winter of 1906 was that Etta, then in the midst of a passionate friendship with Gertrude, would have done anything to be of service to her.

As Gertrude moved out from Leo's shadow, she glowed with a strange and powerful presence that surely would have won Etta's heart if it had not already been vanquished. Ernest Hemingway later described Gertrude's sexual attraction as rare and strong. He said it remained "unequivocal" when she was sixty and he just nineteen.

Gertrude once wrote, "It is one of the peculiarities of American womanhood that the body of a coquette often encloses the soul of a prude and the angular form of a spinster is possessed by a nature of the tropics." The tightly laced Etta Cone was that spinster.

⤳

In March 1906, Claribel returned to Paris for a visit and found her younger sister's apartment on the rue Madame now dotted with bizarre images, as if Etta had become a member of the same strange cult that captured the Steins. Etta must have struggled to describe adequately the places she had been and the things she had seen. But Claribel soon saw one of them for herself—Gertrude and Etta took Claribel to visit Picasso at the Bâteau Lavoir.

The elder Cone sister had spent the preceding years in Frankfurt doing research in pathology. As a doctor, she had had but one patient and that, she said, was quite enough. She spent the rest of her medical career at the microscope.

Life's tawdry side held little attraction for Claribel. The Paris she knew was the Louvre, the Comédie Française, and the splendrous neighborhood just south of the Boulevard Montparnasse. Now she would descend into a sort of distorted mirror universe. It was the opposite of everything she thought acceptable, but one her younger sister found romantic.

Picasso was still working on Gertrude's portrait, and neither he nor his model seemed to mind that the project was taking so long. On arriving with Etta and Gertrude at the rue Ravignan, Claribel was assaulted by the same smells and feelings that had once bothered Etta but did so no longer. Etta had grown used to the Bâteau Lavoir and the strange people who congregated there.

There was Max Jacob, who looked debauched in his ratty suit, thin tie, and top hat. His room smelled of smoke, paraffin, incense, old furniture, ether, and cocaine.

Other artists with studios in the building, and the women who were either "models" or "wives" (but likely neither), roamed the halls with dazed looks that might have derived from hashish, opium, or absinthe. The artist Claribel was taken to see—young enough to be her son—was very much a part of that opiated subculture.

Picasso spoke little English, and because Claribel spoke neither Spanish nor French, what little communication they had was likely through Gertrude, who somehow had a rich exchange with Picasso that transcended language.

During this period, Picasso's most frequent costume was a one-piece blue suit—the type worn by Parisian laborers. His hair, though strictly parted, was disheveled. His hands were perpetually stained. He appeared more street urchin than ground-breaking artist—more boy than man.

By contrast, Claribel was regal. Her soft-waved hair created a crown around her head. Her body, broad and erect, was draped in fine fabric that reached the floor. She held her head aloft in evident self-regard, and let a slight smile play on her lips. At the age of forty, she was someone to be reckoned with and, standing amid the debris of his wretched art studio, the twenty-three-year-old Picasso immediately recognized her for what she was. He called her "The Empress."

Following the introductions, Gertrude and the sisters handed the artist the comic pages from an American newspaper that they had saved for him. Gertrude situated herself in a one-armed chair for her portrait session.

Claribel and Etta began sifting through drawings strewn on the floor, setting some aside for a second look. By the end of their visit, the Cones had purchased eleven drawings and seven etchings for 175 francs, the equivalent of about $2 each. Picasso took the money and placed it in his wallet, which he carried in a breast pocket, fastening the pocket shut with a safety pin.

It is unclear what the older Cone sister thought of Picasso, the Bâteau Lavoir, the apparent depths to which her younger sister had sunk, or the company Etta kept. It may have been difficult for her to understand that her upright sister, clad in silk shirt waists, long dark skirts, and veiled hats, would consider the outcasts of the Bâteau Lavoir to be her friends.

But Etta was apparently able to tolerate artists' foibles that would have scandalized her own set back home. The same Etta, so intrigued by the sordid tales behind Renaissance paintings, willingly condoned, and perhaps even delighted in, the loose living of her artist friends in Paris.

$\backsim$

In March of 1906, Paris played host to another salon— the Salon des Indépendants. Once again Matisse caused a furor at the exhibition with just one painting, *Bonheur de vivre* (Joy of Life). Matisse had begun work on it while the controversy was still raging in the fall over his Salon d'Automne entries. His new work was bold for its size—about 5 1/2 feet by 8 feet—and for its content.

The painting was based on a pastoral tradition, where

figures appeared languorous in the landscape. But Matisse's version was considered by most who saw it to be crudely executed. His central figures were outlined in thick dark lines, his sense of perspective adhered to no law, and his images were overtly sexual. The painting was more a caricature of tradition than a new interpretation of it.

Even Signac, who had previously supported his fellow artist and had also purchased one of his paintings, said *Joy of Life* showed Matisse had "gone to the dogs." He was so angry at Matisse "that he went so far as to pick a fight with the painter at the café where the exhibitors and the members of the hanging committee met after the opening." Once again, Matisse was condemned by the official Paris art world, but not by Leo Stein. Leo found the controversial painting to be the most important of its time, and he bought it.

Etta may have helped facilitate that purchase. In the midst of the drama, sometime in 1906, Etta bought her first Matisse oil painting, *Poterie jeune de Provence* (Yellow Pottery from Provence). It was a rudimentary Matisse, with blocks of vivid oranges and reds and blues hastily and thinly applied to canvas. The painting had a half-finished look, with portions of the under-drawing still evident, and a large patch of canvas untouched.

The work had no relation to the bold painting in the Salon des Indépendants, but purchasing it was a significant step for Etta in part because it involved much more money than she had thus far spent on a single piece of art, and in part because it would be her first of many Matisse paintings (the actual purchase price is unknown.)

There is some question, too, concerning when exactly she purchased the painting, or whether she purchased it directly from the artist or from the Steins. If Etta made her purchase from the Steins that spring, it may have been to help Leo raise the money needed to buy *Joy of Life*. It would have been a very expensive purchase for him, and he wanted it badly even though his "funds were limited."

In later years, the Steins often turned to the Cone sisters as a source of ready cash by selling them pieces from their collection. *Yellow Pottery from Provence* may have been the first of those transactions. Etta no doubt was also caught up in the storm around Matisse as a result of the Indépendants show, and would have wanted to come to the rescue in whatever way she could.

In April, the circle surrounding the Stein households began to make plans to disperse for the summer. On April 18, Sally and Mike had learned of the earthquake in San Francisco, and a few weeks later headed back to the U.S. to take stock of the damage. That journey was historic, if for no other reason than they brought with them a Matisse, which became the first of the artist's paintings ever to reach America.

Meanwhile, Leo and Gertrude departed Paris for Italy. Various artists were heading south—Matisse had already left for North Africa, and Picasso would soon go to Spain. Claribel and Etta left Paris, too, for Germany, to prepare for a trip around the world with their older brother Moses and his wife Bertha.

Etta left Paris reluctantly. As the time approached for her trip back to Frankfurt with Claribel, she began to complain of stomach pains. The complaint was one that most often surfaced when she was forced to do something she did not want to do. Etta used illness as a way of indicating what she could not say. But it was a muffled plea that went unrecognized, and she went along with Claribel anyway.

John Stuart Mill wrote, "All the moralities tell women it

is their duty and all the current sentimentalities that it is their nature to live for others; to make complete abnegation of themselves and to have no life but their affections." Etta did just that. And though her affections may have been strong for those she left behind in Paris, her regard for her family took precedence. She was especially attendant to Moses, whom she idolized.

Ironically, Etta received a marriage proposal that winter from one of the young men who frequented the rue de Fleurus' Saturday nights gatherings—Mahonri Young, an American grandson of Brigham Young, then living in Paris as a sculptor. But, though she found him "particularly agreeable," Etta turned him down. Years later, she explained that she had never met anyone who could equal her brother Moses.

Nursing what she called her "bum gut," Etta stayed with Claribel at their Frankfurt lodgings on quiet Beethoven Street, near the Senckenberg Institute where Claribel worked. Etta had moved from the vibrant circle of revolutionary artists and the smoke-filled and cluttered studios of Paris to the utter calm of a wealthy residential neighborhood set far from the center of Frankfurt. What music there was, played deep inside the massive homes along the tree-lined street. The art was equally private and proper. Compared with what Etta had left behind in Paris, it was dead.

Throughout her German summer, Etta received letters from Gertrude, entreating her to come back to Paris in the fall. Gertrude was spending the summer in Italy working on yet another book—this one a sort of history that would be called *The Making of Americans*. Once again she wanted Etta to type her manuscript. Etta said she would probably return to Paris by the fall of 1906, but cautioned, "Goodness knows how long we will be there as when I leave Frankfurt I shall no longer be my own boss. Goodbye to little Etta's freedom, but somehow I never did mind being bossed by my biggest brother . . . ."

Gertrude also kept Etta up to date on the Bâteau Lavoir, where the financial struggles of their friend Picasso had not abated, despite their support. Etta responded: "Poor little Picasso! but then I'd swap all around with his health and genius, were it possible, but as it is not, I've just got to fight it out to the end and it's not unhappy I've been lately pain & all included and it's not America either that I'm hankering arter . . . Well, adios, with much love and sort of glad at the prospect of seeing you soon even if I can do no typewriting as wants to."

The plans for the Cone family trip changed during the summer of 1906. While Etta was convalescing in Frankfurt, her brother Moses and his wife Bertha arrived in Italy. Etta's "ulcer" did not allow her to join them, and in fact she did not meet up with them until that fall, when they traveled north and she traveled south to come together in Paris.

During the weeks before the planned December rende-vouz in Vienna between Etta, Moses, Bertha, and Claribel, their social calendar in Paris was full of dinners and parties and afternoon visits. It was no doubt with some alarm that Moses, like Claribel, viewed the circle in which his younger sister traveled.

Sunday newspaper supplements at the turn of the century were full of stories about the free life in Paris and the "dudes" and "mashers" who preyed upon single women. In popular literature, the amorality of the artist's life was legend. Now Moses saw that Etta had been living among that set and realized that he indirectly had financed it.

That fall, Paris was abuzz with news from the art community. Cézanne died, and Picasso and Matisse met for the first time at the rue de Fleurus, a full year after Leo purchased his first works from each artist. "It may seem very strange to everyone nowadays that before this time Matisse had never heard of Picasso and Picasso had never met Matisse," wrote Gertrude. "But at that time every little crowd lived its own life and knew practically nothing of any other crowd. Matisse on the Quai St. Michel and in the Indépendant did not know anything of Picasso and Montmartre and Sagot."

Picasso's companion Fernande documented the meeting between the two artists. Matisse, now thirty-seven, appeared to be a "grand old man of art" compared with Picasso, whom she described as looking like a small gangster. According to Fernande, the older artist was a "great western" and "sympathetic character," with regular features and blazing red beard. Behind his big spectacles, she said, he seemed to mask the exact meaning of his expression.

Whenever he talked about painting, Matisse chose his words deliberately. He argued, affirmed, wanted to convince. Fernande called Matisse "clear, of an astonishing lucidity of spirit, precise, concise, intelligent. Perhaps much less simple than he wished to appear ... Very much the master of himself at his meeting with Picasso, who was always a bit sullen and restrained at such encounters. Matisse shone imposingly."

The twenty-five-year-old Picasso, according to Leo's account, "had nothing to say except an occasional sparkle." And when he didn't know what to say, he burst out laughing. The younger artist came away from the meeting convinced he and Matisse were as different as the "north pole" and "south pole."

As different as they were personally, professionally they

were following similar timetables. Within a year of each other—Matisse in 1906 and Picasso in 1907—they completed the paintings that became their signposts, indicating the direction each artist later took in his mature works. For Matisse, it was *Joy of Life*, which he exhibited in the spring of 1906, and which, when, barely dry, Leo immediately bought.

For Picasso, it was his *Demoiselles d'Avignon* (Young Women of Avignon), which has been called the "first truly 20th century painting" for shattering the human form and perspective, and "effectively ending the long reign of the Renaissance." Remaining in his studio for a dozen years, rolled up or turned to the wall, it was not publicly shown until 1937.

# Blowing Rock, 1908

*Make up your mind to a brief disappointment. Life is full of them.*
*We have all got to be broken in; and this is a mild beginning for you.*
—George Eliot, *Daniel Deronda*, 1876

*I*n December 1907, Etta and her family left Paris for Vienna to meet up with Claribel and to start their world tour. Etta's year of independence was over. If traveling with Claribel alone was difficult, it was much more so with Moses and Claribel. Both were used to having their own way, and both had very firm ideas of what that way was.

In the years after Moses and his brother Ceasar began the Cone Export and Commission Company in New York, they developed a textile empire. The Cone family business owned three cotton mills in North Carolina, and Moses was referred to in press reports as the "denim king" because his mills turned out the largest denim production in the world. He expanded his Flat Top Manor estate at Blowing Rock, North Carolina, to include man-made lakes, formal gardens, forests, and orchards.

And, fully in charge of the large Cone family since the death of his parents, Moses even went so far as to dictate the careers of two younger brothers. He decided, for example, that there should be a doctor and a lawyer in the family, and since he apparently did not consider Claribel suitable in the role of physician, he directed his brother Sydney to study medicine. Bernard, he decided, should be the lawyer in the family.

Despite Moses' firm grip on family members and family matters, one younger brother caused something of a problem. Solomon, four years younger than Claribel, was a womanizer and a gambler—tax assessors eventually determined he had an annual gambling "turnover" of $30,000, and lived, according to rumors, with a "bullet behind his left ear." His brothers finally bought out his share of the family business because he was "forever putting his friends in trouble, both customers to whom he made impossible promises and his associates who were embarrassed by them."

If Moses felt it necessary to control everyone around him, Claribel was just the opposite, at least while traveling. She utterly exasperated Moses with her perpetual tardiness and lack of regard for her traveling companions. While Moses was interested in ancient "dynasties and the size of entombed kings' treasuries," Claribel was interested in "sanitation conditions in foreign hospitals."

A photo of the group taken in India that year shows them on top of an elephant with an Indian driver. Bertha looks vaguely disturbed, Moses fierce, Etta not quite happy (she's attempting a smile), and Claribel bored.

In fact, the only concession Claribel seemed to have made to her surroundings was that she was astride an elephant. Otherwise, she was dressed head to toe in dark fabric, as if the heat of the subcontinent did not exist.

During a journey down the Nile, an English-speaking sultan took a fancy to Claribel, and offered to buy her from Moses. The Cone patriarch might have been inclined to accept, if only to have a more pleasant journey, but in the end Moses did not strike a deal.

Luckily, the group did have something in common—they were all great shoppers. Moses purchased stone Buddhas for his North Carolina estate. Etta and Claribel bought fabrics, brass, wood carvings, saris with gold thread, and Hindu jewelry.

In Turkey, the two sisters bought dozens of towels; in Japan, ivory and lacquered ware; and in China, imperial robes and ceramics. In fact, the journey's bounty proved to be the start of another aspect of the Cone collection—jewels, textiles, and artifacts.

Etta's letters from the trip were surprisingly cheerful considering the many compromises she must have made along the way. Their journey took them, among other places, to Budapest, Constantinople, Athens, Jerusalem, Cairo, Canton, and Shanghai.

On February 6, 1907, from Cairo, she wrote to Gertrude, "Every whit of my oriental blood rejoices in hot sympathy for these charming people, and if my brother weren't so dead set against leaving us out here or in Europe I might be a harem-lady, who knows?"

In the same letter, Etta indicated that a major piece of information had reached her—her place as Gertrude's typist had been taken by a San Francisco woman who had just arrived in Paris.

Alice B. Toklas had initially been invited to Paris by Sally and Michael Stein on their return from San Francisco after the earthquake in the spring of 1906, but Alice didn't make the trip to Paris until the following winter. When she did, she stepped in to fill the spot Etta left vacant.

As Gertrude's assistant-companion, she began correcting proofs of *Three Lives* and typing Gertrude's latest manuscript, *The Making of Americans*. For the rest of their lives, the two women were inseparable.

From her great distance, Etta did not know what Alice's arrival meant to her relationship with Gertrude, so she continued to write her warm, flirtatious letters. From Cairo she wrote Gertrude, "I am most jealous that it's you and not me what's got a Renoir. Guess I'll take out my joy in viewing it (happy thought) in your atelier ... P.S. Has my successor done her duty by my place what she usurped and does she your typewriting & takes she care of that nice Mikey man.

"I am sometimes envious, but I guess I am greedy, cause so far, this trip has not been at all a bad stunt. It's not Ameriky I am hankering arter and every night my sister says: Etta, I don't expect to like American life & I lays low and says nothing & only hopes."

In Darjeeling, she wrote Gertrude, "I am hating the idea of America more everyday and unless it all turns out different from what I anticipate, I don't expect to tarry long in the U.S."

In a Rosh Hashanah greeting Etta sent Gertrude, she wrote, "Happy New Year to you, you heathen, but I like you even if you be a heathen & I wish I had you a little nearer, but it's a good thing I haven't, or you'd get too much material for your novels and it would keep you busier than is good for your health."

From China, she wrote Gertrude yet another letter, this time saying: "Now do be amiable and send me some good hot Italian breezes to Baltimore, 2326 Eutaw Place, my brother Sydney's home, where my mail must come for the present. My wanderings promise still to be a perpetual motion proposition, for there is no happy home awaiting the Cone sisters and no prospect of one. Good bye. Take much love and get the typewriter in good condition in case—but I don't know ... ."

Etta's uncertainty about her future was no doubt linked to

Moses' health. The trip had been partly designed to give him the rest that he wouldn't have had if he had remained in the United States attending to business.

But by the time the group reached port in San Francisco, Moses was ill and Etta put her plans to return to Europe on hold. And though Etta would never mind coming to the aid of her brother, she wrote Gertrude, "I hate, I despise Baltimore . . . ."

Claribel apparently regarded the city of her youth more favorably. She took what Etta called a "bachelor apartment" in the new Marlborough apartments, built next door to the family's one-time home on Eutaw Place.

The Marlborough was as close to a European-style apartment building as Baltimore had at the time. Its massive facade, ringed by a wrought-iron balcony near the top, would have fit quite neatly in Paris. Claribel did not invite Etta to join her there, but she did ask her younger sister to help set up the apartment.

After completing her chores for Claribel, Etta spent the winter in North Carolina, but fully planned to return to Paris that spring if Moses were well enough for her to leave without worry. Etta's Paris fever was heightened in January 1908 by a letter from Gertrude—it contained Picasso's self-portrait, along with the artist's handwritten greeting, "Bonjour Mlle Cone."

Etta commented: "I love Picasso and have him & his full tummy before me always & I am just hungry for the nice good old times ... I am going to Balto & get entangled in hateful old clothes & teas & dinners & such like . . . ."

Shortly after, Etta wrote Gertrude, "I shall sail sure as fate on May 2 for I am wild to see you'ns and Italy and all that I love best in the world outside of this tiny little group down here. Your postal with all the nice signatures gave me pleasure and if I don't get back to Italy and Paris soon I'll go crazy . . . ."

Throughout that fall and winter, Etta had also been writing to Gertrude of her new passionate friendship with a woman named Ida Gutman. Ida, a prominent woman in Baltimore's cultural set, had married into a retail Baltimore family, and, while considered one of the city's beauties, was also said to be "mad as a March hare." Etta described her "love of Ida" and how her "heart still beats hot when her letters come." But she complained she saw very little of her. "The poor thing," she lamented, "is so walled in with an excited household."

It is difficult to imagine that Etta would have written of her love for another woman if her relationship with Gertrude had not already ended. It could be that since leaving Paris, Gertrude had written Etta about Alice in similar ways. But, in any case, by the time the Cone sisters were once again on their way to Europe, the attachment between Gertrude and Etta had died away and become simple friendship.

In May 1908, the sisters reached Rome. Shortly after, they met up with Gertrude and her new friend, 31-year-old Alice B. Toklas, in Florence.

⤳

Gertrude's new companion was small and birdlike, with gray-green eyes and a light growth of hair above her top lip—in sum, an unattractive woman. Gertrude, by contrast, positively glowed with health and vigor. Years later, Alice wrote a brief description of the first meeting with the Cone sisters. "Gertrude took me in Florence to lunch with Dr. Claribel and Miss Etta Cone, whom she had known first in Baltimore and then in Paris. Dr. Claribel was handsome and distinguished. Miss Etta not at all so. She and I disagreed about who should pay the lunch bill."

Despite Alice's account, the reunion of the Cone sisters with Gertrude in Florence was doubtless a lively catching-up session, with stories to tell on all sides. Gertrude learned of the Cone family journey, and the two sisters learned of the many recent developments in Paris.

Much of the talk was about the new pecking order in Paris' artistic community, where major shifts were occurring. With his death in 1906, Cézanne was finally gaining the recognition denied him in life—Leo went so far as to describe him as "the man of the moment."

That title, it seems, actually belonged to Matisse. Those interested in radical art were now turning to Matisse for guidance, and regarding him as leader of the avant-garde. But as early as 1907, Matisse felt Picasso threatening his new position at the front of the radical line.

Matisse called Picasso "unsympathetic as a man and less than negligible as a painter." And he accused Gertrude Stein of going to the rue Ravignan not out of interest in art but for "the spectacle she saw there."

Despite his apparent dismissal of Picasso, and perhaps in response to the younger artist's growing consequence, Matisse began and completed in 1907 what would be his most controversial painting to date, *Nu bleu (Souvenir de Biskra)—(Blue Nude—Memory of Biskra)*.

The *Blue Nude* was regarded at the time as nothing short of hideous. The painting was based on a distorted bronze reclining figure that Matisse also produced that year. The sculpted figure's upper body was massive, and what were traditionally the soft curves of a woman's body became jutting angles in Matisse's hands.

But the figure in the painting, which was based on the bronze, was even more tortured. It was twisted around itself in a painful pose, its flesh outlined in black and shadowed in blue.

The Parisian art world was coming to expect the unexpected from Matisse, but his entry of the *Blue Nude* at the spring Salon des Indépendants "served to increase Matisse's popular reputation for gratuitous ugliness and iconoclasm." Once again, Leo bought the scandalous canvas, but it would be his last Matisse purchase.

Just as Picasso and Matisse began attracting a wider audience, Leo began to lose interest in both artists. He was particularly brutal about Picasso's "pink" or Iberian period. He said the work was "deplorable," accusing Picasso of borrowing from African art because he lacked his own ideas.

For Matisse, Leo's support was no longer as critical as it once had been. Now, a sufficient number of younger artists were interested enough in his work that he started a formal school. The "Académie Matisse" attracted a range of students, nearly all of them foreign, and including American expatriate Sally Stein. But the artist gave the school up after a short time because he said he was depressed by the students "doing Matisse."

The prospering artist also moved his family from the Quai St. Michel in 1908 to the Hôtel Biron near Les Invalides, the same building where sculptor Rodin took up residence. The Matisse family began to dress in expensive clothing.

Perhaps the best evidence of Matisse's growing artistic success, however, came in April 1908. Matisse took part in his first show in America, which photographer Alfred Stieglitz staged in his New York gallery at 291 Fifth Avenue. Though the show's contents were relatively modest (the works were all drawings), the response from the American critics was rabid.

"On the strength of these things of subterhuman hideousness, I shall try to put Henri Matisse out of my mind for the present," wrote J. Edgar Chamberlain in the *New York Evening Mail*.

In June 1908, the New York journal *Scrip* reported: "Like nearly all the other very modern Frenchmen . . . he feels that sickening malevolent desire to present the nude (especially women) so vulgarized, so hideously at odds with nature, as to suggest . . . the loathsome and abnormal, and both with a marvel of execution and a bewildering cleverness that somehow fills one with a distaste for art and life."

James Gibbons Huneker, a *New York Sun* writer, called Matisse's women "memoranda of the gutter and brothel."

It was these less-than-reassuring accounts in the New York press that the Cone family read, and sent overseas to Etta, who must have felt at least a little discouraged. The critics' implication was that she was squandering part of her inheritance on an artist ill-deserving of her support.

⌒

In Florence, Etta looked forward to returning to Paris to see first-hand the works that had simulatneously brought Matisse more criticism and more fame. She also was anxious to see the Picassos that Leo had so strongly rejected.

But the Cone sisters did not make it to Paris that summer. In August, they returned to America. They had received letters from Greensboro about Moses' failing health, and Etta herself received letters from Moses telling her how much he missed her.

In June, Etta wrote to Michael Stein from Florence, explaining why she could not visit Paris: "It is the dream of my life to have a home of my own in the vicinity of yours (in Paris), but my eldest brother, who has placed me on an absurdly high place, is not at all well, he wants me near him . . . for with the love I have for that brother, the sacrifice doesn't count."

In September, Etta was already caring for her brother. But three months later, on December 8, Moses died at Johns Hopkins Hospital of a heart-related illness. He was buried at Blowing Rock. The bulk of his estate went to his wife, Bertha, and the remainder was divided among his brothers and sisters.

↬

Claribel left for Europe in the spring following Moses' death, but Etta remained in North Carolina. Ostensibly, she remained there to console Bertha, but her letters to Gertrude indicated that Etta herself was devastated by her brother's death. And once again her distraught emotions manifested themselves in physical ailments. She complained of stomach troubles, nerves, and insomnia. She said she was a "slave" to veronal, an addictive, hypnotic sleep aid.

In April, Etta wrote to Gertrude, "I have meant to write before for several times I simply longed for a talk with you. Somehow it's hard to pull myself together and honestly I feel so indifferent whether I live or not and in this mood I have to face the summer in Blowing Rock."

Through the summer and fall, Etta's letters show her to be increasingly unhinged.

**July 25:** "My silence only means that there is no good in telling you the truth of how miserable I am, but I always knew that the death of my eldest brother would be hard with me ... In the meantime I am walking all alone over these roads— usually average 10 miles a day, but it makes me sleep & thats all I want of it."

**August 22:** "... honestly Gertrude, you cannot possibly know how unhappy I am & you could not have realized how I adored, almost worshipped my brother & how I fought hard against depending on him & his exaggerated approval & love for me, for next to sister Bertha he cared for me & sometimes—but what's the good to write this when it gives me such pain."

**September 26:** "There is no need to deny it but I have gone through the greatest trials that I could have had in this life, and all I want now is to be able to look at my future with calm, for I seem such a worthless sort of creature these days."

And finally, in December, she wrote Gertrude: "My brother's death almost unbalanced me ... The most terrible trial that could have come into my life has come. I miss my brother's intense devotion and approval of me. I miss—well the only people in the world who could give me something that I know I need are you and Mike and Sallie."

And, "I wish, oh I do wish I could typewrite for you ... I shall come to Europe surely next year if I live."

Etta did live, but she did not return to Europe for several years. Moses was dead, Claribel was abroad, Gertrude had a new typist, and Etta, immobilized by grief and longing, was quietly returning to her family caretaker role as the helpful younger sister, with only memories of that other life to sustain her.

# Claribel

# Frankfurt, 1910

*"No, I don't wish to touch the cup of experience. It's a poisoned drink! I only want to see for myself."*
—Henry James, *The Portrait of a Lady*, 1881

*I*n 1909, in the spring following Moses' death, Claribel left the United States again for a tour of Europe. She was not as shattered as Etta by the loss of her eldest brother. But, unbeknownst to her family, she had suffered a personal set-back abroad that changed her view of herself and of the world.

From 1903 to 1906, Claribel had conducted pathology research at the Senckenberg Institute under its director, a poet/scientist named Eugen Albrecht. Eight years younger than Claribel, he respected her professionally and personally, at least judging from her writings.

In fact, Claribel's mention of Albrecht in her letters is the only time in her life she expressed any sentiment approaching love for a person outside her family. In most cases, Claribel referred to other people as barely tolerable nuisances, but she heaped accolades on Albrecht.

She wrote Etta that she was "most terribly flattered by his praise—especially as he is so awfully critical as a rule, and the men in the laboratory, who say how difficult Albrecht is *zufassen* [face to face], look at our daily morning confabs behind closed doors with wonder and awe ..."

And in another letter, she confided, "I cannot hear from too many people of Albrecht's interest in me—for it is one of the most flattering and charming things that has ever happened to me in my life—to be approved of as a woman and as a worker by one of the most talented yet critical and learned men in the world ..."

Albrecht, no doubt, brought about in Claribel a completely different—and more positive—state of mind. Her effusive letters from that period in Frankfurt praise even a rain storm. But Albrecht died in 1908 of tuberculosis, which he contracted in the laboratory. It is not clear if Albrecht's death was a contributing factor, but Claribel never again worked at the Senckenberg, even after returning to Frankfurt in 1909.

Within two years of Albrecht's death, the Women's Medical College of Baltimore, with which Claribel had been affiliated as a lecturer and professor since 1895, would also close, setting her professionally adrift.

That condition, however, was nothing very new to her. Even at the height of her medical career, Claribel had published only a few articles—on gross and cellular pathology and physiology—and admitted she was "usually too late to claim any innovation." She told an interviewer who asked about her publications, "I never get my work into shape ... There are so many other things to do."

From 1908 on, her scientific career finished, Claribel immersed herself in opera, the symphony, books, art, and travel.

In a speech to a women's group in Baltimore, Claribel once discussed American women traveling abroad. She divided them into three categories—pseudo workers, the dutiful, and the idlers. To describe the last group, she quoted Robert Louis Stevenson: "Idleness has as good a right to state its position as industry itself. It is a sore thing to have labored along and scaled the arduous hilltops and when all is done find humanity indifferent to your achievements."

Claribel, the woman listed in one publication as the sole example of a Women's Medical College graduate who did "credit to both their alma mater and themselves," was offering a justification for living the rest of her life as an aimless wanderer. Having reached that decision, she luxuriated in its liberty.

Her 1909 trip to Europe was with company. But her trip the following year, in 1910, was alone. Her letters indicate that Claribel, now forty-six, increasingly relished her solitude and kept up whatever dialogue was necessary through missives to her younger sister Etta, who was shuttling between North Carolina and Baltimore.

"There is a sort of intolerable loneliness in being with people you do not like—a loneliness much greater than that of being alone—for in being alone there are the possibilities of all sorts of other companionships—when you have time to think of them—whereas a bad companion is an actual unpleasant fact . . ."

"Do you know as to *Oberammergau* [a passion play], I do not want a companion—I want to enjoy the performance—I want to feel the reality of it and I do not wish to have my thoughts distracted by the conversation or comments of some uncongenial or half congenial person. I enjoy Wagner operas now because I learned to know them when alone.

"You do not know what good friends I am getting to be with myself and when I have to shuffle off this mortal coil—and go to the worms (or the fishes!) I shall be truly sorry as I now feel the world is very beautiful."

As the middle Cone sister grew older, she became more physically striking. One interviewer said, "Dr. Cone has often been said to be like George Eliot, and indeed, in her large, dark eyes, her wavy hair and her strong features may be traced some resemblance of the great novelist, with the advantage greatly in Dr. Cone's advantage, however, for she is a remarkably handsome woman." She was described by an admirer as simply "the only lady who combines great dignity with an easy grace."

Claribel's figure swelled—beyond what was then called matronly to just large—but she carried her bulk with a majesty that made her as impressive as a queen. Much to her amusement, she was often mistaken for a noble Russian or English woman. And, in fact, at some point, she adopted a slight accent that her relatives called a kind of Irish brogue.

Claribel's European itinerary in 1910 took her back first to Frankfurt and Beethoven Strasse. The scientist in Claribel was inextricably drawn to Germany. By the first World War, Germany had won almost twice as many Nobel prizes in science as any other country. Claribel was also drawn to Germany's orderliness, its austere grandeur, and its formality. In Germany, she could live life without being touched by it.

Claribel engaged in an endless series of visits with acquaintances. But though her letters indicated she appreciated—even relished—the regard of those around her, she wrote of people as if they were some sort of alien phenomenon that she occasionally encountered but did not fully understand or even like.

"Do you know every now and then it dawns upon me that people do like to be thought of—I am so busy and free—occupied all the time in my work—that I do not stop to think of this enough ... and oh the good human ties I am always throwing aside—not seeing them—for what I call

my pleasure in work—well—when I get to be an old lady—
if I get to be an old lady, which I very much doubt strange to
say—but nevertheless I shall finish the sentence—when I
get to be an old lady—and can no longer work—then I shall
take time to be human—and I can be very human indeed
when I have time to think about it."

What "work" Claribel was doing at the time is unclear,
but it could be that she regarded handling the many necessities of life as a travail equaling employment. In her later years,
she carried around with her a hand-sized notebook in which
she made countless lists of things to do and people to write
to or see. She even included "list-making" in her "to-do" lists.
Note-taking alone may have consumed a significant portion
of her day.

Claribel was also famous for being a late riser and, when
finally up, for dawdling into the early afternoon. And she
spent a good part of each day writing letters. Claribel ostensibly wrote to Etta, but the missives she mailed were not so
much letters as daily journal entries, many of them poetic and
nearly all of them beautiful.

From Frankfurt, Claribel traveled to Munich, where she
began her love affair with that city, attending "music-music-
music-every evening and theater.

"Oh how I love this random wandering ... I have not
been so happy for a long time as I am now. I was thinking this
as I wandered about the streets this morning. And now I realize
that I am not happy in America—how I hate those cramped,
narrow, crowded, high above civilization—lonely (lonely)
rooms on Eutaw Place—this I am just beginning to realize."

After an extended stay in Munich, Claribel tore herself
away in late August to travel to Weimar, Eienach, and the
Wartburg, whose natural beauty inspired her as much as
Munich's bustling streets and rich cultural menu. Dr. Claribel

Cone, who had spent her adult years viewing life in a laboratory, had suddenly awakened to its wild charm.

"How awesome it was at times to stand in a deep ravine between rocks so close together that they almost seemed to crush you—or threatened to do so as you passed under and between them—above your head—which let the daylight through in splashes—shredded and spots—and then green sunlight now and then green because of the mossy covering and the overhanging trees above—and the sound of splashing, gurgling water.

"I think without exception it is one of the most poetic incidents I have ever experienced—and as I entered the drachen schlucht [Drachen passageway]—at the beginning of the walk I passed a man and a young girl—the man walked slowly—and stopped a bit—the girl was young—and erect—they entered the ravine just a bit ahead of me—but soon I overtook, then passed them.

"And I saw that the man had a scholarly book (perhaps his step was scholarly—I think his walk was rheumatic)—he looked about 56 or 60 years of age—then as the water gurgled under the footpath—made of narrow birch branches strung together, crosswise—I heard the man in a deep rich mellow voice with a cultured accent begin to quote Shelley ... He was not at all sentimental—he repeated it in fact as he would have done to me or anyone else—it was the occasion that called it forth and not his companion—that was only a passive element in the incident."

In that same letter, Claribel described an encounter with a boy who played the banjo. She felt an affinity for the youth, yet chose to proceed on her walk alone. In the self-reflective mood that Weimar wrought, the strangeness of her choice was not lost on Claribel.

"At the crossroads we parted. Now why did I deprive

myself of a pleasant companion when I might have had agreeable company all the way!—throughout life—that is what I do—and have been doing—there is something subtle —and indefinable—that impels me to be alone—it interests me to send people whom I might like away from me."

There is no indication in any of Claribel's writings that she was ever close to anyone outside her family, except perhaps Albrecht. She seemed content to share the world or her experiences with no other person—she had no need for that sort of validation. For Claribel, other people were of value only if they could be useful to her or if they could appreciate her genius.

As luxurious as Claribel's solitary travels were, however, they were not to last long. She was joined by Etta, and a companion joined her in Europe in 1912.

⤳

Claribel's younger sister, now forty-two, had suffered greatly in the years following their brother's death—both physically and emotionally—and now found it necessary to travel with a nurse. Etta met Claribel in Frankfurt accompanied by a twenty-five-year-old unmarried attendant named Nora Kaufman. The group spent the summer in Italy, and by the fall they were in Paris.

Drastic changes had come to the rue de Fleurus. Alice now lived with Gertrude and Leo—she was given a small room called the "salon des refusés." Leo and Gertrude quarreled more. He thought her writing was "rubbish," and she disapproved of his romance with an artist's model, Nina Auzias, who had been known in the quarter for singing in the street.

In the past, Leo had been the one to hold court during Saturday evening salons, while Gertrude sat quietly in a chaise lounge. But increasingly, Leo sat in another room during the sessions and primarily discussed diseases of the stomach. With the help of Alice, Gertrude was now the doyenne of the lively gatherings.

Leo explained the change simply: "When my interest in Cézanne declined, when Matisse was temporarily in eclipse, when Picasso turned to foolishness, I began to withdraw from the Saturday evenings."

Leo's final rift with Picasso came when the young artist discovered Cubism. The term "Cubism" was coined in 1911, at the Salon des Indépendants, by the same critic who six years earlier had called Matisse a *"wild beast."* The Cubists' leading influence was mathematician Maurice Princet, who frequented the bars in Montmartre, and whose wife, Alice, left him to marry André Derain.

Maurice Princet, said Leo, talked about infinities and fourth dimensions, and "Picasso began to have opinions on what was and what was not real, though he understood nothing of these matters." But those opinions became Cubism.

Gertrude, unlike Leo, admired Picasso's new work. What he was doing in paint, she decided, she was doing in words, which must have irked Leo to no end. He said of Picasso, "It is not the lack of ability that puts me off, but the silliness."

But the artist's fortunes no longer depended upon Leo's support. Having attracted many collectors, Picasso was now visibly well off. In 1909, he had moved from the Bâteau Lavoir to the Boulevard de Clichy, where he ate his meals in the dining room, served by a maid in a white apron. When the movers came to collect the few items from the filthy rue Ravignan, Fernande heard them speculate, "Surely these folks have won the jackpot."

Matisse, too, was faring far better now than when the Cone sisters had last seen him six years before. He had not subscribed to Cubism. Matisse, said Leo, was "too intelligent and too sincere" for the movement.

Instead, he continued his own pursuits, which brought him increased notoriety and some new collectors. Matisse also signed a contract with the respectable Bernheim-Jeune Gallery and moved his family yet again—this time to Issy les Moulineaux, southwest of Paris.

The Cone sisters visited him there during their 1912 tour, and they must have been struck by the harmony of the setting. Matisse was robust and healthy. His at-home studio looked out upon a garden of brilliant flowers. He had two dogs as companions and a horse for exercise. In the gentle air and absolute quiet of the French countryside, he and his family appeared the picture of domesticity.

The Matisse household, however, was not entirely happy. With his family settled in the country, Matisse continued to travel to Paris to work with models. For some time, he had been having an affair with a Russian Jewish student of his, Olga Merson, who had posed for a Matisse portrait and sculpture in 1911. Olga is possibly the inspiration for the red-haired nymph approached by the nude male in the erotic *Nymph and Satyr* from 1908-09.

Whether Madame Matisse knew of her husband's indiscretion is not clear. It is also not clear if the Cone sisters were aware of it. But they freely exchanged gossip with Sally Stein, who, like Olga, was a one-time student of Matisse, and who no doubt knew of the affair. There would have been no reason for Sally to have spared the Cones the news of Matisse's dalliance.

Despite his success, Matisse the artist was still viewed in some sectors of Paris as a menace. Urinals in Montmartre were covered in the graffiti: "Matisse has done more harm in a year than an epidemic! Matisse causes insanity!" Someone altered hundreds of emergency bulletins distributed throughout the quarter. Rather than warning of the dangers of white lead, they now carried—because of the defacement—a warning about Matisse.

And in the United States, Matisse's work continued to be greeted with outrage from critics and collectors alike. The artist had had his first American sculpture show in March 1912—this time, as before, at Stieglitz's gallery in New York. Critics were unanimously appalled by the work. Arthur Hoeber of the *New York Globe* said the sculpture looked "like the work of a madman, and it is hard to be patient with these impossible travesties in the human form . . . Indeed it is unbelievable that sane men can justify these on any possible grounds."

Some American collectors, just beginning to be interested in Matisse, were warned off by American artists. Gertrude Vanderbilt Whitney considered purchasing the sculpture *Le Serf* at the Stieglitz show, but was dissuaded by portrait painter Howard Cushing. (The Cone sisters later purchased the piece.)

And Isabella Stewart Gardner was warned away from Matisse by a former Museum of Fine Arts Boston official who said John Singer Sargent considered Matisse's painting "worthless."

The Cones, however, remained faithful. They also followed Leo's lead and shunned Picasso's new work. Two camps had developed—Gertrude and those who preferred Picasso, and Leo, Sally, Mike, and the Cones, who preferred Matisse.

By 1912, Gertrude backed her loyalty with money, and bought her first Picasso painting, a Cubist piece, which she defiantly hung in the rue de Fleurus. She and Picasso, she believed, were artistic soul mates. Both fantasized about being so famous that if thieves broke into their homes, they would steal his paintings and her writings rather than silver or coins.

The Cone sisters soon got a taste of Gertrude's Cubist-inspired writing. During a visit that fall to the rue de Fleurus, Gertrude announced she had captured the sisters in a word portrait she called *Two Women*. The tortured prose went round and round in an endless and repetitive series of phrases that, taken as a whole, were somehow meant to elucidate the Cone women. Claribel said she was "enchanted" by Gertrude's work, though she admitted she had no idea what Gertrude meant by it, and took the floor to read parts of it aloud. Gertrude said Claribel did so with great aplomb.

Claribel read: "There were two of them. They were each one of them rich. They each one of them had what they wanted. Martha when she was wanting. Ada when she was going to be wanting. And they both had not what they were wanting. The older Martha because she was not wanting it and the younger Ada because she could not come to want it.

"They both of them were spending money that they had and they were both of them very different one from the other of them. They were both of them doing what they were doing that is to say Martha was doing what she was doing that is to say she was not changing in doing what she was doing, that is to say she was going on and that was something that she was saying was a curious thing, that she was doing what she was doing and not changing and not doing that thing."

A photograph of that reading would have shown Claribel, with mischievous smiling eyes, large and resplendent in fine but dated clothing, in the midst of a group of admiring younger women reciting incomprehensible prose that would not bring Gertrude widespread recognition for another twenty years. And all around the group of ladies were the pictures that had made the rue de Fleurus famous.

By 1912, the plaster in the Stein studio had begun to crumble, but the decay was barely noticeable because of the hundreds of images that covered the walls. Leo had collected works by Matisse, Picasso, Vallotton, Cézanne, Daumier, Renoir, Manet, Bonnard, Manguin, and Toulouse-Lautrec, among others. The image of the women, in their dark turn-of-the-century garb, sitting among paintings that would still be considered bold fifty years later, is an incongruous one, made more so by Gertrude's indecipherable prose.

The sisters returned to America again at the end of 1912. Etta had taken an apartment in the Marlborough, near Claribel's, and the two sisters began filling both apartments with odds and ends picked up during their travels. Etta's apartment contained the few paintings and drawings she had acquired. Both homes were enlivened by the brilliant textiles they had collected on their world tour.

Claribel, however, was bored. She occasionally spoke to women's groups in the city and attended cultural events, but she lacked the freedom and stimulus in Baltimore that she had had in Europe. As in Gertrude's word portrait of the sisters, Claribel was "wanting."

A flu epidemic hit Baltimore during the winter of 1913, sending Etta to her bed and indirectly causing the sisters to miss the one art event in America that might have aroused Claribel's interest. The famous Armory Show, held in February in New York, was the official introduction of modern European art to the United States.

Thousands of people lined up to see works the Cones already knew intimately. Leo and Mike and Sally had loaned several pieces to the exhibition, including Matisse's *Blue Nude*. And the dealers along the rue Lafitte had also contributed several works.

The art world in America was as horrified by the exhibition as the French crowd had been eight years earlier, when first glimpsing Matisse's *Femme au Chapeau*. One American critic labeled the Cubist grouping the "Chamber of Horrors."

And, once again, the press reviled Matisse. A *New York Times* critic wrote, "We may as well say in the first place that his pictures are ugly, that they are coarse, that they are narrow, that to us they are revolting in their inhumanity." The academic mural painter Kenyon Cox wrote in the same newspaper, "many of his paintings are simply the exaltation to the walls of a gallery the drawing of a nasty boy."

Etta and Claribel surely read about the uproar, because it only increased as the exhibition traveled. In Chicago, students made a copy of Matisse's *Blue Nude*, which Leo owned, and burned it in effigy. But the controversy—as controversy most often does—benefitted the artists. In this case, it sparked interest among America's intelligentsia, who now rushed to buy the ridiculed work.

〜

In the summer of 1913, the sisters were back in Europe for their annual visit. But Claribel decided hers would be an extended stay this time. She would not return this time to Baltimore. She would live in Germany instead.

Etta could have stayed in Paris while her sister remained abroad, but she did not. By the fall, she and her nurse-attendant, Nora Kaufman, were aboard ship heading back to the United States. Perhaps Etta recognized that the Paris of 1913 was not the Paris that loomed so large in her memories. The innocence and conviviality of the early years were gone.

That fall, Leo prepared to move out of the rue de Fleurus. He told the collector Albert C. Barnes, "I can't stand Gertrude. She's crazy." Leo took the Renoirs, Matisses, and Cézannes for his house in Florence, and Gertrude kept the rest.

During that same period, a depressed Matisse was having trouble working. He said the success of Cubism, which was at its peak, left him "virtually alone." Because he had chosen not to join that particular school, it threatened to eclipse him.

In fact, when he entered the café La Coupole on the Boulevard Montparnasse one evening, he was greeted by an unusually excited crowd. But, he soon learned, the uproar was not for him. The gathering had mistaken him for Picasso.

For his part, Picasso's moment had come. He had left Fernande and moved to Montparnasse with his latest love, Eva, to begin a new life. But, Gertrude said, Picasso never laughed any more.

The bohemian and naïve world of the Bâteau Lavoir and the rue de Fleurus had vanished. The artists and writers were no longer in the business of indulging themselves and each other. They had found respectability and a place at wealth's table.

# Munich, 1914

*We had seen three days of the German army by now; and it seemed*
*to me ... that the whole world had turned into a gray machine of*
*death ... And over it all lay a smell which I have never heard men-*
*tioned in any book on war—the smell of a half million unbathed*
*men, the stench of a menagerie raised to the nth power.*
                    —Will Irwin, writing in *Colliers Weekly*, 1914

*P*icasso's "Empress" roamed the streets of 1914 Munich
with a freedom and leisure she lacked in every other city.
Claribel had just enough acquaintances there to keep her
social calendar full, but no obligation to see any of them. For
her, it was a perfect existence that revolved around music, the
opera, and the cultural heart of Bavaria.

Munich in 1914 was the city of Thomas Mann and the
country's poets, and the center of Germany's modern art movement, then led by the director of the Bavarian State Gallery.

Wassily Kandinsky and Alexej Jawlensky also lived there,
as did Paul Klee, Franz Marc, and other members of the expres-
sionist movement known as *Der Blaue Reiter* (The Blue Rider).

It was also home to a destitute young Austrian who had
taken an attic room above a tailor shop in the bohemian district of Schwabing. Adolf Hitler, still struggling to be an

artist, supported himself by selling postcards.

The year Claribel took up residence in Munich, the city was celebrating the 25th anniversary of the reign of Kaiser Wilhelm II, and was bursting with nationalist pride. On August 1, 1914, a declaration was read to the public from the steps of the Feldherrnhalle in the Odeonplatz.

Germany was declaring war on Russia. The kaiser was forced into the conflict, the declaration said, when Serb nationalists, two months earlier, assassinated Austrian Archduke Franz Ferdinand. The Archduke, before his death, had assured Austrians that Germany would come to Austria's aid if the Serbs' ally, Russia, was brought into the conflict. By July 30, Russia mobilized along Austria's border, and Germany seemed to be standing by its pledge to defend its ally against the great Russia.

United States news reporters stationed in Munich sent home urgent dispatches.

"This city is feverish with excitement over the prospect of war. We arrived from Berlin and Dresden, where the mobs in the streets and processions of students singing *Die Wacht am Rhein* *[Watching Over the Rhein]* and other war ballads were of such magnitude that old residents said nothing like them had been seen since the beginning of the Franco-Prussian conflict of 1870.

"We had just been driven out of the famous picture-gallery by the four o'clock closing bell, when we found excited throngs eagerly calling for immediate and complete mobilization of all reserves and indicating that the great European war had come."

One American writer said the first reports of war "gave an impression . . . [that] Europe by some dark enchantment had become a witches' cauldron brewing mephitic shapes."

By August 4, France had declared war on Germany, Germany on Belgium, and England on Germany. Some 70,000 Americans traveling in Europe were caught in the conflict.

"Suddenly," wrote one reporter, "the paralysis of civilization that war brings left them stranded. Waiters left the dining rooms for 'mobilization,' trains were diverted to become troop carriers, traveler's checks were worthless and boundaries between countries became impassable."

The correspondent for the *New York World* reported, "In their eagerness to get away from the perils of war, Americans even abandoned all their belongings, fought for places on the last train from Paris and arrived in London starved and moneyless. President Wilson means to provide them gold and ships to bring them home."

Claribel, however, did not join her countrymen in the mad rush to leave Europe. After the first few heady days of war and mobilization, Munich calmed down and life returned to much of its pre-August 1st character. In fact, during the first years of the war, Bavaria would be spared most of the hardship the rest of Europe suffered. Germany was the aggressor, pushing its troops across other countries' borders.

In Paris, however, the evidence of war was everywhere. Search lights, mounted atop the Eiffel Tower, roamed the sky for the enemy. For Paris' artists, life fundamentally changed. "Paris is dark at three in the afternoon," Max Jacob wrote. "Each day is like Sunday; absinthe has been outlawed, there's only one kind of bread to eat, hardly any films to see, and no one dresses up or plays music."

Picasso remained in Paris, living with Eva in a plush apartment, but their life was made gloomy by the zeppelin alarms and the cemetery the apartment overlooked.

Braque, Derain, Apollinaire, and Lèger left for the front, and Matisse tried to enlist in the service, but was rejected. He moved his family to Collioure and then returned to his studio in Paris where, unable to paint, he spent the first year of the war playing the violin.

Gertrude and Alice had been in England when the war broke out, but eventually made their way back to Paris, and then headed south to Palma de Mallorca, where the war played out in a bizarre burlesque. A German governess hung out her country's flag every time there was a German victory, and the Allies' supporters on the island did the same when their side won.

In America, the New York Stock Exchange shut down after Germany declared war on Russia. It did not re-open until that December. President Woodrow Wilson had vowed to remain neutral, and declared October 4, 1914, "Peace Sunday," instructing Americans to pray for an end to the conflict.

But despite the distance and the prayers, the battle continued, and soon its direct effect on the United States was felt. As one of its first acts of war, Britain cut the only German cable linking the United States and Germany. Britain also seized and examined all German mail bound for America.

For those, like Etta Cone, cut off from family and friends in Munich or Berlin, who hoped to get a glimmer of what might be happening to them there, the news reports were no help either. Correspondents traveled with the Allies and practically all their reports were censored.

It was as if Claribel, in her insulated way, did not exist. Nor, apparently, did she recognize the danger she was in. Her "Day's Work" from the start of the war lists: "1. get red buttons. 2. write check for $1,000 to pay for antiques. 3. tip room maid 50 cents." Claribel lived in the eye of the storm, yet was undisturbed by its turbulence.

In September 1915, she wrote Etta. "My dearest sister: I think very often of you and hope you are well. Take things a bit easy. That is the only way to make life worthwhile. I say this and have just finished writing for 3 1/2 hours part of a long list of things I mean to do (or hope to do) this winter in Munchen. My schedule of work if I finish 1/2 of all this I shall be satisfied. A man's reach should exceed his grasp else what's a Heaven for? Here it is wonderfully beautiful."

In 1915, Claribel was 51 and living the life of a bohemian above a shop. There is no indication she ever knew any of the painters of *Der Blaue Reiter* living in Munich, or purchased any of their art, but Claribel was apparently in contact with poets.

In one letter to Etta, she wrote of a Hungarian poet who had her read his work aloud and told her she gave it just the right emphasis and expression. And she said "over here they put me in the category of Poetry-Art. And when I say I have never written a line of poetry in my life, they say, not in that sense."

She had also grown philosophical about the war. In apparent response to a question from Etta about her loyalties, Claribel wrote in July 1915, "I am strictly neutral my dear sister. Please do not mistake that. But being in the midst of so much suffering, so much heroism and so much nobility of soul and self-sacrifice, I cannot but feel deeply sympathetic and sincerely interested in the cause of the German.

"This does not mean however that I cannot sympathize equally as much with all the tried peoples of the earth—who are suffering through this mistaken notion of upholding one's own dignity—I cannot lend my acceptance to a situation which makes it necessary for human beings to slay each other in order to make wrong right.

"But as all of the nations appear to be guilty of this error, I must complacently accept the situation and simply feel deeply for those poor maimed bodies and wounded souls that are the result of such a system of error. I speak of all the nations—for as Thomas Paine said years ago—'War is murder, all the more heinous for being gloried in.'"

The kaiser was still in Munich, the operas were plentiful, the beer gardens full, and the good life persisted. Claribel was enchanted by existence there. Except for news reports of soldiers killed in war and a steady stream of men in gray green leaving for the front, life in Munich was untouched by the horrors unleashed in Belgium and France. It was as if the war ripping the continent apart were nothing more than a distant drama.

By October of 1916, Claribel had moved out of her apartment for the comfort of the Regina Palast Hotel. She was concerned about the cost, she wrote, but said the landlord at her previous lodging, an "eccentric hysterical little woman," made continued residence there impossible. The new quarters Claribel took up were in a luxurious hotel billing itself as the most modern in Europe.

It was a large building with 240 rooms overlooking the Maximiliansplatz in the heart of imperial Munich. To the southwest was the Justizpalast, and to the northwest the Arco Palais, Palais Ludwig Ferdinand, and the Leuchtenberg Palais. The wide boulevard in front of the hotel had two massive fountains on either end. In between were landscaped paths frequented by the city's wealthy residents. Claribel's suite included three rooms with a private bath and balcony.

Her daily routine included twenty minutes of exercise involving steps she copied from Isadora Duncan's dancing, visits with relatives and friends in Munich, and talks with other hotel guests. Among them was a soldier who she said was interested in psychic research. Claribel, he told her, should have been an actress.

In fact, her life in Munich amounted to something very close to that. She thrilled at being a mystery to her tablemates, who wondered about the imposing figure among them, all alone in the great city. But her ultimate thrill, she wrote Etta, was an encounter with King Ludwig himself, who apparently mistook her for visiting royalty in the lobby of a concert hall in Munich.

Claribel, it seems, had heard the royal party being

announced. "Along with the rest of the guests I bowed. The procession continued and I returned to the occupation of fastening the laces of my sleeve. My head being bent I did not see what was happening. Presently I was conscious of someone standing before me—and heard a voice say *Ich hatte Sie Nicht gesehen*, (I had not seen you). There stood the king— with outstretched hands—charming, apologizing for having failed to acknowledge my bow."

In 1917, Claribel's family tried to persuade her to return to the United States. Ceasar Cone used political connections in President Wilson's administration to arrange for Claribel's return home in the American diplomatic corps' private train. Pressure was building for the U.S. to enter the war, and if that happened, Claribel had to be out of Germany, Ceasar reasoned.

But despite Ceasar's efforts, Claribel refused to budge. She would not go, she said, because she was not permitted a private compartment on the train—for herself and her ten or fifteen trunks—and "she would not change her habits just because of a world war." The normally calm and kind Ceasar "hit the roof."

Claribel wrote to her brother Sydney, "I thank you for wishing me to come home. I try somehow to arrange to come—but I seem to have taken root here and believe I am thriving. Physically I feel better than I have felt for a long while. Is it the climate or the life I lead here I do not know. I have such interesting personal experiences and meet such interesting people."

For Claribel, Munich was a stage grand enough for her performance. And the thought of leaving her richly appointed hotel suite in a dynamic city for what she called cramped rooms in the cultural backwater of Baltimore made the shadow of war a mere minor obstacle to her staying.

But she soon discovered the ramifications of her decision.

In February 1917, Claribel received letters telling her that Ceasar had died. She tried to respond, but her letters were returned. Claribel found herself cut off from any communication with America. The United States had entered the war, and she was living in hostile territory.

～

It had taken President Wilson three years from the start of the European war to commit U.S. forces. Even after the Germans torpedoed the *Lusitania* in 1915, he chose to remain out of the conflict, saying the United States was "too proud to fight."

But repeated German attacks on merchant and passenger ships, and growing anti-German sentiment among the American people, weighted the scales in favor of war. By February 1917, the United States had severed diplomatic relations with Germany, and on June 5, American men were registering for the draft to fight the battle in Europe.

War hysteria gripped the United States. The great German gun "Big Bertha" was trained on Paris, dropping shells from seventy miles away, and Americans vowed not to be victims of a similar attack. Thirteen percent of the U.S. population at the time was of German birth or descent, and that large group became suspect.

In the U.S., a general hysteria and suspicion fed rumors that German-born Americans, loyal to Germany rather than the U.S., had laid solid concrete foundations in the cellars and garages of their homes, enabling them to hide guns and other weapons that they planned on sending their countrymen across the ocean. Fearing that the German-Americans might also take up arms against the U.S. within its borders, U.S. citizens invaded the homes, posse-style, to root out these German armaments and sympathizers. As the war continued, anti-German sentiment grew more bizarre—Americans refused to use the words sauerkraut, German measles, or dachshund.

Soon food shortages began and rationing was initiated. In 1918, U.S. Food Administrator Herbert Hoover, later to become president, called for wheatless Mondays and Wednesdays, meatless Tuesdays, and porkless Thursdays and Saturdays. He also proposed a per person limit of two pounds of meat per week, and issued twelve rules for public eating places that included no bread until after the first course and a maximum half ounce of butter per person.

In Baltimore, industry was booming because of the war. The city became a hub for steelmaking and shipbuilding, as well as a center for ammunitions and explosives manufacturing. In fact, just several blocks from Etta's apartment, a firm was making ammunition that would be used to attack the German army.

The war in Baltimore not only brought new commerce, but also widespread mistrust. Police searched the homes of unnaturalized Germans, and the telephone company asked its employees to sign a pledge of patriotism.

Given that atmosphere, it can be safely assumed that questions were raised about the Cone family's loyalty—their sister, after all, was still living in Germany, the country to which the entire family traced its roots. It would have been impossible to explain that Claribel remained in a belligerent country because it was too inconvenient to leave.

But whether questions were raised specifically about the Cones is not known. What is known is that the previously harmonious mixing of gentiles and Jews along the Eutaw Place corridor began to break down during the war. The Jewish community had many ties to Germany, and though supportive of the Allied effort, was less virulent in its attacks on Germany than its gentile neighbors.

Etta, viewing her own war-time situation, could only have imagined the worst for her sister in Germany. There was no fighting on U.S. soil, and yet its food-deprived people had been whipped into a frenzy. What could Claribel be suffering inside Germany, which had been isolated from the rest of the world and engaged in fierce battles for three years?

In fact, the war was finally becoming a reality for Claribel. Denied access to her own U.S.-based money, she was forced to borrow funds from her relatives in Germany. Long lines had begun forming at Munich food stores, and schools were closed to make room for the returning wounded. Italian planes had dropped scattered bombs on the city, and there was a flu epidemic and a housing shortage.

From her perch at the Regina Palast, she watched the grand city bow to the pressure of battle and war. The glorious façades remained the same, but Munich was wounded from without and rotting from within.

The Schwabing taverns that once echoed with the verses of poets were home to new groups obsessed with the politics of the extreme left and right. The leftists wanted to bring Bolshevism to Germany and to do away with its firmly entrenched class system. The rightists, in search of the glory days of old, wanted to rid the country of those elements they believed had made Germany weak.

In 1912, in a published book called *If I Were Kaiser*, Dr. Cheinrich Class ominously predicted, "Jews who had not obtained German citizenship would be expelled from the country ruthlessly and to the last man."

That theme was taken up by rightists in the Schwabing taverns. Alfred Schuler called for "an apocalyptic purging of all Jewish elements from the world" in order to purify it. The tide of the war was turning against Germany, and some factions of its society were looking for someone to blame.

# Munich, 1918

*We're turning everything upside down, we're tearing it all to pieces.*
—Weiss Ferdl, 1918

$\mathcal{J}$f Germany seemed a dark place in 1917, it was a completely black place in 1918. Pride in Germany's war-machine had given way to demonstrations demanding an end to the fighting. In November 1918, Munich's streets were filled with a hundred thousand people demanding the overthrow of King Ludwig and his government, as well as an end to the war.

As the crowd marched, its numbers swelled. The army soon joined the protest. The rumble of thousands of feet and the chant of the disenfranchised proved to be too much for Ludwig and his royal family, who fled Munich. The crowd was triumphant. Like the czar in Russia the previous year, the German king had been toppled from his throne by a popular uprising.

The demonstration was choreographed and led by the drama critic Kurt Eisner, who, with no previous political experience, was declared minister president of the newly freed state of Bavaria. Soldiers waving red flags raced through the city, occupied the rail station and the ministries, and set up machine guns on street corners. Almost overnight, the relative calm of wartime Munich was shattered by social revolution.

Claribel's hotel was in the middle of the chaos. From her balcony, she could see government buildings and royal palaces, and she could watch the throbbing, shrieking masses below. But at the core of the "new Bavaria" movement was a kind of idealism that might have even appealed to her. Kurt Eisner, a Jewish intellectual, had stated with great eloquence his decision to end the suffering of global war. Despite the guns and the soldiers, the appeal had a touch of nobility about it that may have piqued Claribel's interest and earned her respect.

Claribel's American family, meanwhile, read news reports that Germany was going to pieces. Unable to contact her directly, they worried that she, too, might have perished in the tumult.

Things were not much better in Baltimore. In addition to local soldiers killed in battle, Baltimore in 1918 had the highest death rate in the United States from an influenza epidemic. Cold weather prevented the burial of flu victims, and rotting corpses piled up. Everywhere was death and deprivation, and there was no reason to assume Claribel, in a Germany far worse off, had been spared the indignity of either.

In fact, she had not, though war and revolution were proving to be great levelers. In Munich, there was an almost total lack of the "things" Claribel and the wealthy upper-class had previously taken for granted. By 1918, Munich's markets were bare, clothing and other essentials unavailable, and money increasingly meaningless. Nearly everyone in Munich suffered.

In a letter written several years earlier, Claribel had said that one of war's lessons to her was that, in peacetime, people ate too much. Munich had been on a war diet for four years, and it looked as though the post-war years were to bring even greater hardships. From inside their grand homes, the city's wealthy watched with apprehension as the world war ended, and a civil war erupted in their midst.

Claribel watched, too.

⤸

For all its death and destruction, the first World War, from the vantage point of Munich, was a relatively orderly affair—it saw the inexorable march of thousands of uniformed troops armed with cumbersome weapons. There were clear enemies and battlefields, clear winners and losers.

But with the outbreak of post-war revolution, rag-tag troops followed dozens of minor leaders, each with its own sets of allies and adversaries. The rules changed daily, and anyone and everyone was a potential victim. The revolution-related violence gripping Munich was being felt intimately—neighbor to neighbor—and it was terrifying.

In the first weeks of November 1918, Germany crumbled. Kaiser Wilhelm fled into exile on November 10, after the German Republic was declared. Fritz Ebert, a former saddle maker, was pronounced Germany's new chancellor.

The next day, on November 11 at 11 a.m., the armistice went into effect, signaling Germany's defeat, and burdening the country with crippling post-war reparations to the victorious Allies. Throughout the country, posters proclaimed the arrival of Bolshevism. A once proud Germany had been brought to its knees. Munich was in an uproar.

New voices were added to the chorus of malcontents. Eisner's government was denounced by a growing band of German nationalists, who blamed him and his supporters for an odious armistice agreement that would cost Germans dearly. The press dismissed Eisner and his followers as "strangers, carpet baggers, and Jews."

But while demonstrators on the left and the right roamed

the streets, shouting their slogans and demands, another, much more insidious group was meeting quietly in the upper floors of a Munich hotel. The Thule Society was Pan-German, nationalistic, and anti-Semitic. It called the revolution in Germany the work of its deadly enemy Juda, and vowed "an eye for an eye and a tooth for a tooth."

Gradually, Thule agents filtered into the Eisner government, and hundreds of thousands of anti-Semitic leaflets were hurled into the streets of Munich from speeding vehicles. The messages bore the Thule Society's emblem—a swastika.

Thule, its labor offshoot the German Workers Party (which would grow into Hitler's National Socialist Party), and numerous German nationalist groups blamed the Jews in Germany for losing the war, and for permitting the influx of Bolshevism immediately afterward. As the confusion of revolution grew, the chief target of the groups' hatred became increasingly clear. To them, eradicating the Jews would bring back the glory of pre-war Germany.

On February 21, 1919, a half-Jewish military officer, rejected by the Thule Society because he was not "pure," assassinated Eisner outside the Diet. Once spilled, the blood began to gush. During a eulogy to Eisner that same morning, an opposition leader was shot and wounded, a guard killed, and another delegate murdered. The new Bavarian government of Kurt Eisner ceased to exist.

A state of siege was declared in Munich, and a worker-soldier-peasant central council assumed governmental power. Placards throughout the city warned citizens to stay indoors, and a 7 p.m. curfew was imposed.

Prominent citizens and aristocrats were arrested and held hostage. Trucks mounted with machine guns roamed the streets. Public buildings, banks, and hotels were occupied by Red troops and armed workers. A group of revolutionaries declared Bavaria a Soviet Republic.

This time, the revolution literally came to Claribel's door. Her hotel, the Regina Palast, was occupied by soldiers who arrived at her suite to conduct a room-to-room search. Claribel must have been terrified. She was a Jew, an American, and wealthy, which made her a target for all sides of the raging street battle. Even the stoic doctor would likely have been rattled by the appearance of the soldiers, who could take from her what they wanted without fear of reprisal.

Whether she acted out of fright, or whether she was actually intrigued by the filthy troops in her doorway, is not known. In either case, she did not panic, but assumed the role of the gracious hostess, inviting the soldiers in. She told them she had nothing they would want and nothing illegal, but they searched her room anyway, and, in a Spanish chest, found some candy Claribel had forgotten about.

Using cooking equipment in her room, she made the soldiers hot chocolate, divided up the confiscated bonbons, and engaged them in a chat. Claribel's tea-time visit with the occupying forces left her unperturbed.

The revolutionists had established their base at the Wittelsbach Palace, a half mile from her hotel. Claribel's balcony was like a theater box seat from which she could view the revolutionary drama unfold. Shortly after the brief and civil intermission with the soldiers in her room, an armed overthrow of the Bavarian Soviet-style government failed, after which street gunfighting erupted. The already bad situation worsened.

The *putsch* ushered in a new group of hard-line Communists who issued decrees for the confiscation of private and corporate bank accounts, business profits, and food supplies. According to one historian, "a state of hysterical panic" gripped the middle and upper classes as armed patrols searched private homes.

By the spring of 1919, the situation became so grave that old residents began packing up their possessions and moving out of Munich. In the "war after the war," Munich was precisely as described—an "insane asylum."

The nationalists, who had been plotting to win back Germany from the Bolshevists, surrounded Munich with 20,000 troops in April and pushed into the city from all sides. Soviet rule fell and martial law was enacted. The liberation of Munich had come, but there was evidence that an even darker chapter would soon begin. In the aftermath of the takeover, the city's streets were littered with corpses, and the victorious troops charged with maintaining order wore swastikas on their helmets.

A general call for doctors was made to help treat the wounded in Munich. Claribel told an interviewer years later it was "with some surprise" that she remembered she was a doctor. The woman who bragged she had had only one patient was rolling up her sleeves and treating the victims of Munich's bloody street battles.

⤸

By August, the first trickle of mail from America began to reach Claribel. The relief she must have felt at hearing from her family can only be imagined. Claribel wrote to Etta, "The close of the war and the opening of the mails was a godsend to me—naturally I was worried until I got word of your well being and of that of our other dear ones. I dread to hear of the changes that have taken place in the two and a half years in which no message came to me from home. I trust that most of these changes have been for the better." Also in her response, Claribel asked Etta to send her 10,000 marks.

The value of the mark plunged drastically during the

post-war years in Germany. On the day the European war ended, the mark was worth 7.45 to the dollar. By 1919, it was worth 35.45 to the dollar. Because of rampaging inflation, the money her family sent Claribel—the requested 10,000 marks—was only enough to pay her hotel bill or her debt to her German relatives. Even if she had received more money, the city's stores shelves were empty.

Oddly, despite the turmoil and deprivation, Claribel was not immediately ready to leave Germany even then. In September 1919, she wrote to Etta that she didn't know when she would be returning to the United States because there was a long list of people awaiting passage.

"This will probably shove my homecoming to the winter. As I do not feel equal to traveling in cold weather I fear I must wait till the spring. As usual I have taken such deep roots into the place where I happen to be living that it will take more than horses to drive me away ... I have gotten so out of the habit of traveling that I scarcely know how to pick up again. I feel much like a person who has sat for a long time in a cramped position and tries suddenly to get up again—you know what that is—well that is my mental state as to moving on—a very cramped one ... ."

That fall, while Claribel resumed her correspondence with Etta, a newcomer in the German nationalist movement began making his first speeches in Munich. Adolf Hitler had joined a small group of nationalists and quickly emerged as its leader.

In September 1919, he wrote his first political treatise— its topic was the Jew. "True anti-Semitism," he wrote, "should consist of a deliberate, planned campaign to deprive the Jews of the rights that they, unlike other foreigners, were enjoying in Germany." In November, Hitler made his first public anti-Semitic speech. He received thundering applause.

As the situation in Munich grew more tense, Claribel took steps to leave. In October, she contacted the Spanish consulate to secure passage, but was told she could only leave if she offered satisfactory "evidence" that a physical disability had prevented her from quitting Germany at an earlier time.

With no sure way of leaving the country, she instead turned to Etta to see if she could provide some of the things she was unable to get and at least make her involuntary stay in Germany more tolerable.

"... you were so kind as to ask can you send me something and if you have the opportunity I will ask you please to send me—a pair of rubber shoes! number 8 probably best. I used to wear 7 but my shoes are so big—(I have one pair of shoes)—that it takes the larger size to go over them. Oh yes, yesterday in preparing my trunks for travel purposes I found a pair of big so-called "ground grippers"—a pair of orthopedic shoes so big and so ugly I had not ventured to wear them.

"But this morning you should have seen the admiration which Emma (my maid) and I bestowed upon this pair of shoes—the "ground grippers"—and the delight with which I acknowledge myself the possessor—the happy possessor—of a pair of shoes and of such quality! I have tried for two or more years to get a pair of shoes ...

"Fortunately I have the habit of keeping my worn out shoes and clothes, and things which even I thought too shabby to wear have appeared like a gift from heaven when the last shred of a bit of rubber would hold the shoe I was then wearing on my foot ... for deep snow I found a big pair of flannel lined men's rubber boots. They are Russian and of good quality."

Times had changed drastically for the Empress. She now regarded the things she had previously possessed in abundance, even taken for granted, such as precious jewels and various physical comforts. In fact, Claribel's letters during the years she

prepared to leave Munich were increasingly about "things"—
not people. She even began to write that the necessary disposal
of some of her things was keeping her from leaving Munich.

In response to a letter from Etta, she wrote, "You are
right—do not let things consume you. But on the whole I find
things so much more satisfactory than people, people are
interesting but you cannot live with them as satisfactorily as
with things. Things are soothing—if they are works of art—
most people are over-stimulating—and nowadays—the people who have suffered war and especially a lost war—are irri-
tating. Some are like a bitter medicament."

That same month, she finally wrote, "I am ready to take
myself out of Germany. But the things! the trunks! the boxes!
the books!"

⤻

While Claribel sorted through her possessions and
packed—two tasks that consumed a full two years—the
streets of Munich seethed. The beer halls that had once
echoed with boisterous revelry were now arenas of political
debate. In February 1920, Hitler's party held its biggest rally
to date at the Hofbrauhaus and attracted 2,000 people.

And that spring, as its membership increased, the party's
name was changed to the National Socialist German Workers
Party. Announcements concerning the group were distributed from trucks and posted on bright red placards in the
streets of Munich.

The ultra-nationalist meetings, previously held behind
closed doors, were bursting out onto the city's boulevards.
Enthusiastic crowds under the spell of Hitler's speeches
spilled from beer halls and marched through Munich singing
pogrom songs. For Hitler, Munich was the "holy city of
national socialism."

Assassinations, random murders, beatings, and kidnappings became the norm in a city that had once been the cultural heart of Germany. Lion Feuchtwanger, in his book *Erfolg* (Success), wrote, "Formerly the beautiful, easygoing city drew to itself all the best talents of the Reich. How is it that they were gone now, and in their place everything that was rotten and evil in the Reich?" Warnings were issued in a Berlin newspaper for travelers to avoid Bavaria. Munich was labeled a "murderer's center."

The ranks of those joining the nationalist forces were growing by the thousands. For Claribel, it was finally time to leave. The Munich of the kaiser, the opera houses, the symphony, and the theater—the Munich she had once loved— appeared to be gone forever. There was no end to the violence corrupting her European home, and a vast increase in hatred directed at her as both a Jew and a foreigner. Claribel, nearly 57, was not up to the fight.

After finally deciding to leave the bulk of her possessions behind in Germany, the solitary traveler booked a stateroom for three on a ship bound for the United States. It would be her first trip home in seven years.

Before leaving Munich, she wrote Etta: "I shall be so glad to see you again my dearest sister and all my dear ones. A lifetime—many lifetimes—wars, revolutions, upheavals, insurrections … strikes … strikes … strikes … all sorts of strikes and all sorts of changes have taken place since we have seen each other, and yet curiously enough I believe we shall both be just the same as before. That seems curious does it not?"

# Abroad Together

# Paris, 1922, Part One

*There is never any ending to Paris, and the memory of each person who has lived in it differs from that of any other. We always returned no matter who we were or how it was changed or with what difficulties, or ease, it could be reached. Paris was always worth it ...*

—Ernest Hemingway, A Moveable Feast, 1964

*P*erhaps Claribel wished that the two sisters would be just the same as before the war, but they weren't—nothing was. The war machine had screeched to a halt, but the vivid memory of its horrors lingered. There was a momentary stillness after the fighting while the world assessed the damage. That done, Europe began its arduous cleanup, and America began a frenetic dance that became the '20s. It was as if the sheer joy of victory set the U.S. on a wild course of speculation and spending.

But the frenzy may have been more the result of fear than joy. America and the world had seen the depths to which modern man could plunge. Americans and Europeans reacted to the horror by making the most of the peacetime, spending each dollar and each day as if it were their last.

The Claribel who returned to Baltimore in 1921 was not

the dark-haired, finely dressed aristocrat who had boarded a ship for Europe eight years before. The woman who appeared at the Marlborough Apartments was a gray-haired, heavy-set creature wearing threadbare clothes, her face lined with signs of suffering. The proud woman who, once, not very long ago, had been mistaken for a queen still resided in that body, but she had been shaken to her roots. The sight must have shocked Etta, so different was this new woman from the Claribel she had known.

Etta, too, had changed. She was now fifty-one and, in the years since her brother Moses' death, she had become a wholly independent woman. She fully recovered from the loss of her brother, though she was still afflicted with strange maladies that may have been psychosomatic. She had grown into a matronly woman whose angular face had softened over the years. Her hair, now flecked with gray, was still pulled back off her face, but it was worn looser.

Everything about Etta appeared more comfortable—as if she had settled into a life that either was agreeable to her or one that she had accepted as such. She fit easily into the role of "Aunt Etta" to her brothers' and sisters' many children, often traveling between Baltimore and North Carolina for extended visits. Etta's household at the Marlborough had grown to include two servants and her younger brother Fred, who took an apartment adjoining hers. She had made a Baltimore home for herself similar to the one she briefly had in Paris in 1906, when she was so happy, and purposely peopled it with those she loved.

Etta offered the returning Claribel a sanctuary in which to recover. The younger sister took charge of the older, nursing her back to health in a setting that must have seemed almost disturbingly calm to Claribel. There were no gunshots or screams, no marching feet or abandoned corpses. For

Claribel, the teeming Munich she had left just weeks before was a terrible other world. That other world, despite her love for Germany, was one to which she would never return.

During her recovery period, Claribel set up house in a small apartment on the sixth floor of the Marlborough, two floors below her brother and sister. She began filling it with the things she had collected in Germany, which one relative described as "mostly junk." The two sisters and their brother Fred decided that Etta's apartment would be the central home for the Cones in the building, and Claribel and Fred would pay to take their meals there.

How to pay, however, was initially a sobering question for Claribel, who worried upon her return that she was now penniless. According to rumors circulating in Germany during the war, the United States had confiscated the funds of any American citizen who remained in Germany during the war. Her concerns turned out to be unfounded.

During the war, firms that manufactured goods to meet military needs prospered. On Wall Street, the companies were called "war babies." The Cone Export and Commission Company was one of them, and Claribel's stock dividends had been piling up uncollected since 1916. One relative estimated that Claribel was now worth about $100,000.

Maybe the news of her wealth helped speed her recovery, for, by the summer of 1922, Claribel was ready to travel again. The two sisters, along with Etta's nurse, Miss Nora Kaufman, prepared for their first journey to Europe together in nine years. Claribel was once again the Empress. She had not lost the weight she had somehow put on in Germany, but she had regained her composure.

〜

Out of consideration for Claribel, who was not as interested in "making a tour" as she had once been, the sisters'
travel itinerary changed slightly. They immediately based
themselves in Paris at the elegant Hotel Lutetia, where Claribel
remained during the summer, while Etta and Miss Kaufman
traveled.

The Lutetia, a relatively new hotel built in 1910, was the
only palace hotel on the city's left bank. It provided the previously poor bohemians of the Montparnasse quarter, now
rich, with a new address. Artists and writers and dancers of
means ate in the hotel's brasserie until late in the evening, and
then drank in its luxurious salon into the early morning.

The hotel was as grand as the Regina Palast, and may
have reminded Claribel of her previous hotel residence. But
despite its size, it had an intimacy about it, and it fit nicely
into the corner of the Boulevard Raspail and the rue de
Sevres. It offered the Cone sisters every convenience, as well
as easy access to the adjacent Bon Marché department store,
where a delighted Claribel wandered amid the abundant supply of goods, selecting items by the dozen.

The Paris the sisters returned to in 1922 was electric.
During the war, a million Parisians had fled the city to the
protection of the countryside. The streets were virtually
empty then, and nine out of ten street lamps were extin-
guished. German bombs had fallen on Paris—on the church
of Saint-Gervais, on the church of the Madeleine, and in the
Seine. The city was left pock-marked and empty.

But with war's end, people once again flooded the streets,
and many of them were Americans introduced to the
romance of the place while stationed there for work or military duty. The dollar was strong and the franc was weak, so
even a down-and-out American writer or painter could afford
to live well in the great city. Paris became a magnet for the

"lost generation"—Americans like Fitzgerald and Hemingway—who arrived there with letters of introduction to gain them entrance into the city's legendary salons.

Etta and Claribel needed no introduction to the salons— they had been part of them from the start. They went back, needing and hoping to discover what fate had befallen their friends.

⮌

The Cone sisters had not seen Gertrude and Alice since 1913. Gertrude, now forty-seven, still lived with Alice in the rue de Fleurus. The two had spent the war delivering relief supplies in a Ford they called "auntie," as part of an American charity effort, the American Fund for French Wounded. Gertrude, it was said, could drive "forward admirably," but could not master the process of backing up.

The pair's small income was diminished during the war— everything, including the necessities of life, had become so expensive—and found themselves forced to scrounge through French markets just to buy food. Gertrude said she and Alice had once been offered German sausage, but she warned Alice away from it, saying, "Take care, it might be Claribel." In a characteristic understatement, Alice called the times "confused."

But Gertrude's passion for writing had not been affected by the confused state of things war had brought—nor had her work become more understandable to ordinary readers. She continued to write despite little recognition for her troubles. She worked at night and left the pages for Alice to patiently type in the morning. In the evening, they received visitors.

Increasingly, however, the crowd was literary and drawn to the rue de Fleurus not by the paintings on the walls but by the sheer force of personality—the very aura—that surrounded the heavy-set woman holding forth from her armchair.

Gertrude would talk to the "geniuses," and Alice would entertain the wives. Sherwood Anderson was among the first young American writers to make a pilgrimage to Gertrude's door. At the end of 1921, with a note of introduction from Anderson, Ernest Hemingway arrived as well.

Leo Stein had spent the war years in America undergoing psychoanalysis, or as one writer put it, pursuing his three major complexes—inferiority, castration, and pariah. Nina, the artist's model who had been his companion, stayed behind in Europe because she could not get the necessary papers for travel. They remained attached through the war years by way of passionate letters, many of which described Leo's sexual escapades with other women.

Upon his return to Europe, Leo declared in a letter to Gertrude that his whole life up to that point had been a "prolonged disease, a kind of mild insanity." But, despite his warm tone in letters and almost conciliatory attitude toward their differences, he and his sister never reconciled. He married Nina in 1921 and continued his obscure existence away from the rue de Fleurus culture he had almost singlehandedly created in 1905.

The artists who had been part of those early years were also changed or gone. Apollinaire was dead, Max Jacob had become a Christian and joined a monastery, and Picasso, who had quarreled and broken with Gertrude, was married.

Picasso's great love, Eva, had died in 1916, and in early 1918 he married the Russian ballerina Olga Kokhlova, whom he had met in Rome while designing a set for Diaghilev's ballet *Parade*. As Picasso's professional fortunes improved, his art became sweeter. No longer doing the analytical Cubism that had made him infamous before the war, he was now mixing

Cubist principles with his old love of circus figures and with his latest influences—musicians and dancers. He also painted portraits of his new wife in a classical style that was nothing less than an homage to Ingres. It was perhaps in reaction to war that the artist who had previously sought to shatter reality on canvas turned now toward the most traditional of subjects.

He and Olga moved into an apartment on the rue la Boetie off the Champs Elysées and near his new dealer, Paul Rosenberg. His life had turned decidedly bourgeois under Olga's influence, and in February 1921 he and Olga had a child, Paulo. Infants became a subject for the revolutionary artist—Picasso had entered a new period.

Matisse spent the first year of the war in Paris, back in his old studio on the Quai St. Michel, without his family and unable to paint. The gray desolation of the city and the despair into which it was plunged left the artist incapable of producing his richly colored works, and so he turned to the violin, which became an obsession.

Matisse, however, may have also been blocked artistically by worry over the fate of many of his works, which had been stuck in Berlin since the war's outbreak. A Matisse retrospective had opened at the Gurlitt Gallery in July 1914, including nineteen paintings the Michael Steins lent. But the Berlin show had been forced to close in August when war was declared. There was no indication when or if the paintings would be returned.

The prolonged lapse without work, however anxious it might have made the artist, proved important and, in some ways, beneficial to him. By 1916, Matisse was painting again, and that year and 1917 are characterized by one of his earlier biographers, Alfred Barr Jr., as perhaps the greatest years of his career. Claribel explained the change simply. The war, she said, had taught Matisse, who had been essentially a decorative artist, to be more complex.

Matisse was working with the Italian model Lorette, and occasionally her sisters, painting interiors that exhibited an intimate sensuality—a feeling of close flesh—that would dominate the remainder of his artistic life. The paintings were portraits of Matisse's world—the sanctuary of his studio or the comforts of his home at Issy les Moulineaux. Like Picasso, he had returned to a kind of traditionalism in his subjects.

But unlike Picasso, who celebrated his new domesticity on canvas, the 48-year-old Matisse spent the war years documenting his desires. The shocking experimentation that characterized Matisse's pre-war works was largely gone. And though the newer works were in no way classical, they were much more accessible than the *Blue Nude*, for example.

In 1916, Matisse wrote to Hans Purrmann after seeing Derain, who had joined the army, "How irrelevant the mentality of the rear must appear to those who return from the front." And, as if in retreat from both the fighting and the soldiers he was not allowed to join, Matisse headed south to Nice.

The move would prove to be one of his career's most significant. In the Mediterranean city, Matisse found the light he needed to sustain him as an artist, though he almost did not stay. He prepared to leave Nice one morning in 1916, after days of continual rain, but the sun came out, he unpacked, and remained for thirty-five years.

Matisse took up residence in the Hotel Beau-Rivage overlooking the sea on the Promenade des Anglais. His routine was unvarying. He rose early, ate breakfast, practiced his violin in a "remote bathroom so as not to disturb the other guests," then painted from nine to noon. The violin, he said, limbered his fingers for painting, but he also worried that if he ever went blind, he could no longer support his family through painting. Playing music on the street was thus his back-up plan, though it proved unnecessary.

His gallery, Bernheim-Jeune, more than doubled its asking price for Matisse's work, which had gained the attention of international collectors, including the Americans John Quinn and Albert C. Barnes.

Almost in inverse ratio to her husband's good fortune, Madame Matisse's had declined. In the year 1917, a melancholy one for her, she began to suffer psychosomatic illnesses. Depressed and rarely venturing out, she became, in effect, the opposite of her husband.

But it was not surprising. The woman who had sustained her husband through extreme poverty felt excluded from his success. He rarely used her as a model any more. Instead, he spent his studio time with exotic young women posed in sensuous settings. Matisse believed his paintings had curative medicinal powers. He once advised a friend to sit among his painted works until he felt better. But Madame Matisse, it is certain, would not recover her spirits in a room filled with the lounging nudes who so occupied her husband.

In the spring of 1919, after the armistice was signed, Bernheim-Jeune staged a one-man show for Matisse. In 1920, three books on Matisse were published, and in 1921 he took an apartment in Nice in the Place Charles Felix. Until 1938, he divided his time between Nice and Paris.

Now that the Cone sisters were back in Europe, the grand gentleman of French painting resumed his friendship with them virtually where he had left it ten years before.

# Paris 1922, Part Two

*Some are coming to know very well that they are living a very dull
way of living. These go shopping. They go shopping and it always
was a thing they were rightly doing. Now everything is changing.
Certainly everything is changing. They go shopping and they are
being in a different way of living. Everything is changing.*
                                  —Gertrude Stein, *Flirting at the Bon Marché*

*C*onsumerism on a mass scale was born in America before
World War One. Encouraged by newly advertising companies
to "buy more," everyone from paycheck-to-paycheck workers
to the idle rich became, with an almost religious fervor, pre-
occupied with "things." Women, in particular, accepted the
advertiser's urgings to shop and buy—if only as a way to
keep America's industrial wheels turning.

Claribel and Etta already had the tendency to acquire,
and now that neither of them had any other occupation, it
became their driving force. For Claribel, shopping compen-
sated for the lack of things she had suffered in Germany. For
Etta, it was a way to buy back pieces of that magical time she
had spent in Paris in 1905 and 1906.

From their inheritance—money and dividends from the
Cone company stock—the sisters took in an impressive

annual income. After calculating how much of that sizeable total could be spent during their summers abroad, they set out to buy. They bought silk stockings by the dozen, shirt waists, hats, handbags, jewelry, antiques, exotic fabrics, ornate boxes, books, rugs, and, most significantly, art.

In 1922, the Cones began building in earnest the art collection that Etta had unconsciously begun twenty-five years before, with the purchase of five Theodore Robinson impressionist paintings. The sisters had not purchased any paintings since 1906, when Etta, under Leo's influence, went on a buying spree, picking up Matisses and Picassos for a song.

But on July 11, 1922, the lengthy drought ended. The sisters paid a visit to the Bernheim-Jeune Gallery and purchased five Matisse paintings, paying as much as 8,500 francs, or about $500, for one of the works—considerably more than the 100 francs Etta had paid for a Matisse watercolor in 1906.

There is no way of knowing for certain which sister purchased which painting—the bills from the gallery are all addressed to Dr. Claribel Cone. We do know that Etta was the sister with the greater command of things artistic. She had also made all the Cone painting purchases up until 1922. And she had been the one to take a chance on unknown artists just after the turn of the century.

But the dominant Claribel, usurping Etta's claim to the territory, came to be recognized as "the collector" of the pair. The two were most often referred to as "Dr. Claribel and her sister, Miss Etta Cone," as if the younger were a shadowy companion who followed her powerful sister into the habit of collecting. But Etta, despite years of independence, did not protest. She assumed once again her submissive role when dealing with Claribel's strong spirit. She "became like a voiceless bird" next to the commanding doctor.

In the past, the Cones had frequently mingled socially

with the artists whose work they bought. Etta made her purchases directly from them, which was, for her, a significant part of the charm of collecting. But now that Matisse had risen in the world to a position of fame, fortune, and representation, the Cone sisters, for the most part, were forced to make their Matisse painting purchases from the two brothers who owned the Bernheim-Jeune Gallery.

The Cones must have been even more of an enigma in 1922 Paris than they had been in 1906. The Jazz Age now gripped the city. Women's liberation had finally come to fashion—the French designer Paul Poiret banished the corset. The cosmetic industry was in full swing, selling powders and creams and colors to heighten the cheeks and eyes of women. And women were taking their long hair out of top knots and buns and cutting it off—the bob was all the rage.

Hemlines went up, necklines dipped down, women bound their breasts to make their profiles long and slim, and the female faces deemed most appealing were small with tiny lips. The new woman of the 1920s—the one considered the most fashionable—was the very opposite of the Cone sisters.

True, at their age, they were no longer expected to follow fashion trends. But to those trends they made absolutely no concessions. Judging by their unchanged appearances, they were utterly unaware of the much-changed world.

Though the well-heeled Cone sisters were certainly welcome guests, they must have struck an odd chord on entering Bernheim-Jeune. The two sisters were almost the same height, with Claribel slightly the wider of the two. Standing side by side, they appeared to be an enormous, almost square block of black cloth. They were described as "colorful in a stodgy way; stout, staunch, individualistic ... their swelling bodices buttoned up to the neck, their full skirts sweeping the floor and hiding buttoned shoes."

To the two brothers who owned the gallery, the Cone sisters must have appeared in the doorway as apparitions from the previous century. But these particular ghosts were a gallery owner's dream. They wanted Matisses, and they wanted them in quantity. On July 24, Claribel marched back into the gallery and purchased a Matisse oil painting, *Le pot d'etain* (The Pewter Jug), for the vast sum of 20,000 francs.

⤺

The sisters did not entirely abandon the artists for the galleries. On July 14, Claribel posed for a portrait by Picasso. The key detail surrounding the sitting—whether Picasso suggested it or Claribel—is unclear. Also unclear is where the event took place. From July to the end of September, Picasso was staying at a villa at the Forêt de Fontainebleau, but he most likely met Claribel in town during a visit to his studio off the Champs Elysées.

Claribel, having not visited a Picasso studio since the Bâteau Lavoir, would have been much struck by the difference between his opulent new setting and his previous abode. In fact, the differences are evident even in Picasso's elegant pencil drawing of Claribel. It is clean, simple, and without any of the haunting shadows associated with poverty that dominated his portrait of Gertrude. Claribel sat on a comfortable wooden armchair with her feet on a pillow, looking like a contented lady of means (and a little like an older, female version of Oscar Wilde).

Picasso, still in the midst of his return to classicism, considered Claribel to be a perfect subject. The Claribel he drew, in ruffles and pendant, was every bit a queen—a figure large enough, in bulk and in spirit, to do justice to his style. Picasso wanted 1,000 francs for the drawing. Claribel hoisted up her skirt, found a pocket in her petticoat, counted out the notes, and handed them to the artist. The woman who had been mistaken for European royalty certainly had an uninhibited American way of transacting business.

Sometime that summer, the two sisters also met up with Matisse, whose schedule put him in Nice in the winter and Paris in the summer. It must have been a joyous reunion, especially for Etta, who had not seen her favorite artist for a decade. Matisse and the two sisters had all expanded across the middle, and gone at least partly gray on top, but they were as exuberant and as full of life as they had been in 1912.

Matisse had much good news for them, including word that the French government had finally purchased one of his paintings. He had settled into a luxurious life of ease and creativity, one that had hardly seemed possible in 1905 when he considered abandoning painting because he was so poor. Now Matisse, and by reflection his paintings, began to "rejoice in the comforts of life that the French cultivate with such care." His subjects—flowers, textiles, objects, and women—struck a special chord with the Cone sisters, unlike any they had with other artists.

Years later, during an exhibit of the Cone collection at New York's Knoedler Gallery, a critic for the *Herald Tribune* wrote: "If it is true, as has been claimed, that the pictures a man buys are, even within the limitations of his education and pocketbook, a most revealing index to his inner self, then the Cone sisters of Baltimore present one of the most fascinating paradoxes in the history of American art collecting . . . Behind the monumental, forbidding, blue stocking exteriors of the two must have beat warm, expansive, even hedonistic hearts."

The critic was right. Despite their austere exteriors, Etta and Claribel Cone were sensualists. They had both suffered —Etta, ill health and loneliness, and Claribel, deprivation

and war. And at the end of it all, they set out together to surround themselves with things rich and deep and beautiful.
Their demands were not great. They did not join the throbbing masses dancing until dawn, or the sexual revolution
boisterously upending tradition in Paris.

They looked for the sensuous life in quiet ways. The
Cones stayed in only the best places and ate only the finest
food. They drank cocktails and sherry and wine in the Lutetia's
glorious salon, and when they smoked cigarettes, one of the
sisters marveled over the fanciful figures the smoke made
in the air, while the other blew her smoke into rings. They
delected over the details of life no matter how minute. In the
weave of a piece of fabric, for example, they saw a rich history
that others missed.

Matisse's paintings were exactly suited to the Cone sisters' taste—they met their every criterion. His canvases were
intricate, potent, abundant, ripe, and sexual. His works gave
a vibrant voice to the sisters' inner lives.

Matisse was under contract with Bernheim-Jeune to sell his
paintings through the gallery, but the contract allowed him to
sell his bronzes directly from his studio. The Cone sisters bought
four bronzes from the years 1905 to 1908. These Matisse purchases indicate the course their collecting career would take.
They could rarely buy one of anything—no matter how costly.
In fact, at some point during the summer of 1922, the sisters purchased duplicates of each of Matisse's four bronze sculptures.
They might have been considering how they would split the
collection if they ever parted—or they simply might have felt
compelled to buy and own more than one.

～

As planned, Etta left Paris with Miss Kaufman that summer for side trips through Europe. If she worried about leav-

ing Claribel behind in Paris, she needn't have. Claribel wrote to Etta, then in Brest, that she was having the time of her life shopping. The Empress was busy roaming galleries, antique shops, and department stores in search of objects that had come to be her most cherished companions. Her purse was open, and she was spending freely. Etta complained to Gertrude that she and her sister were "being drowned in things."

Claribel later said, "As a matter of fact ... I didn't even know that the things I had could be called a collection until people began to use the term in talking to me about them. Ever since I was a small girl and picked up all the shells I could find, reveling in their color and in their forms, I've been acquiring beautiful things. I've picked them up here and there all over the world, some of them at first hand, some from dealers. I took beauty where I found it ... ."

Before the two sisters left Paris that fall, they arranged for Michael Stein to send back to Baltimore the many items they had purchased. From that point forward, he was to serve as a kind of manager for them on that side of the ocean, in the same way their brothers functioned on the other side, in America.

The Cone sisters had grown increasingly close to Michael and Sally Stein, in part because the attraction of the rue de Fleurus had faded. Leo was living in Italy, and Gertrude's social life was designed to achieve just one end—"the furtherance of her literary career." *Vanity Fair* magazine ran a picture of Gertrude that summer. She was trying desperately to get published in the *Atlantic Monthly*.

But Michael Stein's services as the Cone business manager in Paris were not entirely altruistic. The Stein family was short of cash, and the Cones had it in abundance. In the 1920s, a new relationship developed between the two families—

whenever the Steins needed money, they sold the Cones a piece of art or furniture. For both parties to the transactions, it was better than going through a dealer. The Steins received cash immediately, and the Cones picked up pieces from collectors whose taste they considered impeccable.

The full evidence of the Cone sisters' 1922 shopping spree could be measured—in seven crates shipped to Baltimore. In them were fifty-seven works of art, including six Matisse paintings, four Matisse bronzes, and twenty-two Matisse lithographs. Also in the crates were one Picasso painting, one Picasso drawing, two Picasso engravings, and one Renoir etching.

"My dear Etta," Michael Stein wrote. "There are seven cases in all. 1-2-3-4 are Claribel's, 5-6-7 are yours ... I had made out the paper of declaration 'Purchased in various antique shops in Paris during the summer of 1922.' That would not do so I made out names as near as I could remember."

On the tariff declaration, Michael Stein wrote, "I further declare that it is impracticable to obtain declarations from the artists as they are either dead or their whereabouts are unknown to me." Stein knew the names and the whereabouts of the artists perfectly well, but he saved the Cones aggravation and money by pretending their crates did not contain a single twentieth century art treasure.

⌒

Back in Baltimore, the sisters anxiously awaited the arrival of their crates. That winter was the first of many spent arranging their homes to accommodate the new items, and showing mystified visitors what they had bought.

Soon Claribel's small apartment on the sixth floor was full, but rather than throw anything out, she took a second apartment. The expansive "museum" she established on the eighth floor near Etta's apartment had at least seven rooms—all needed and used—to house her acquisitions.

⌒

The world outside their Marlborough apartment windows had changed. The streets previously disturbed only by the clatter of horse-drawn carriages were now noisy with the roar of cars and honking horns. The houses in the neighborhood, once urban palaces for the city's wealthiest families, were slowly being broken up into multiple-family homes. The German-Jewish community was moving out.

Prohibition, which was aimed at boosting society's morals, had accomplished just the opposite. A few blocks to the west, Druid Hill Avenue—which W.E.B. Du Bois had called one of the finest black streets in the United States—was now considered a vice district. Nearby Pennsylvania Avenue, which showcased some of the best black musical talent in America, was home to speakeasies, prostitution, and cocaine.

The Cones' small neighborhood was changing, but the sisters seemed unaffected by the drift. They focused increasingly on their treasures. Each spring, after a winter of securing their European acquisitions, they set out to buy more.

# Paris, 1923-1924

*I know a large part of myself is in the clothes I choose to wear. I've a great respect for things! One's self—for other people—is one's expression of one's self; and one's house, one's furniture, one's garments, the books one reads, the company one keeps—these things are all expressive.*

—Henry James, *The Portrait of a Lady*, 1881

*I*n the spring of 1923, having returned to Paris with her sister, Claribel Cone faced a new challenge—filling her museum back home. Whether unconsciously or by design, the Cone apartments in Baltimore began to look like the Stein homes in Paris. The two sisters covered their walls with paintings, and furnished their rooms with exotic pieces and antiques in the same manner their friends had when they began their collections in 1905.

But the Cones had a long way to go before their walls were as full of art as the rue de Fleurus or even Mike and Sally's at the rue Madame. The sisters were arguably limited in what they could buy. Their Baltimore apartments were comprised of tight, intimate rooms. Thus, theoretically, they could only purchase smaller pieces. And what art they did hang on the walls competed for space with their many chests of drawers, cabinets, bookcases, and buffets.

The sisters, however, felt largely unencumbered by these limitations. They easily found, and bought, pieces to suit them, regardless of size.

In June 1923, back at Bernheim-Jeune, they purchased six more Matisse oil paintings costing a total of 73,500 francs, or about $4,000 (in 1923 dollars). Etta's purchases tended toward lovely domestic portraits: *Violiniste et fillette, Divertissement* (Violinist and Young Girl) of 1921; *Jeune femme a la fenêtre, soleil couchant* (Young Woman at the Window, Sunset) from the same year; and *Femme au pull-over rayé, violin sur la table* (Woman in Striped Pullover, Violin on the Table), which Matisse finished in 1922.

But Claribel struck out for something bolder. In addition to two still lives, she purchased the Cones' first Matisse odalisque, *Odalisque debout, tambourin dans la main droite* (Standing Odalisque, Tambourine in her Right Hand), which Matisse painted in 1922. The painting dripped with sensuality. In some quarters, it was even called pornographic.

Its subject aside, the odalisque was a daring purchase merely because it was a Matisse. In 1922, the Detroit Institute of Arts became the first American museum to purchase a Matisse. The acquisition was considered so audacious that the museum released a bulletin assuring visitors the artist was "wholesome, human, sane and well ordered."

Matisse, now fifty-four, called his odalisques "the bounty of a happy nostalgia, a lovely, vivid dream." But they were also the result of a very tangible reality. In 1920, a local movie agency had begun supplying Matisse with nubile young actresses to serve as models for his erotic canvases. More than once, models with whom he conducted affairs surfaced later in lustful images. But his new series of odalisques, painted in a type of bedroom setting, had a bordello feeling that was undeniably carnal.

Matisse's friend, the French poet, novelist, and journalist Louis Aragon, said Matisse's nearsightedness forced him to sit close to his models—sometimes so close that his knee pressed against their knee. In one photograph, Matisse is shown with one hand touching the model while he worked with the other.

But it was not entirely trouble with his eyes that brought the painter so near his subject. "When I paint or draw," said Matisse, "I feel the need for close communication with the object that inspires me ... A cake seen through a store window does not make you salivate as much as when, having entered the store, you have your nose on top of it."

In Matisse's sculpture, the contact between artist and model went even further. Of one model, he said, "She was a pretty girl, a perfect model. I touched her body, my hands enveloped her forms, and I transmitted into clay the equivalent of my sensation."

Baltimore's nationally known columnist and critic, H. L. Mencken, wrote, " ... the truth is, as everyone knows, that the great artists of the world are never Puritans, and seldom even ordinarily respectable. No moral man—that is, moral in the Y.M.C.A. sense—has ever painted a picture worth looking at. ..."

Perhaps the Cone sisters shared that view, and ignored the rumors designed to tarnish the great artist's reputation. In any case, the sisters must have recognized in his works the intense sensuality they conveyed. The seemingly prudish pair bought their favorite artist's new paintings. In fact, in the summer of 1923, they bought art only by Matisse.

In July, they purchased two more Matisse oil paintings. Etta bought a Matisse from 1899 that Leo had owned, and in September she purchased her first odalisque, *Odalisque debout reflétée dans la glace* (Standing Odalisque Reflected in a Mirror) from 1923—for 19,000 francs. The painting was of a bare-breasted woman with a fleshy midriff, in pantaloons, facing full front—a sliver of her reflection in a mirror.

The Cones spent an estimated 121,500 francs on Matisse paintings—or about $6,700—during a single summer. The average American at the time earned about $760 a year.

In fact, the sisters, on a sped-up course of spending, didn't really know—and didn't much care—how much money they had. Periodically, though, they faced reality, realized they were running low, and wrote their brother Bernard, asking him to deposit more cash into their accounts in Greensboro.

In July, Etta set off for Venice with Miss Kaufman and left Claribel to her Parisian pursuits. Claribel detailed her every move in voluminous letters that she sent to Etta's Italian hotel, where they were dutifully kept. But Etta's responses were not saved, so the existing correspondence is a monologue by Claribel on the people she saw and the things she bought in her sister's absence.

The letters show a remarkably brisk schedule for an enormous woman of fifty-eight. In the afternoon of July 23rd, for example, she lunched with Pierre and Margot Matisse, the artist's children, took a taxi up to Clichy and bought a rug, attended the opera, took a car drive, and then signed up for a trial Berlitz course.

On July 24th, after lunch with Michael Stein, she visited antique shops. And on July 25th she shopped, causing a stir in the various stores she visited, which were most pleased to have her business, but must have wondered at the ways of this strange American woman.

"Went to Ararat's . . . Ararat is away—but madame was there—they had nothing new—but because I got her to upset things a bit I bought a Persian dagger and a Japanese gold lacquer inro ... From there I went to the Bon Marché and bought a few things—I took my nice interpreter to the purse department, sent up for my old friend Mr. Dupré at the head of the purse work rooms—asked for my salesman who speaks English—Mons.

"Just—and when all the clerks and the head of the purse department, and the head of the working room and the interpreter were surrounding me—I told them what I wanted— and they all smiled and seemed glad to see me and remembered me quite well—because I had caused them so much trouble last year ... they all seemed awfully glad to see me come back—strange to say—I suppose it was an evidence that their work gave satisfaction to one so 'difficile.'"

Bon Marché's sales staff undoubtedly found her difficult. But Claribel's imperial manner and free spending combined to make her a charming and valued customer. She was becoming even more of a character than she had been before. Her more marked eccentricities made her all the more flamboyant.

She ordered silk stockings and handkerchiefs by the dozen and had them monogrammed and numbered so she could rotate their usage. She wore two extra blouses under a new dress during fittings at the dressmaker to make sure it would be roomy enough. She had over 120 Liberty scarves on approval at her hotel room at any given time. And once, when she saw Miss Kaufman wearing a sweater she admired, instructed Miss Kaufman to buy her a dozen just like it.

Claribel ordered multiples of everything—three sets of shoes, three copies of a book. Her brother Sydney once found her sick in bed with three thermometers in her mouth.

In Paris, Claribel surrounded herself with things—and people, if she chose. But the people, always peripheral, mainly served as facilitators in her quest to acquire things. "I find my chief objection to all these people is not that they have faults (which all of us have of course) but that they and their personalities get in my way," she wrote Etta. In fact, her misanthropy was an accepted part of her personality.

During a drive together, Gertrude asked Claribel whether she liked Paris, to which she replied, "Very much."

"And do you still like the Germans better than the French?" Gertrude asked.

"They are all human beings to me," said Claribel.

"Which means that you do not care much for either of them!" Gertrude replied.

⤸

When the sisters returned to Baltimore that autumn, they were struck again by the meager cultural life of their native city. Compared to Paris, Baltimore surely seemed a deadly dull and backward place. It was not merely a relative thing, either. A.D. Emmart, then a literary and art critic for the Baltimore *Sun*, described the city as "sedentary, uneventful and ingloriously safe." He called it "middle aged in spirit."

Baltimore was not cosmopolitan enough to support even one large continental restaurant. It had just three book stores, and only two second-hand bookshops. The opera season listed just three nights. And the director of Baltimore's only art school called modern art "poppycock."

To that environment, the Cone sisters retreated for the dreary months of winter, which in Baltimore meant a steady cold rain that only occasionally turned to snow, and, most of all, a bleak grayness from November to April.

The sisters might have become involved in an important project that winter—the Baltimore Museum of Art was just opening its doors for the first time. The new museum, one would have thought, would have been anxious for the kind of publicity it could receive by exhibiting the budding Cone collection. But while the museum was happy to receive the sisters' donations of money, it was uninterested in their art. The sisters' collection, concluded museum officials, was too avant-garde for the provincial city.

Their fellow Baltimoreans saw the Cone sisters as alien creatures—eccentric if not downright crazy. A Maryland doctor wrote, "The very few Baltimoreans who knew or had heard of them were apt to regard the sisters as a single legendary figure" who collected "disturbing" modern art in large amounts under the guidance of "somewhat questionable" bohemians— Gertrude and Leo Stein.

Miss Kaufman relayed to the sisters some of the stories she heard about them, but rather than get angry, they laughed. They were unique—as unique as the art that hung on their walls.

Claribel began to drape her body in her collection. She wore numerous colored shawls, exotic jewelry around her neck, and a silver skewer in her hair, which she also used as a letter opener. At private dinner parties, she wore a red velvet gown trimmed in gold lace. In public, she and Etta always wore dark floor-length skirts with black silk petticoats equipped with pockets that held valuables.

Etta did not top off her dress with the exotic, as Claribel did, and when the two were spotted in Baltimore at the symphony, which Claribel attended as often as three times a week, their appearances contrasted sharply. In fact, those differences told their stories at a glance. The majestic and bejeweled Claribel sat dozing a few rows in front of Etta, taking up two seats—one for herself and one for her possessions—while the retiring younger sister sat quietly behind her in a single seat, always in the shadow of her older sibling.

Etta's life still revolved around her older sister and her younger brother, Fred. She ran her own household, as well as theirs, arranging all their meals, and serving as hostess whenever guests visited.

As recreational pursuits, Etta lavished time on her art collection and read. Every Wednesday at 11 a.m., she played piano with a woman named Cecilia Gaul, a former Franz Liszt student debilitated by a fear of performing. It was a quiet but full life, and yet it is not clear if it satisfied Etta.

Claribel did what Claribel had always done—busied herself with minutia. She carried around with her a palm-sized note pad, on which she wrote lists of things to do and things she had done. She noted what time she went to her own apartment on a given day, and how long she slept during an afternoon nap. She even wrote a note to herself that she should write herself a note. She did not use a key to enter Etta's apartment—she always rang the bell, most likely because it was easier than fumbling with the lock.

And her relations with her brother and sister were not always easy. She angered Etta by consistently arriving late for meals. On one of her note pads, Claribel recited the dialogue of a fight with Fred.

"Please do not get the book sticky, Fred."

"Damn it! Shut up!"

"Well, you are holding the honey very near the book."

"'Go to the devil,'" he replied before throwing honey, pencil, book, and paper on the floor and leaving the room in a rage. In summation, Claribel noted, "They did not break but made the floor sticky."

By the end of the long winter, in their increasingly cramped apartments, the sisters were eager to escape to Paris. The real question was why they had ever left France in the first place.

⌒

Paris had seen two significant marriages while Etta and Claribel were away in Baltimore. Mike and Sally's son, Allan, married a dancer named Yvonne. And Matisse's daughter Margot married the art historian Georges Duthuit. The Cone sisters were fond of both Allan and Margot. They had known the Stein boy since he was a child.

Margot Matisse, always attentive to the Cone sisters, sometimes worked as an intermediary between them and her father. Sometimes she designed frames for the Matisse pictures they bought. During the summer of 1924, Pierre Matisse, the artist's son, was also married, and the Cones fell in with the happy families during that summer of joy in Paris. In fact, the harmony of the season was only diminished by a letter from Gertrude at the end of June asking Etta to buy the manuscript for *Three Lives*, which Etta had typed nearly twenty years before.

"I want to tell you something a propos of the thing you mentioned in connection with the autographed *Three Lives* selling for $13," Gertrude said. "It seems that the latest passion of the art collectors in America is the buying of manuscripts ever since Quinn made such a success with Conrad and *Ulysses* manuscripts that he bought through the editors of the transatlantic.

"Some one has suggested my selling the manuscript of Three Lives for a thousand dollars, I don't suppose that you want to pay any such price for a manuscript but since you had a connection with that manuscript I want to tell you about it before I consider doing anything. I think it's kind of foolish but I wouldn't want you to think that I would sell it to any one else without telling you about it first, *a bientot* Gtude."

Gertrude, needing money, was trying to coax Etta into parting with some of hers. When the Steins were short of money, the Cones had bought more than a few paintings from them. But, for Etta, this particular proposition was different. It crossed the line into indelicacy. She felt hurt, being offered—and at such a high price—the very thing she had typed lovingly and without charge. Etta, who referred to the manuscript as "partly" hers, now saw a $1,000 price attached to it. The incident was evidence of just how far apart Gertrude and Etta had grown.

To be sure, Gertrude was now a "famous personality"—just as she and Picasso had fantasized when they were younger—and had a habit of rejecting old friends who could no longer be of any use to her.

But Etta's estrangement from Gertrude was also Alice's work to some extent. She was territorial when it came to Gertrude, frequently and purposefully driving away those who had had intimate relationships with Gertrude. She would eventually drive off Hemingway, too. And she had already cut off Gertrude's American friend Mabel Dodge. Alice could easily vanquish Etta.

Etta responded a day later to Gertrude's letter. "I do indeed appreciate your kind thought of me in realizing my personal pride and interest in your *Three Lives*," she wrote. "I simply have to face the truth and that is, that I am seriously considering putting all I can spare of what I have left of my income into a Renoir painting. This, with other expenses somewhat heavier than usual are handicapping me a bit this year."

In fact, Etta did not buy a Renoir that year, but she could not come out directly and say she was hurt by Gertrude's proposition—though it was common knowledge among her close associates that she was.

She would have been even more hurt had she understood the duplicity of the Stein family's relations with the Cones. Michael Stein, who had gained the sisters' utmost trust, also

$\mathcal{E}$tta Cone began collecting in March 1898 by authorizing a bidder to use $300 to buy as many Theodore Robinson paintings as he could at an estate sale in New York. Her money bought five paintings.

*Theodore Robinson, Mother and Child, mid-1880s, oil on canvas. BMA Collection.*

*c. 1895. BMA Collection.*

*H*erman and Helen Cone moved their eight children to Baltimore in 1871 from Tennessee and made their home on Eutaw Place, among the city's wealthiest families.

*M*oses Cone, the eldest of the Cone siblings, was called the "denim king" in the press because the Cone mills produced the world's largest supply of denim.

*BMA Collection.*

*C*easar Cone began the Cone Export and Commission Company with his brother Moses, and gave Claribel and Etta an annual income for life.

*BMA Collection.*

$\mathcal{E}$tta Cone played the piano throughout her life and used the medium of music to establish some of her closest friendships.

c. 1900. *BMA Collection.*

$\mathcal{I}$n 1901, Etta Cone, her cousin Hortense Guggenheimer (not pictured), and her friend Harriet Clark traveled to Europe on the first of Etta's many trips abroad.

*BMA Collection.*

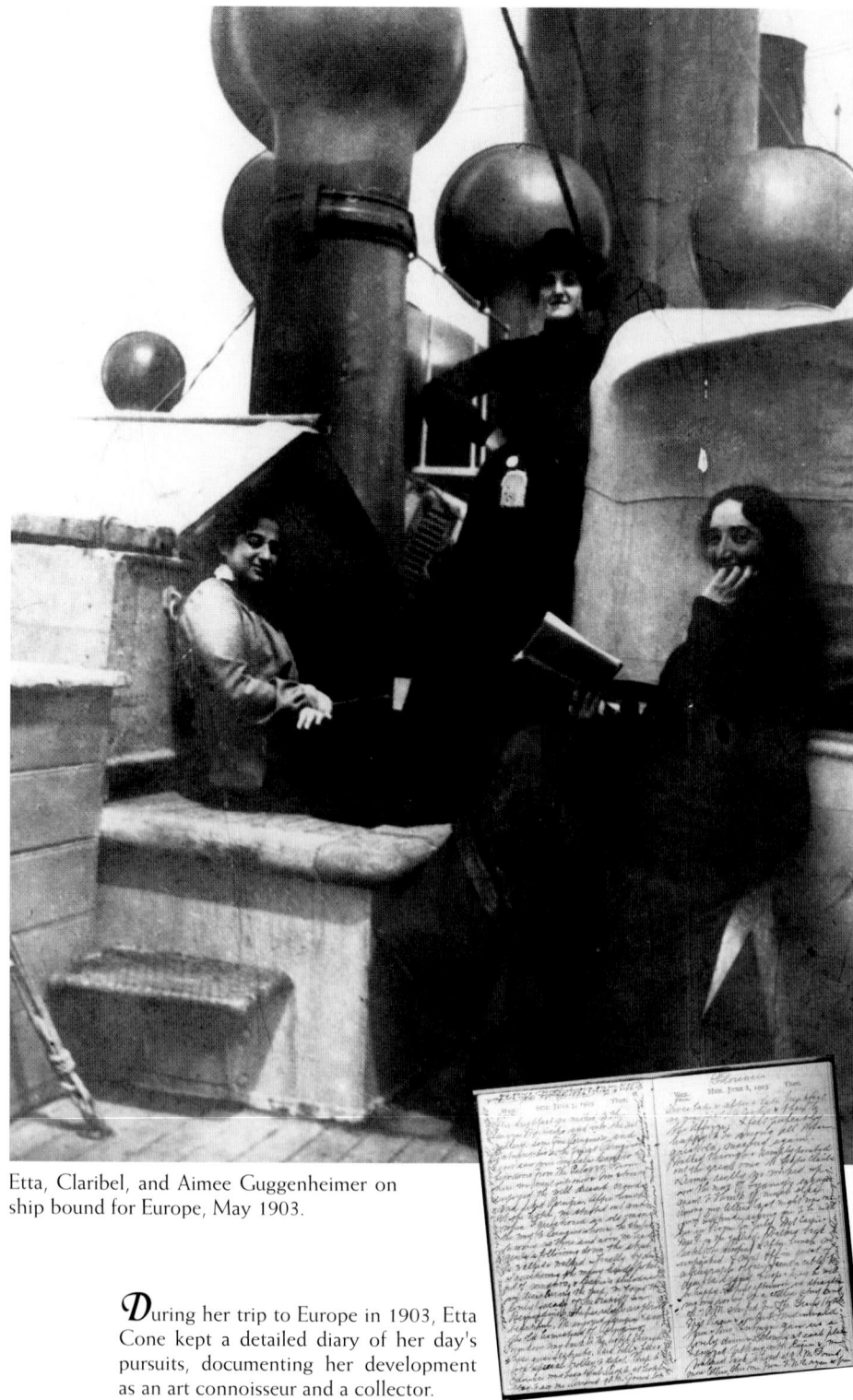

Etta, Claribel, and Aimee Guggenheimer on
ship bound for Europe, May 1903.

*D*uring her trip to Europe in 1903, Etta
Cone kept a detailed diary of her day's
pursuits, documenting her development
as an art connoisseur and a collector.

*Florence, 1903. BMA Collection.*

$\mathcal{G}$ertrude Stein, Etta Cone, and Claribel Cone (left to right) met in Italy in 1903 during the first of the sisters' many trips abroad together.

$\mathcal{M}$ichael Stein (right) took care of his younger brother Leo and sister Gertrude after the death of their parents, providing them with a modest income for life through the sale of their father's railroad franchise. The three eventually settled in Paris, Leo and Gertrude at the rue de Fleurus, and Michael and his wife Sally around the corner on the rue Madame, early 1906.

$\mathcal{L}$eo Stein introduced Etta Cone to the new artists in Paris in 1905, a period when one historian said Leo was "possibly the most discerning connoisseur and collector of 20th century painting in the world."

*M*ichael Stein and his wife Sally were among the first Americans to support Henri Matisse, filling the walls of their Paris apartment with his works. It was Sally Stein who introduced Etta Cone to Matisse. *Left to right: Michael, Sally, Matisse, Allan Stein, and Hans Purrmann, late 1907.*

*BMA Collection.*

*M*oses Cone and his wife Bertha accompanied Etta and Claribel on a world tour that took them to Egypt, China, Turkey, Greece, and India. During the trip, the Cone sisters began building their textile collection, which was considered at one point the second most important in the world.

India, 1907. *BMA Collection.*

Claribel trying on Near Eastern robes, about 1903.

BMA Collection.

During a visit to North Carolina in June 1908, Etta Cone received a letter from Gertrude Stein in Paris that contained a self-portrait by Picasso. Etta declared, "I love Picasso and have him & his full tummy before me always..."

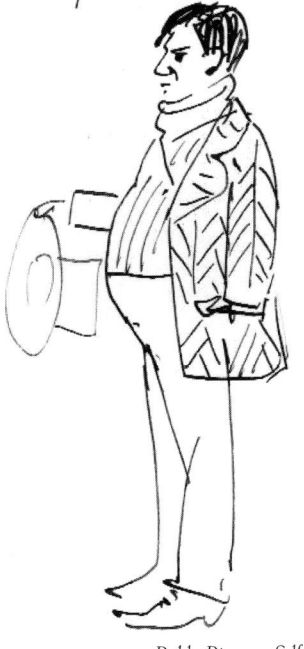

Pablo Picasso, Self-Portrait (Bonjour Mlle Cone), 1907, pen and ink on paper. BMA Collection.

c. 1915-1916. BMA Collection.

Claribel, living in Munich during World War One, thrilled at being mistaken for royalty as she roamed the great city.

Gelatin Silver print. BMA Collection.

Alice B. Toklas (left) and Gertrude Stein, rue de Fleurus, Paris, 1922.

*G*ertrude and Alice lived at the rue de Fleurus, which at the turn-of-the-century was the center of the radical in art, but after World War One primarily attracted a crowd interested in writing.

Birth Place of Marechal JOFFRE at Rivesaltes april 1917

*1917. BMA Collection.*

Alice B. Toklas and Gertrude Stein spent part of World War One delivering aid in France in a car they called "Auntie."

*Claribel* returned to Europe after the war with a mission— to devote her life to collecting.

*BMA Collection.*

Claribel, whom Picasso had called "The Empress," posed for a portrait by the artist in July 1922. When it was time to pay him, she hoisted up her skirt and pulled banknotes from a hidden pocket.

*Pablo Picasso, Dr. Claribel Cone, 1922, pencil on paper. BMA Collection.*

$\mathcal{E}$tta Cone purchased her first Matisse painting just weeks after meeting the artist for the first time in January 1906.

*Henri Matisse, Port de Collioure, 1906, watercolor on paper. BMA Collection.*

$\mathcal{T}$he painting Etta Cone purchased in 1925 (opposite page) is considered the most magnificent of Matisse's 1924 interiors, and remained Etta's favorite Matisse painting throughout her life.

*Henri Matisse,*
*Interieur, fleurs et perruches,*
*1924, oil on canvas.*
*BMA Collection.*

$\mathcal{E}$tta purchased her first odalisque in 1923. It was a daring painting for even a male art collector because Matisse's paintings were considered by some to be nothing short of pornographic.

*Henri Matisse, Odalisque debout refletée dans la glace, 1923, oil on canvas. BMA Collection.*

*Paul Cézanne, Mont Sainte-Victoire Seen from the Bibemus Quarry, c. 1897, oil on canvas. BMA Collection.*

𝒥n 1925, Claribel purchased the painting for $18,860—10 times the annual salary for an average American worker that year, and the most she ever paid for a work of art. The painting has been referred to as the most important in the Cone Collection.

*Henri Matisse, Nu bleu ("Souvenir de Biskra"), 1907, oil on canvas. BMA Collection.*

Claribel Cone purchased the painting that was considered so outrageous it was burned in effigy in Chicago in 1913. It was still considered daring when she bought the painting at a Paris auction in 1926.

$O$n Sept. 20, 1929, Claribel Cone purchased this painting during a stay at Lausanne. The work, with its subdued tones and still imagery, was an unusual choice for a collector who loved virility in art. Claribel died the day she bought it, at age 65.

*Gustave Courbet, The Shaded Stream at Le Puits Noir, c. 1860-1865, oil on canvas. BMA Collection.*

*T*here is some indication Etta Cone purchased from Gertrude Stein's collection this Picasso painting shortly after Claribel Cone died. It would have spoken to Etta's mood following the loss of her closest friend and relative.

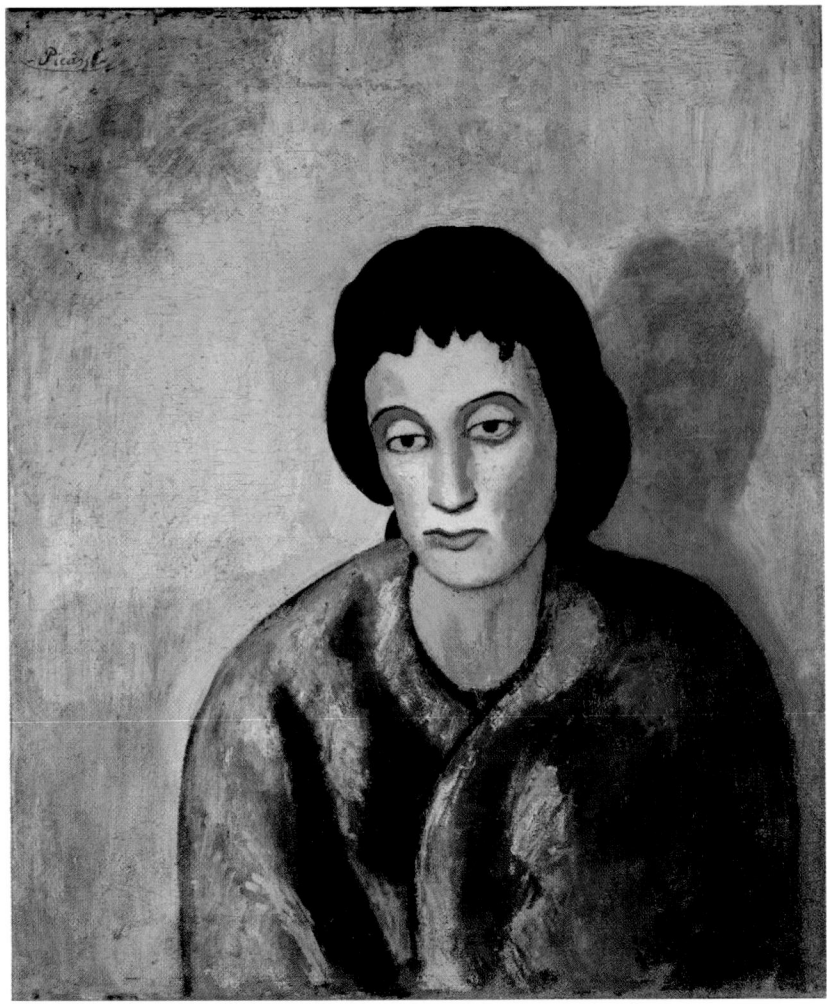

*Pablo Picasso, Femme aux franges, 1902, oil on canvas. BMA Collection.*

*Henri Matisse, Le robe tilleul, 1929-31, oil on canvas. BMA Collection.*

*H*enri Matisse surprised Etta Cone in Nice in 1933 by having a model stage a performance of the painting Etta had purchased the year before. One relative said the surprise left Etta "bubbling like a schoolgirl."

$\mathcal{E}$tta Cone purchased the painting most often referred to as "The Pink Nude" in 1936, possibly as a counterpart to Claribel's "Blue Nude." Matisse gave Etta 22 photos documenting the development of the painting.

*Henri Matisse, Grand nu couche, 1935, oil on canvas. BMA Collection.*

*Pablo Picasso, Allan Stein, 1906, gouache. BMA Collection.*

𝓔tta Cone's collection of French art began in 1905 when she purchased some Picasso drawings for a few dollars. It ended in 1949 with the purchase of a Picasso work from that period for $15,000. But she did not live to see the final piece make its way to the Cone Collection. She died before its arrival.

$\mathcal{E}$tta purchased a Matisse self-portrait from the artist during her summer visit to Europe in 1937. Its style was not unlike portraits Matisse had completed of Etta and Claribel Cone three years earlier.

*Henri Matisse, Self-Portrait, 1937, charcoal and estompe on paper. BMA Collection.*

$\mathcal{W}$hen Henri Matisse visited Etta Cone in 1930, he agreed to do a portrait of her late sister Claribel—and also one of Etta. He worked on the project for three years, developing the sisters' characters on paper in four drawings of Claribel and six of Etta.

*Henri Matisse, Etta Cone, 1931-1934, Charcoal or crayon on paper. BMA Collection.*

*Henri Matisse, Dr. Claribel Cone, 1931-1934, pencil or charcoal on paper. BMA Collection.*

*Henri Matisse, Poesies de Stephane Mallarmé, 1932.
BMA Collection.*

*A*t Matisse's request, Etta
Cone purchased in 1933 the
original drawings, printed and
rejected copper plates, three
proof volumes, and the signed
first copy of the printed edition
of his illustrated book, *Poesies de
Stephane Mallarmé.*

*O*ther original drawings from Matisse's signed, illustrated book, *Poesies de Stephane Mallarmé. BMA Collection.*

After her sister's death, Etta Cone focused on building a collection of modern French art, which she kept in her Baltimore apartment.

*Baltimore, 1930s. BMA Collection.*

In December 1930, Henri Matisse visited Etta Cone at her Baltimore apartment. It was the first time he had seen his paintings and sculpture in her home. He was quoted later as saying it was the perfect setting for his work.

*December 17-18, 1930. BMA Collection.*

*T*he Cone sisters' Baltimore apartments held a treasure in modern art, textiles, and jewelry. Clockwise, from top left: Front room in Claribel Cone's Apt. 8B; front back room in Claribel Cohen's Apt. 8B; Etta Cone's Apt. 8D; study in Etta Cone's Apt. 8D.

*BMA Collection.*

acted—without disclosure—as an agent for Gertrude and Alice in cajoling the Cones out of their money.

Shortly after Etta refused to buy Gertrude's manuscript, Michael wrote Gertrude that he would try to "work" Etta "for MSS of the 3 lives." In another case he wrote Alice, "The Cones came last night & Sally at once got busy for Gertrude. She has sold 9000 francs worth without the Favre pictures. Pretty swifty as Allan would say. . . ."

For all their eccentricities, the Cones were loyal, devoted friends and would have been shocked to think that the Steins, especially Michael and Sally, were anything less. In letters, Claribel described them as family. In fact, Claribel scolded Etta in a letter that fall, holding up the Steins as models of excellent behavior.

"You train people to take you pretty much for granted and they count—not what you do in your favor—but what you do not do against you," she wrote. "The Steins are an example of a principle I have observed—the people who do the most for you are always the people who evidence most pleasure in little attentions you show them."

Claribel even took into account Michael Stein's supposedly delicate sensibilities when considering whether to invite him along to see George Bernard Shaw's *Mrs. Warren's Profession,* a play about prostitution. "I am not quite sure," she concluded, "but that the play is a bit too *'intime,'* shall we say naughty, for Mike to see."

In truth, the Cone sisters never understood the Steins. Claribel was too disinterested in her fellow human beings to recognize their scheming. Etta was not shrewd enough.

# Lausanne, 1926-1929

*Now that I stop to reason about it, it is silly foolishness this*
*collecting of things! ... But it must have some solid foundation ...*
*deep in the hearts of people—for look at the thousands who are*
*moved by the same impulse. It is the craving for beauty that is such*
*a vital function of the human soul. Or perfection—some say that*
*is one way of finding the path to god. Is it?*
— Claribel Cone, in a letter to Etta Cone, Sept. 2, 1924


*W*hat had started so long ago as an interesting pastime
had become, for Etta, a high-stakes career. The same was true
of Claribel. The two took advantage of their long winter
months in Baltimore to study the paintings in their own collection, attend lectures on aesthetics, and teach themselves
art history by reading the hundreds of volumes that became
part of their vast library. Michael and Sally Stein continued to
whisper suggestions, trying to steer them toward one artist or
another—or toward something their own family had to sell.

And artists in search of patrons increasingly sought to
woo the sisters. But though they were sometimes taken in by
the efforts, the character of the collection belonged to no
one but the Cones. They became almost one person—single-
minded in the pursuit of art.

Each of their prime qualities was reflected in the collection. The strength of the larger-than-life Claribel showed itself in the bold works she bought, whereas Etta's gentleness and timidity were evident in her choices. Together, their collection worked like the rarest of marriages, which combines the strengths and weaknesses of each partner to produce a better whole. Either one of the sisters' collections alone would have been too much of one note. Their collections, when put together, created a special harmony.

Between 1925 and the fall of 1929, Etta and Claribel bought ninety works of art, firmly establishing their reputations as the world's most important contemporary collectors.

During the summer of 1925, the sisters made two of their most important purchases.

Ironically, none of the works purchased from the rue de Fleurus that summer turned out to be very important. A Marie Laurençin oil from 1908 called *Group of Artists* was costly at 10,000 francs, and important for its sentimental and historical value, rather than as a work of art. It was a portrait of Picasso, Fernande, Apollinaire, and Laurençin as they appeared during their Bâteau Lavoir days.

Claribel also picked up a bronze mask by Picasso. But otherwise she bought from Gertrude mostly insignificant works by the artist Louis Favre, a less talented version of Matisse whom Gertrude and the sisters had befriended.

Meanwhile, Claribel did not share her younger sister's antagonism toward Gertrude over the manuscript for *Three Lives*, and wanted to help pull Gertrude out of her financial quagmire. Records indicate she spent 19,000 francs that season, or about $1,000, on art she bought directly from Gertrude.

~

Claribel also made purchases outside the Stein fold, one of which has been referred to as the most important painting in the Cone collection. It was Cézanne's *La montagne Sainte-Victoire vue du Bibémus Quarry* (Mont Sainte-Victoire Seen from the Bibemus Quarry). At auction in Paris in late June 1925, it was purchased by Bernheim-Jeune during the Gangnat sale, possibly at Claribel's request. The elder Cone sister bought it from the gallery the day after the auction for 410,000 francs or, according to Claribel's calculations, $18,860.

The price of that single painting was more than ten times the average annual salary in America, and the most the Cones had ever paid for a work of art. It must have alarmed the Cone brothers, who watched Claribel and Etta seemingly fritter away their fortunes on art.

At one point, Claribel cabled the Cone Export and Commission Company in New York, "Bought pictures. Cable me through American Express, Paris, twenty-thousand dollars in Dollars. Claribel Cone, Hotel Lutetia." She diligently jotted down that the cable cost her 86 francs.

After 1922, Etta, in her art purchases, ventured away from Matisse only once, and that was in November of 1922, when she bought a Degas pastel. In 1925, she continued to remain faithful to her favorite artist by buying only two works—one a painting by Matisse's daughter Margot, and the other a work by Matisse himself, which she purchased from the artist's son Pierre. The painting was not as expensive as Claribel's Cézanne—a mere 70,000 francs—but Etta's latest Matisse, *Intérior, fleurs et perruches* (Interior, Flowers and Parakeets), was considered the largest and most magnificent of his 1924 interiors.

The painting was a burst of pattern and color—part still-life, part interior—that must have looked to Etta like an invitation into Matisse's world. A rope draws a curtain aside and beckons the viewer into the warm red glow of the artist's room. At almost 4 feet by 2 1/2 feet, the painting was thus far the largest the Cones had purchased, and would remain Etta's favorite Matisse painting throughout her collecting career.

The two major purchases of 1925 showed the sisters to be collectors with a discerning eye and a keen knowledge of their artists. Still, the Cones bought not what others considered important, but rather what they liked. If the two coincided, all the better. Their collecting was chiefly the combined act of love and liberation. It gave the sisters, and especially Etta, the freedom to act extravagantly and without censor on the large and brightly lit stage of the international art world.

Most of the players on that stage were men. Most women buying art were doing so with the help of advisers. But that would never do for the Cone sisters. They not only wanted to call the shots on what to buy, but they even wanted to dirty their hands in actual negotiations, and when possible, buy the work directly from the artist.

Pierre Matisse, the artist's son who became a picture dealer, said the Cones "very freely followed their own curiosity." He added, "Many collectors just buy a few things and let it go at that. But the Cone Collection was always developing. They were very enthusiastic, very consistent."

⌒

In 1926, Claribel turned sixty-two. Though she would not admit it, she was finding it increasingly difficult to cope in Paris with the rigors of her "second career"—as a shopper. She had begun to lose things. Her constant roaming around the enormous city, which seemed to grow increasingly congested each year, had become more difficult.

Claribel weighed about 270 pounds—Etta slightly less. They were so large they had to be pushed into taxicabs backwards. And so as not to be "posteriorly touched," they were helped into cabs with wooden sticks called "pusher hands," which were carved in the shape of a palm and fingers, and were kept in a special lace bag. Paris, they decided, was for the more portable, so that year they settled on an easier base for their summers abroad, in Lausanne, Switzerland.

It turned out that the brother of the artist Felix Vallotton (Paul) had a gallery in Lausanne and was eager to dote on the two sisters. They returned the favor by buying art through his shop. Claribel was entertained with gossip about the extra-marital romances of the artists—Bonnard's mistress, Felix Vallotton's flirtation with an American girl (which Claribel said made him more interesting than his paintings), and Swiss artist Ferdinand Hodler's decision to leave his consumptive wife and run off with her nurse.

The dinners and talks helped Claribel pass many a pleasant summer in Switzerland. She was convinced Vallotton cared for her and Etta like a brother. "He is really devoted to us, not only commercially," she wrote. While her trust may have been well-placed, he was certainly eager to do what he could for his two summer clients. After all, they spent thousands of dollars each year at his gallery.

Michael Stein learned of the relationship and saw a business opportunity missed. "My Dear Folks"—presumably he was writing to Gertrude and Alice—"While in Lausanne Claribel became quite intimate with Vallotton the picture dealer who is a brother of Felix and on that account it was possible to interest her in the portrait and I think she will take it for 10,000. Where is it? Is there any way I can get it?" The portrait in question was a not very remarkable 1907 painting by Felix Vallotton of Gertrude.

Michael Stein knew his mark all too well. Claribel purchased the painting from Gertrude in October 1926 for

10,000 francs. Like the Laurençin, the Vallotton portrait was of more interest for its personal and historical value—because it was *by* a friend, *of* a friend—than as a work of art. But if Michael hoped to unload more Vallottons on the Cone sisters, he would have to wait. Claribel ended that year's shopping season with a single purchase that established the Cone sisters as collectors to be reckoned with in the eyes of New York and Paris dealers.

The winter before, the sisters had hosted a rare visit to Baltimore by Matisse's son, Pierre. Though the art collection of the late John Quinn was heading to auction, Pierre said the estate's executors had asked him if any American collectors might be interested in the Matisse works before they went on the block. In fact, Pierre Matisse had made a special trip to Baltimore to act as an agent, in case the sisters wanted to buy any of the work. While flattered by the attention, the sisters rebuffed his efforts, much to his surprise, and he left without making a sale.

But in October, at the auction of Quinn's estate, Pierre found himself bidding against Claribel for one of the pieces Pierre had tried unsuccessfully to sell her that winter—Matisse's bold *Blue Nude*. The painting, first owned by Leo, and later purchased by Quinn, finally fell into Claribel's possession when Pierre kindly dropped out of the bidding. Michael Stein facilitated the purchase for Claribel, at a price of 120,760 francs.

The painting, though nearly twenty years old, was still considered grotesque and outrageous. If a male collector had purchased it, he would have been considered bold. But for a woman—especially a sixty-two-year-old woman dressed in Victorian garb—to claim the writhing nude as her own was more remarkable still. And, Claribel's *Blue Nude* also had something that neither Leo's nor Quinn's had had. Claribel alertly noticed that Matisse had never signed the painting. He cordially did so, in the lower right hand corner, at her request.

Claribel considered two points when purchasing a work of art: did it represent an artist's best style, and/or would it decorate her living room? Surely the *Blue Nude* would fall into the former category. It had been burned in effigy in 1913, and would never be mistaken for decoration. And yet when it was hung in the Marlborough amid the Cones' other paintings, it fit easily.

By the time the *Blue Nude* became part of the Cone collection, the two sisters' apartments had become more than a little crowded—with things. There were Renaissance and Queen Anne furnishings (mostly reproductions, which they bought thinking they were real), Oriental rugs, bronze sculptures, Persian cloths, Turkish scarves, African and Asian objects, boxes, and chests.

Some paintings were stacked. Etchings were piled in trunks and in a bathtub. Drawers held more treasures—fabrics and jewelry. And everywhere on the walls were paintings and drawings in their elaborate frames. The overall impression was not of a museum but of a home whose every article had a rich history. *Blue Nude* was only the latest story.

The sisters kept their purchases separate, Etta's in her apartment and Claribel's in her "museum," which Etta needed permission to show—Claribel's living quarters were completely off limits. In fact, no one but her nephew Sydney saw the place for years. He was hired to do secretarial work for Claribel—making four sets of all her records.

When he first entered her apartment, he was horrified by what he found. The furniture, trunks, books, magazines, and newspapers filled all available floor space—except for a trail to the bedroom so narrow that Claribel could navigate it only with difficulty. "She would complain that the dressmakers were not what they used to be," Sydney said. "But we suspected that her floor-length skirts over the several underskirts might have caught and torn on the sixth-floor apartment's trail."

In January 1927, Etta, sans Claribel, paid New York an extended art-hunting visit. While there, Etta received a letter from her sister, in Baltimore, that caused her concern. Claribel wrote about falling asleep "Oriental fashion" in a velvet night dress after pausing for a smoke on a Persian rug—with all the lights in her apartment burning. Without her there in Baltimore to keep an eye on Claribel, Etta worried, her older sister was apt to self-immolate. Claribel, for her part, knew she was a terrible burden to Etta, but didn't care. It was, she felt, her prerogative as an older sister and as a "personality"—and an aggressive personality at that.

Despite her worry, Etta continued her trip and stopped at several galleries in New York. Though impressed by a Van Gogh flower piece at Henry Reinhard, Etta had reservations about making the purchase, and must have voiced them in a letter to Claribel.

Claribel replied, "If I were considering putting $4,000 in a picture I should wish to see it several times before deciding to buy it—if it were for myself this is what I should say:—Van Gogh is very great—he was one of the biggest influences on Cézanne and certainly on Matisse—and many of the later men—everything that he has done is strong and virile (almost too virile sometimes)—and his paintings are attractive—I wonder whether he will remain 'the fashion' as long as I live—for he seems a bit less in the limelight than he was some years ago—so much for his name—

"But for the particular picture you have in mind of that I should say if it is pretty (which you say it is) attractive, and if it is decorative and pleases you—why care a darn what anybody else says of it ... and if it gives you a thrill why I guess the thing for you to do is to take it . . . a Van Gogh is not to be sneered at: a good Van Gogh is an addition to any collection."

Etta bought the piece, which Meier-Graefe confirmed was authentic. Years later, with the help of Theo Van Gogh's son, Vincent, she discovered to her dismay that the painting was a fake. Aside from purchasing some faux furniture, it was the only instance during the Cones' long collecting career that they fell victim to forgery.

In the 1920s, the sisters grew increasingly close to George Boas, a philosophy professor at Johns Hopkins University. When he first arrived in Baltimore, said Boas, he was "warned that of course I might visit the Cone collection if I wished but that its owners were beyond doubt mental cases."

He didn't heed the warning and came to know the sisters intimately. He said their home was a sort of refuge for a certain type of person who came to Baltimore but felt culturally adrift. For that traveler, said Boas, the Cone apartments felt like home.

"Though both Etta Cone and her sister Dr. Claribel had clear cut personalities, traits which were far from nebulous, and talents which could easily have brought them before the public, they both preferred the peace of their homes and the small confidences of their friends . . . They simply sat there and saw.

"They never used their pictures as a background for themselves, but submitted themselves entirely and persistently to their pictures. One went to see the Cone collection; one came away with a vivid image of two beautiful people."

The summer of 1927 saw the two American sisters yet again in Europe. But, as Americans, they were hardly alone. American tourists, taking advantage of France's near economic collapse and the strong dollar, were staging a second invasion of the country. The 1927 American Chamber of Commerce reported 15,000 Americans living in Paris that year, but the unofficial figure was closer to 40,000.

The "new American" was not the hero who had helped France defeat Germany in the first world war, but a brash and reckless visitor who used Paris as a playground. In fact, only a very select group of Americans was welcomed by the French. Among them that year was Charles Lindbergh, the shy solo pilot who proved New York was only thirty-three hours from Paris when he arrived by plane at La Bourget.

Etta and Claribel no doubt considered themselves closer to the Europeans than to the new generation of Americans tearing up the town. Claribel spoke of Americans as "a good natured crude people." The sisters would not be taken for that. The years had turned them into continental dowagers, equally comfortable in a number of countries, and concerned primarily with things cultural. For the Cone sisters, things cultural meant primarily art.

In June, they stopped in Paris, where Claribel picked up thirty-three pieces at the Bernheim-Jeune gallery, including four Matisse lithographs, four Van Gogh gravures, two Modigliani gravures, and two Picasso gravures.

At their next stop, Lausanne, Etta diversified her purchases, selecting works by Othon Coubine, Henri-Edmond Cross, Rodin, Degas, Vallotton, and Signac. Claribel bought an Odilon Redon, a Van Gogh, and an Egyptian bronze cat, which she found especially delightful because of the mystery surrounding its origin.

Claribel, still in the market for a Matisse, hinted that she was looking for one of his older pieces, something like the interior with parakeets that Etta had purchased a few years before. "If Matisse has something, I want one as brilliant as your lovely red interior—but Matisse has seen the heyday of his virility and I fear is toppling downward."

Etta would never voice such criticism of Matisse, but Claribel had her doubts. "It is a question how many artists of the post-impressionists group will be handed down to posterity as famous," Claribel wrote, "and whether Matisse will be among them. He is a leader now, but who can say? Only time with its strong focusing lens can give us the proper perspective." She added, however, "We hope and believe in Matisse." By the end of the summer, she had overcome her reservations. She found and purchased a Matisse painting that she liked—a still life—for 32,500 francs.

Through 1928, the sisters continued to buy more and varied works. In that year alone, Claribel purchased thirty-one works of art. It was as if she were racing against an unseen clock, filling up her home as fast as she could with as much as she could buy. She may have feared that the same weariness that had forced her to retire to Lausanne would soon force her to remain in Baltimore and effectively end her collecting career.

⤶

Claribel had once been romantic about death, threatening to die young while in Munich. Now she was practical about it. Her main concern was how to distribute her precious things.

In April 1929, during a visit to Greensboro, North Carolina, she drew up her will. She bequeathed her entire art collection to Etta, writing, "It is my desire in respect to the above Art Collection that in so far as is possible, or practicable, the same be kept in tact as one individual collection. It is my suggestion, but not a direction or obligation upon my said Sister, Etta Cone, that in the event the spirit of appreciation for modern art in Baltimore becomes improved, and if the Baltimore Museum of Art should be interested in my said Collection and desire to be named as appointee hereunder to receive said Collection after the death of my said sister, Etta Cone, that said Baltimore Museum of Art be favorably considered by her as the institution to ultimately receive said Collection. My second preference for an appointee would be the Metropolitan Museum of Art, of the City of New York."

Claribel must have been relieved that she had completed her will when she did. On her next visit to Europe, while Etta and Miss Kaufman traveled in Germany, Claribel, convalescing in Lausanne, felt a pain in her chest.

She wrote what she thought would be a final letter to Etta: "My dear Sister Etta: Last night I had a pain in my heart—the first one I have ever had. This morning my pulse omitted a beat on several occasions—for that reason—and in view of the fact that I have reached the age at which the eldest members of our family die I am writing this letter to say good-bye to you my dearest sister who have always been so good to me (Also to my very dear Brothers, Sisters, nephews and nieces). When one begins to grow feeble one is a useless member of society—so I should say I go without regret—except for the momentary pang of regret (this blot is ink—not a tear although it should be that!) it may be to my dear Brothers and Sisters.

"Give my best love to all—to my brothers, sisters, nephews and nieces and grand nephews. I should like you dear Etta to select from my things—or to buy for each of them something they may like. Of course for you and the Collection I should wish the suitable things saved . . . I expect to write again! You see I am only one of the many millions who have passed on. (will have passed on.) Say goodbye to Miss Kaufman for me. C... I love my family both in Greensboro & Baltimore very much although I am too lazy to express it."

The letter was premature—Claribel didn't die. When Etta and Miss Kaufman returned to Lausanne in August, Claribel was weak, but well. Miss Kaufman returned alone to the United States, while the two sisters spent time alone for the first time in years.

In the world's eyes, they had become like a husband and wife, forever associated with each other but never really alone together enough to learn what the other truly felt. In Baltimore they had Fred, the household help, Miss Kaufman, Miss Gaul, their extended family, and the friends they had made.

In Europe, when they were together, they were in the center of swirling activity that increasingly involved young family members. Now they had time to sit quietly together.

The sisters, still as different as two souls could be, had nonetheless been constant companions since Claribel returned from Germany eight years before. It had not been easy for Etta—Claribel was a trial for even the most patient person. But living near and with her older sister had given Etta's own life direction. Claribel was an anchor — half-child, half-husband.

In the next quiet month, they wandered the streets of Lausanne together, taking boat excursions on Lake Leman, and shopping for trifles. But the sisters did not buy art. Not until September 20, 1929 did Claribel buy a painting, and the one she selected was entirely unexpected. It was Gustave Courbet's *Rivulet du Puits Noir* (The Shaded Stream at Le Puits Noir).

For a collector who had always loved virility and color in her art, this was an odd choice, because it had neither. It was a dark and utterly still painting. Its subject was a patch of shallow stream. With a spot of light in the background, it seemed as if the sun had just one place to break through the overgrown foliage. There was a serene decay evident in the painting's lush brown tones, and almost the smell of summer's end. The viewer was invited into the painting by the stream's wide mouth, but there was no exit.

Claribel died of pneumonia the day she bought that painting—two months shy of her 65th birthday.

# Etta, Alone

# Baltimore, 1929

*She did not plan; she merely let herself go, and the overwhelming life
in her did the rest. It is only when youth is gone and experience has
given us a sort of cheap courage that most of us realize how simple
such things are.*

—F. Scott Fitzgerald, *The Crack Up*, 1931

$\mathcal{W}$hen her brother Moses died, Etta fell apart physically and emotionally. But she was twenty-one years older now,
and better able to cope with the mechanics of burying her
loved one—her lifetime companion.

Brother Fred had arrived in Lausanne shortly before
Claribel died, so he was of some help making all the necessary arrangements—transporting Claribel's body back to the
U.S., and sending out personal messages announcing her
death. But Fred, always the least capable of the three, may
have been more of a hindrance to Etta than if she had been
entirely alone.

Claribel's body, it was decided, would be placed on a
train that would go directly to the *Statendam*, for return to the
U.S. Given a choice, Claribel in life would have traveled back
to the U.S. on that very ship. So it was only fitting that she
was entrusted to that vessel in death. Etta and Fred headed

back to Paris to wrap up business there before joining Claribel's body on the *Statendam*.

At the Lutetia, Etta had letters of condolence awaiting her from friends in Europe and the U.S. The death of Claribel, for those who knew her, was like losing a precious and irreplaceable ornament that was difficult to care for, but always gave delight.

She had been larger than life—in some ways, more a character than a person—who exuded romance and fascination. She had treated life as if it were created for her personal amusement, and managed to share her pleasure with the people she knew. Her laugh, her smile, her wit were all sparkling, even into old age. Claribel's friends acknowledged that the world would be a lesser place without her.

Matisse wrote Etta, "My Dear Mademoiselle, I know that words lose every meaning in the face of great emotion but allow me to tell you of my sad surprise in learning by letter from my family of your sorrow. I think of your great sadness knowing your attachment to Dr. Cone and imagine how much her rich and distinguished character enhanced your days. Believe me that I share your grief, my dear mademoiselle, and want you to accept the expression of my affectionate and devoted feelings."

Etta replied, "My Dear Monsieur Matisse, Your letter full of appreciation for the character of my sister profoundly touched me. Permit me to express myself frankly in saying that your acquaintance and work were one of the great influences in the life of my sister, as well as in mine."

Gertrude wrote from the south of France, "My very dear Etta, I have just had word from Mike of the death of Claribel and it has saddened me terribly, I was awfully attached to her, oddly enough just the other day we were telling that delightful story of Claribel and the box in her room with the two old bon bons and the Bolsheviks in Munich, everything she did had an extraordinary quality all her own.

"I had not seen so much of her in recent years but she made a very important and rather wonderful part of my Baltimore past, and Dr. Marian Walker and I were talking of it all and of her in it when she was here just a couple of months ago, and so strangely enough Claribel had been very near me this last summer, and now Etta you know how I understand your loss and feel for it, do take my love and my fondest thoughts of Claribel, Always, Gertrude."

Death being the great healer, Etta was able to respond to Gertrude with grace, putting aside whatever differences separated the two old friends. "I do appreciate your understanding sympathy," she wrote Gertrude, who was then in Bilignin. "Your realization of my sister is also a comfort to me. She always admired you profoundly. I should like so much to hear you talk of my sister, someday when I am more calm within. I thank you for your very kind letter. With my love for you and Alice I am, Your sincere friend, Etta Cone."

While Etta waited for the *Statendam* to begin its journey to America, she consoled herself, or distracted herself, by making a few additional purchases—an activity of which Claribel would have heartily approved. Her choices offer some indication of her state of mind. The pieces purchased —nostalgic, sweet, and comforting—were from the years that had meant so much to Etta.

She bought four Matisse bronzes. Two of the three were casts of Matisse's *Tête d'une jeune fille* (Head of a Young Girl) from 1906, one of which she gave to Sally and Michael Stein. The second two were *Tête du'un enfant* (Head of a Child) from 1905. She purchased two casts of the piece instead of one— in just the same way she and Claribel had done when Claribel was alive, as if she were reluctant to give up the habit.

That fall, Etta may also have purchased a Picasso "blue period" painting from Gertrude's collection. Gertrude was in Aix, so if Etta did buy the painting, she would have done so through Sally and Mike. Picasso had painted *Femme au frange* (Woman With Bangs) in 1902, at the height of his mono- chrome period.

The lone woman in the painting is the embodiment of despair and grief. Her expressionless eyes stare straight ahead from the painting's blue shadows, but appear to be fixed on emptiness. If the Cones, consciously or not, purchased paint- ings that reflected their inner lives, then this Picasso would have mirrored Etta's emotional state that autumn.

Etta and Fred finally made their way to the *Statendam* to escort Claribel's body back to the U.S.. The trip had a poignant finality about it. It would be the last time the two sisters would cross the ocean together. It would be the last time trunks of Claribel's things would be shipped to Baltimore to take their place in her apartment-museum. It would be the last time Etta's life would revolve around caring for her tremendously vibrant older sister.

$\backsim$

While Etta suffered her personal grief, America mourned the crash of Wall Street. In every way, the post-war high life of the '20s was over.

Wall Street had started to rattle on October 24. The mar- ket plummeted as people cashed in their stocks for money that simply wasn't there. By October 28, the tremor had become an earthquake, and the market fell through the floor. A six-hour time difference between New York and Paris iso- lated French brokerage houses for a time, but soon U.S. citi- zens in Paris with large stock investments learned they were suddenly insolvent.

"Americans who had been dependent on remittances from home joined the queue at the embassy for emergency funds to return to the U.S.," said the reports. "The cafés and hotels of Montparnasse emptied out."

In Paris, what Parisians were calling "Le Krach" all but depeopled the city of the invading American hordes. In 1914, it had been the start of the war. Now, the Americans whom Parisians had loved to hate no longer had pockets overflowing with money. The franc was worth more than 25 to the dollar, but the favorable exchange rate could not help the generation of Americans who had lived on credit—and were now dying of it.

Though in the middle of the financial upheaval, Etta was untouched by it, much like Claribel years earlier in Germany. The Cone brothers had taken steps to shore up their stocks by guaranteeing deposits in the North Carolina Bank & Trust Company's Textile Branch. Her finances secure, Etta was able to glide through the crash, nursing her personal loss of Claribel, while those around her succumbed to the panic.

When Fred, Etta, and Claribel's body arrived in Hoboken, New Jersey, the harbor was covered in a dense fog appropriate for the occasion. Etta's younger brother Julius and his wife Laura, along with Ceasar's widow Jeanette, met them at the ship. They all boarded the train that would bring Claribel's body home to Baltimore for her final rest.

Despite arriving in Baltimore at 10 in the evening, Etta insisted that Claribel's body be taken immediately to the family mausoleum, a simple, elegant structure built for the Cones at the Druid Ridge Cemetery, in a suburb of Baltimore. There the family was met by a rabbi, who conducted a burial service by the light of a kerosene lantern.

The brilliant Claribel was dead, but Etta was not willing to give her up. She told her servants to give nothing of Claribel's away. Everything, she said, should remain in her rooms at the Marlborough, just as when she was living. Her clothes were to be hung in her closet, fresh flowers were to be placed in the rooms, and her trunks were to be left as they were—packed and ready for another European trip.

Despite the effort to preserve Claribel's spirit, the Marlborough apartments were almost unbearably silent. The small rooms that once overflowed with Claribel's presence were now empty. No longer would the doorbell ring out, announcing Claribel's invariably late arrival for a meal.

Etta was left to contemplate the future in the rooms whose life emanated only from the walls and the tabletops, which were covered in noisy paintings and animated objects that she and her sister had lovingly gathered. Etta might have realized for the first time then what purpose the collection served. It was her personal reservoir of beauty, love, devotion, and memory.

If Baltimore had not appreciated Claribel in life, it seemed to in death. By November 22, the Baltimore *Sun* was writing glowingly of the lady and her collection. The editor of the *Sunday Sun* wrote to Jacob Moses, a friend and distant relative of the Cone family, informing him of the newspaper's plans to run a page or two of the Cones' paintings in order to show "our own appreciation of the importance of the collection."

The city had not suddenly grown sophisticated enough to understand or even like the collection. The newspaper was taking its cue from Claribel, who, in her published will, had warned that the collection would be left to Baltimore only if the city exhibited a greater appreciation for modern art. A greedy Baltimore began a campaign, led by its leading newspaper and its rather sophisticated art critic, to prove itself worthy of the sisters' bounty.

The *Sun's* November 22, 1929, headline read "Cone Art Unit May Pass To City Museum ... Suggests However, Baltimore's Appreciation Must Improve." The paper's art critic, A.D. Emmart, wrote on the same day in a separate article that the collection of Dr. Claribel Cone "is unquestionably one of the richest and most stimulating and individual accumulations of art which ever has been brought together in Baltimore."

Emmart also issued an apology on behalf of his fellow citizens for their lack of understanding of the new art. "Baltimoreans have had very little opportunity, ever, to see in their native city any extended exhibition of the work of men and women who have made a new world and a new history in art ... The failure to understand and to enjoy proceeds most times from an unfamiliarity, a lack of preparation, a fear before the unknown."

The following year, for the first time ever, the Baltimore Museum of Art, with Etta's consent, exhibited pieces from the Cone collection—giving Baltimore audiences a chance to become acquainted with at least some of the works of art she considered her most valued companions.

⤴

Etta spent a long winter receiving visitors in her Baltimore apartment. They invariably sought to comfort her in her grief, and to discuss the collection, but the visits were more distractions now than anything else. Having at some point decided that her life's job was to carry on the collecting, but with more of a purpose, Etta plotted her next move.

She decided to fill in the gaps of their collection, making it an accurate and full representation of modern French painting. It would be a labor of love, but the task would also give her life the direction it lacked, now that Claribel was gone. It was also a project Claribel would have never undertaken—she wouldn't have had the patience.

By spring, Etta had decided to return to Europe to embark on her new mission. A letter from Margot Matisse about her father's work that year no doubt sparked an interest, adding to Etta's desire to leave Baltimore.

The Steins were also eager to resume selling to her. Michael wrote to Gertrude in a letter that year "... I am practically sure that Etta is not prepared for any big deal this year: but shall try to pull off a small one ... ." Apparently the Steins were not overly concerned about their friend's recent loss—except as it might derail their sales plans.

Etta's records of purchases that spring and summer indicate that Michael Stein scored his "small" deal. Etta purchased fourteen Picasso drawings, most likely from Gertrude's collection, for 50,000 francs.

But Etta did not buy any paintings. Perhaps they were too alive for her mood that season. She did, however, buy sculpture, including the remarkable Matisse *Grand nu assis* (Large Seated Nude).

The figure was no longer the beautiful, sensuous, lithe thing of his paintings, but a woman with an almost masculine form exuding strength, self-assurance, and ease. The sculpture was a stylistic departure for Matisse and a change for Etta, who had previously confined her choices to the serene and lovely. The purchase was one Claribel would have made, and perhaps that was what Etta had in mind at the time of the purchase.

In August, Etta was in Luçerne where a cousin, Siegfried Rosengart, had opened a branch of Berlin's Thannhauser Gallery. To the restless and lonely Etta, Luçerne was a cool and neutral oasis that held all the ingredients for a happy stay. No personal history there would prompt sad memories, as in Lausanne, but Luçerne offered the same easy life she had experienced with Claribel in Lausanne.

It was a place that rose early to the peal of church bells. But the pace was not a hurried or rigid one—champagne was a breakfast beverage choice that could be indulged in without raising eyebrows. And Luçerne had the added charm of Siegfried, who was as eager to discuss art as Etta was.

Etta took a suite at the National Hotel, the most monumental of the great hotels along Lake Luçerne. But while most visitors cast their gaze toward the crystalline, green-blue lake and the picture postcard view of the mountains facing the National, Etta focused on the rear of the hotel. In the shadows of the massive structure, just across the street, was Siegfried's shop.

Every morning at eleven, Etta would sweep her skirts around the corner of the hotel, away from the crowds of vacationers, and into the sanctuary of the gallery. It was not necessarily Luçerne that held her, but the proximity of art and conversation—conversation that usually centered on her collection. Since Claribel's death, Etta had lacked an intimate with whom she could discuss the thing she cared about most in life. In her cousin Siegfried, she found that person.

That summer was to be the first of her annual visits to Luçerne. As if to mark her place, she bought a Manet pastel on canvas, *Femme au Chapeau* (Lady in a Bonnet), from Siegfried's gallery for $17,500. It was the most Etta had ever spent on a work of art and nearly rivaled Claribel's Cézanne for extravagance.

The summer was also a turning point for Etta—she was making her first trip to Europe since 1905 without Claribel's company. She somehow managed to get through it—even enjoy herself—despite her sister's absence. At the age of sixty, and forced to come into her own, Etta emerged from under Claribel's shadow.

But the year 1930 was to become still more important for her for yet another reason. When she returned to America, a November letter awaited her. "My father," wrote Margot Matisse, "has agreed to make a large decoration for the Barnes Foundation in Philadelphia and is obligated to travel to America. He thinks he will arrive in New York about the 18th of December and go directly to the foundation. But my father would be happy to be able to come to visit you if you are in Baltimore at the end of December and if the visit would not inconvenience you."

Etta never dreamed that the great artist who was always her favorite would see his works in her home, or take the time to pay her the honor and tribute of a Baltimore visit.

There would be no inconvenience, she immediately replied. Etta Cone would happily receive Monsieur Matisse.

# Nice, 1933

*Art has often been concerned with religion, and something often said*
*of religion can also be said of art, that it is what man does with his*
*loneliness.*
    —Leo Stein, *Appreciation: Painting, Poetry and Prose,* 1947

*I*f ever there were doubts that Etta would continue the
tradition of collecting, which was generally and mistakenly
regarded to be the province of her late sister Claribel, Henri
Matisse's visit to Baltimore on December 17, 1930, dispelled
them. Etta was only one of two collectors the great French
artist sought out during that American visit, and he left
Baltimore agreeing not only to do Claribel's portrait, but one
of Etta as well.

The following morning, the Baltimore *Sun* featured
Matisse's visit prominently, describing him as one of the world's
most important living artists and remarking—as had so many
others—that the reserved and kindly gentleman did not at all
match his artwork.

A *Sun* reporter interviewed Etta's personal maid, Minnie
Harvey, who said, "Oh, Mister Matisse is a nice man, an easy
gentleman to serve. Of course, Miss Cone knew what he liked
and gave him nothing but the best."

But the appearance in Baltimore of the French master did more than just confirm Etta's intention to collect. More importantly, it brought her and Matisse closer together. He had now seen first-hand the loving care that his works received in Etta's home, and he had glimpsed, for the first time, the true nature of the collection the sisters had amassed.

It was not at all like that of Albert Barnes, whom he had also visited and who kept his art behind the limestone walls of his mansion, protected by a piked iron fence. Barnes' collection was on a grand scale, large enough to match his eccentricity and his ego. Etta's collection was as intimate as the room in which Matisse labored in Nice. It was a true and fitting home for his works.

With Claribel gone, Matisse also emerged as a kind of collecting partner with Etta. Siegfried Rosengart said Matisse would put aside three paintings for Etta each year, and if she could not decide which to take, she would ask Matisse, "What would you like us to have in our collection?" Rosengart said the buying and selling from then on became a "unique collaboration" between the two.

When Etta was in Paris, Matisse sometimes accompanied her to the framers, taking care to meet her at the Lutetia if his daughter Margot was unavailable. Etta, in turn, would await his visits with special glee. Her nephew, Harold, who accompanied her to Europe, said she ordered azaleas for her hotel room and arranged them in a silver pot for the artist's visits, because she said he liked the interplay of silver and petals. Matisse would dine with her, entertaining her young nephew with antics like balancing ashtrays on top of wine bottles.

Matisse and Etta, now intimate friends, were bound together by their long personal history, and by their love of his art. She once complained to him about his rising prices: "After all, Monsieur Matisse, I helped make you." To which he replied, "No, Mademoiselle Cone, I made you." In fact, the two longtime friends "made" each other.

During the winter of 1931, Etta basked in the joy of having hosted Matisse at her Baltimore home. "The visit of your father has given me pleasure that is impossible to express," she wrote to his daughter Margot. "He was at our home like a member of my family and my only regret will always be that my sister did not have the pleasure."

"My father was very touched by your reception of him and enchanted with the moments he spent with you—he has told us about it in great detail," Margot answered. "Upon his return my father showed us the photographs of the doctor [Claribel] which he brought back. He wanted to be relieved of all agitation from moving, to be at last in the right frame of mind for work, to study the photographs with a drawing in mind. It is, I believe, the best method in order that his effort will give the best result."

The move Margot referred to was to a larger studio. When Matisse returned to France from his visit to Etta and to Barnes, he was obliged to rent an abandoned film studio in Nice large enough to accommodate the Barnes murals. He would spend the next three years working on projects that were wildly different in scope—the Barnes paintings, at one extreme, and a commission to illustrate a book of poems, *Poèsies de Stéphane Mallarmé*, on the other.

The Barnes murals were huge and robust, big enough in size and subject to command attention in a public space. The Mallarmé drawings were intimate and quiet works, not meant to dominate, but rather to enhance, the poet's words. The two projects simultaneously consumed Matisse.

Despite that heavy workload, he took on a third project— his small commission from Etta. In 1931, he began his drawings of the Cone sisters, making study after study from memory and photographs of his two loyal collectors. He worked on the drawings for three years.

~~

While Matisse was busy in Nice, Etta decided to embark on a project of her own—one that she saw as a tribute to Claribel. Etta wanted to publish a catalogue of their collection and, seemingly without regard to cost, she began the book in 1931 with the help of her cousin Siegfried in Luçerne.

It was not to be a minor listing of the Cone collection works, with merely a smattering of pictures. It was to be a large volume—with full-page images of each work and a face-page detailing the history of each piece. The project was a massive one that consumed not only Etta, but Siegfried, as they struggled to document the ever-growing collection.

In March 1932, Matisse wrote to Etta that he wanted to visit her again when he was in America—this time to install the Barnes murals. He completed one set in France, only to discover that the measurements given him were wrong, so he had to paint yet another set of murals. The job was an enormous undertaking for the aging artist.

When he finally arrived in the United States in the spring of 1933, he was exhausted. He did not visit Baltimore, but wrote Etta from New York, "Dear Mademoiselle, I leave New York without having come to Baltimore. I arrived the eleventh of May and leave the 29th after having installed in Marion the marvelous decoration. Dr. Barnes is very content. He will open the foundation for a few days at the beginning of October but you can always ask to visit it. I am very tired and am obligated to return to rest . . . Believe, dear mademoiselle, in the expression of my respectful and entirely devoted sentiments."

Etta was no doubt disappointed that Matisse did not visit,

but she was even more concerned about the artist's health. They were both getting on in years. She herself was "always tired," she wrote daughter Margot. "The visits with artists and curators have become very frequent. The contact with intellectuals gives me great pleasure but it distracts me from accomplishing the work that I have begun."

During the winter, Etta worked on her catalogue. During the summer, she bought. For Matisse, her patronage during those years was particularly important. The Depression put a halt to most collecting. Even many of Matisse's most important buyers, including Barnes, held back during the 1930s.

By 1933, a quarter of the U.S. labor force was unemployed. The national income had been cut by half. The suicide rate, though reaching its highest level ever in 1931, was surpassed in 1932. Many Americans were desperate. Squatter camps called "Hoovervilles" had sprung up in almost every major city, and were occupied by people who had lost everything.

Outside Etta's windows in Baltimore, one in eight of the city's residents had no work. Bread lines had opened in nineteen locations. But, as if oblivious to her surroundings, Etta continued to spend vast sums on art. In fact, she purchased three of Matisse's four most important paintings between 1930 and 1935. And in 1933, at Matisse's request, she purchased the drawings for the Mallarmé book of poems.

The artist wanted to keep all of his work on the book together, so he asked Etta to buy 250 items—the original drawings, printed and rejected copper plates, three proof volumes, and the signed first copy of the printed edition. He trusted that Etta, more than anyone else, would care for the materials and not disperse them.

Etta was thrilled with the drawings, which she purchased, for a huge 140,000 francs, in March 1933. The transaction coincided with what was probably the lowest point of American capitalism. She wrote to Margot, "It is the most beautiful illustrated book I have ever seen." Acting on the artist's behalf, almost as a fiduciary would, Etta guarded the set in her Baltimore apartment, and rarely displayed it.

⤳

The just-purchased Matisse line drawings of nudes were charged with eroticism, and explicitly carnal. Image after image depicted women intertwined in sensuous repose. Their bodies were soft and submissive and sated, and could never be explained away merely as an artist's device. The man who did the drawings desired the bodies he drew, and that desire leaped off each page.

One of the great mysteries concerning Etta was how she could surround herself with a virtual harem of nude and semi-nude women and still maintain her image as the prudish spinster from Baltimore. At sixty-two, she was purchasing art that was sexually bold, even by current standards. And yet she lived her life as if she had just stepped out of a Jane Austen novel, hungering for "approbation."

In her dress, she was still covered neck to ankles with pounds of fabric. And she still kept her sexuality hidden. Even through the 1920s, when lesbianism was considered cosmopolitan, she confined her relationships to "passionate friendships." She once told a great niece that people believed there was "something between Gertrude and Alice," but she did not think so. "After all," she asked, "what can two women do?"

Contrary to her protested naiveté, the art that Etta purchased showed she had a keen sense of the erotic, especially the voluptuous images produced by Matisse. In pretending that she knew nothing of carnality, was she simply trying to keep her true nature and the depth of her knowledge hidden from her family?

Most likely. Even Alice B. Toklas, who undoubtedly did have "something" with Gertrude, was prudish in her language. She was known to use the word "compromise" instead of "seduce," "outspoken" in place of "shameless, "impure" rather than "bisexual," and "inadequate" in lieu of "dead drunk."

✍

That summer, Etta headed back to Europe, this time in the company of her sister-in-law, Laura, and Laura's two children, Edward and Frances. Etta's traveling was no minor undertaking. She brought with her as many as twenty pieces of luggage that had to be counted at several points along the journey to make sure none had been misplaced.

She was met at the Paris train station by Raymond Wahl, whom she hired each summer to act as her chauffeur. He would drive her in his black Minerva wherever she traveled. At the end of the season, he would deposit her at the train station for the start of her return trip to Baltimore.

Etta always stayed at the Lutetia in Paris—if possible in the same room each year, but at the very least on the same floor so she could be attended to by Rachel, a housekeeper who knew her habits. Every morning began with a group breakfast, during which she and her companions would plot the day's activities.

Etta allowed herself one excursion per day. She kept her passport, money, and valuables in pockets in her numerous petticoats, which she referred to as her "underground."

She traveled with a raft of purses, setting aside one for each day of the week—and dozens of keys, which were invariably lost but then found by her traveling companions.

Her nephew, Harold Cone, was charged with making the

"strange men check"—looking under beds and in the closet for possible intruders, and warming the toilet seat in case any "strange men" had recently sat on it.

That summer would take the group from Paris to Luçerne, and then Luçerne to Nice, where she was to visit Matisse. While still at work on portraits of the sisters, he had come down with acute nephritis. He was living in an apartment on the third and fourth floors of 1 Place Charles Felix near the city's old port. The location was crowded with flower merchants, fish salesmen, and farmers selling vegetables. The street sang out with activity, but inside, the 18th-century building was quiet. Etta went to the apartment and wrote of the experience to her brother Fred.

"My visit was a joy. One of the first things he said was 'When I am able to work the first thing I shall do is to make the drawing of Dr. Cone.' Then he said, 'I have a surprise for you' and presently I turned and there sat the model in the yellow taffeta dress with the large yellow hat on, just in front of the window—the exact reproduction of my latest painting. His bedroom (which is his studio when he is well) was the scene of this picture.

"Needless to say I was thrilled. Well Mons. Matisse would not listen to my plan to leave (Nice the next morning today) for as he explained Marguerite would arrive *demain* and she would show me the original decoration for the Barnes Foundation.

"Also he insisted that Laura and the children come to see him this afternoon, so according to the master's voice here we are. Poor fellow, he has had several stones in the kidney and says he has been over fatigued. I know it was the result of his hard work."

When Etta returned to her family in Nice to describe the visit and the "master's" request, she was "bubbling like a school girl," euphoric not only about Matisse's staged performance for her of *La robe tilleul* (The Yellow Dress), but his wish to visit with her family. The next day the visit took place, but not before Etta was shown the original set of Barnes murals, which had been rejected because they were not the correct size.

"Raymond took us to the studio where we saw the original design for the Barnes' salon," wrote Etta. "It is a wonderful production and even Laura and the children got great pleasure from seeing it.

"Next we went home with Mme. Duthuit and my little family party was presented to Matisse, who was still in bed. We were having a very happy visit when the doctor came in. He [Matisse] begged us to await the doctor's departure, but he stayed too long so we left."

During their visit, Matisse made it clear that he wanted Etta to buy the murals rejected by Barnes and install them in a building she would construct to house the Cone collection. But she realized that even if she could afford the expense of building a museum—and buying the murals—she did not have the energy for the project.

A little dejectedly, Etta and her family moved on from Nice to Italy, where they received another invitation—this one from Gertrude, who wrote, "My Dear Etta, If you should be coming back this way from Italy and it is a pleasant way to come, we would be very pleased to see you. If you are near Geneva or Chambery or Aix les Bains it is all very near us, and we would be very glad to have you and your family lunch with us."

Ever since trying to sell her the original *Three Lives* manuscript, Etta's relationship with Gertrude had been polite but distant. The two occasionally exchanged letters, and sometimes Gertrude would ask why she and Alice did not see more of Etta.

But in the years after the war, Etta and Gertrude were no longer friends. They had become mere business acquaintances. Etta would buy what Gertrude had to sell. Gertrude's new life revolved around furthering her writing career and, increasingly, farming at Bilignin in the south of France, where she had taken a second home with Alice.

Gertrude had become a legend of sorts. In 1926, Alice clipped Gertrude's hair in something approaching Roman style. It made her look even more the oracle when she sat in the increasingly shabby rue de Fleurus and held forth before a bevy of young writers. But while her reputation as a character grew, she still could not interest a major publishing company in the eighteen books she had written.

All that changed, however, in 1932, when she wrote *The Autobiography of Alice B. Toklas*. All in 1933, Harcourt Brace and Company bought the book, she was finally published in the *Atlantic Monthly*—it serialized the book—*and* she became almost instantly famous. Gertrude had had to wait until she was fifty-nine years old for the publishing world to recognize her genius. But now, she was a major celebrity.

She had sent a copy of the manuscript to Etta, no doubt delighted with the fact that it was to be published. And though Etta wrote back, saying she was pleased to have been mentioned in the book and also happy to read its serialized version in the *Atlantic Monthly*, she didn't have the courage to say what she really felt. She was distressed by the gossip that Gertrude circulated in *The Autobiography*. Etta joined a long list of people who criticized and scorned Gertrude's literary triumph, citing her indiscretions and outright lies.

Leo, who had been working on a book of his own called *Others, Do They Exist?*, called Gertrude's book "a romance . . . little related to the facts" and a "stupid brag and general bosh." He said, "There is almost nothing in the period before the war with which I am not acquainted and there is nothing that she has written that is true."

Hemingway never forgave her for the lies she wrote about him in the book. Georges Braque, André Salmon, Tristan Tzara, and Matisse all signed an article published in *transition* that charged Gertrude with representing the epoch they had lived through "without taste and without relation to reality."

Etta showed no concern for Gertrude's depiction of her in the book—as a kind of provincial simpleton. But she did object to Gertrude's public disclosure that Margot Matisse Duthuit was actually the artist's illegitimate daughter. Margot herself, it was believed, did not know that the woman she had always called "Mother" was not really her biological parent. Etta learned during her summer abroad in 1933 that the book was going to be translated into French, which meant Margot would surely read it. Etta could not forgive Gertrude. She said Gertrude "can't help telling everything she knows."

Etta was still upset about the book when she received the good-natured invitation from Gertrude, which she promptly declined. "Dear Gertrude," she wrote in reply, "Your very kind letter followed us ... I thank you for your kind invitation for my family and me, but as our route from here will be directly to Paris, we shall not be able to accept, and I am sorry."

Etta added, somewhat disingenuously, "Your autobiography of Alice Toklas is one of the most interesting and the best of the literature of today. With all good wishes for your continued success I am as always, Your sincere friend, Etta Cone."

Explaining to her family members her decision not to visit Bilignin, Etta said Gertrude was not worthy of meeting them.

# Baltimore, 1934

Lent by—*that was their identity as far as the general public knew, and that was their desire ... The Cones were satisfied to embody themselves in their collection, as if it were sufficient expression of their personalities.*

— George Boas, in unpublished notes to his foreword/
introduction for the Cone Catalog, circa 1933-4

$\mathcal{I}$n 1934, a movie ticket in America cost 35 cents, a night at the opera about $1.50, and a signed etching by a popular living American artist about $5.

That same year, Etta bought a Van Gogh landscape for $9,900. Her brothers, again concerned that she was spending too much money on one type of "investment," urged her to diversify. Etta's annual income, according to tax records, was then about $60,000. She spent most of it on paintings and sculpture.

But for Etta, the art was not an investment—it was her life. Her every relationship outside her family revolved around art. Collecting was both her occupation and her passion.

"Etta bought because she couldn't resist," Siegfried Rosengart said. When talking with her about art, he added, he entered into a kind of intense romance from which he often came away exhausted. Art consumed her as much as the artists whose work she bought.

On the other side of the creative coin, she was the person who hungered for and appreciated what the creators produced. She was the ideal collector of artists' dreams, sought after because her support enabled them to be free to paint or sculpt. She dispensed money in large enough amounts that artists could immerse themselves in their creative pursuits, able to ignore everything but reproducing their vision of reality. And she shared their vision—lived in that vision—in her cluttered apartment high above Baltimore.

Etta was no longer known as Dr. Claribel's sister, but as an art collector and connoisseur in her own right. Major museums in the United States courted her, sending either their directors or top-ranking representatives to try to win her collection for their facility.

The Baltimore Museum of Art enjoyed an edge, partly because Etta became friendly with the museum's new curator of prints, Adelyn Breeskin, who shared her enthusiasm for the new art. In fact, Etta lent works from the Cone collection to the Baltimore Museum for exhibition in 1934.

But the museum's advantage did not stop others from trying. Alfred H. Barr Jr., who believed the Cone collection to be too good for Baltimore, visited Etta on behalf of New York's Museum of Modern Art.

The Philadelphia Museum's curator, Henry Clifford, made frequent pilgrimages to the Cone apartments.

The Museum of Fine Arts Boston, the Brooklyn Museum, the Art Institute of Chicago, the Cleveland Museum of Art, the San Francisco Museum of Art, Harvard's Fogg Art Museum, and Washington, D.C.'s National Gallery of Art— all sent representatives to Baltimore to woo the younger Cone and win the prized Cone collection for their cities.

The treasures the sisters held had become widely recognized in the art world, in large part because of the completion of Etta's catalogue project. With the help of Siegfried Rosengart, Etta had assembled an approximately 400-page volume with 125 plates, featuring the works she owned of Matisse, Picasso, Cézanne, Coubine, Courbet, Degas, Derain, Van Gogh, Manet, Marquet, Pissarro, Redon, Renoir, Robinson, Rodin, Signac, Sisley, Vallotton, Vlaminck, and Zorach, among others.

The book was "dedicated to the memory of Dr. Claribel Cone by her sister Etta Cone." It opened with Matisse's portrait of Claribel, followed five pages later by Matisse's portrait of Etta—as if Etta were still sitting several rows behind Claribel at the symphony. From among the ten drawings he did of Claribel and Etta, Matisse himself had selected those he wanted reproduced in the volume, and as always, his instructions were followed.

George Boas, the Hopkins philosophy professor, wrote the book's introduction: "There was never in the minds of the Misses Cones a desire to rival the great museums. There was simply a desire to own these specific pictures which pleased their sense of beauty. Their collection therefore is as much a testimony of themselves as of the history of art.

"The brilliance of Dr. Cone's perception, those flashes of wit, those penetrating observations which made her so engaging a conversationalist, are personified by the pictures hanging on her walls and when one enters her apartment one still feels the personality of its owner as if she were about to greet one in person. Her taste ran to power rather than serenity; it was she who acquired the examples of Matisse's fauve period.

"Her sister's selections, on the other hand, seem to a spectator to be a quieter and more classic type. Her taste leads her to works of art beyond the phases of experimenta-

tion, to pictures which have already reached the point indicated, almost attained in the canvases which belonged to Dr.
Cone. The result is that the united collection is extremely
well rounded, neither too rough nor too smooth. If one may
use a musical metaphor, every suspended chord is resolved
and yet there is no monotony."

Etta printed about 1,000 copies of the catalogue, sending
them to nearly everyone she knew, and to all the major museums, universities, curators, libraries, and key art world nota-
bles. It was no small gift—the table-top book weighed about
seven pounds. But, more importantly, it was a portable representation of Etta's life's work.

The letters of appreciation and surprise from those who
received the catalogue poured in from around the world. Alfred
Barr Jr., for example, declared the catalogue "magnificent."

Every letter of appreciation sent to Etta for the gift of the
catalogue was rapturous, though some correspondents admitted that, while they were delighted with the book, the art, in
all candor, remained incomprehensible to them.

A Van Gogh nephew said he was so surprised by the
huge package, shipped to him from Germany, that he at first
feared Hitler had sent him a bomb disguised as a parcel. But,
in the end, he was delighted by the catalogue, he said.

Etta was triumphant. Her career was at its peak. She had
not only bought something, but now she had made something
greater from what she bought. Siegfried suggested she print an
additional 500 copies, this time to sell, but Etta refused. The
book had been printed in Germany, and she did not want any
more to do with a country that was now controlled by the
Nazis. She even had the book's printing plates destroyed in
order to make a subsequent run impossible.

Gertrude, too, was still basking in a publishing triumph
when Etta learned she was embarking on a U.S. lecture tour

designed to promote her book. For the first time in thirty years, Gertrude would return to the country she left, along with Etta, in 1904. Etta, apparently ready to put aside her differences with Gertrude, tried to arrange a lecture date for her in Baltimore.

In February 1934, Etta wrote Harcourt Brace and Company, Gertrude's book publisher, that Hopkins did not have the money to pay Gertrude to lecture there. Gertrude's price was $200, a pittance compared with what Etta paid for paintings. But she apparently was not all that interested in bringing her friend to town—she easily could have sponsored the lecture herself, but did not.

Still, Etta wrote excitedly to Gertrude about her coming trip. "Many museum directors have been here this winter and many of them were thrilled to find the bronze and portrait of you in this collection," she said in an April letter. "I always apologize for the Vallotton portrait, for it is not you." It was as if Etta had been caught up in the Gertrude mania sweeping the United States, and, at least for the moment, forgotten how difficult their relations had become.

Gertrude and Alice arrived in America on October 17, 1934. In New York, Times Square pulsed with the flashing message "Gertrude Stein has arrived in New York ... Gertrude Stein has arrived in New York." The two women were greeted by a rush of press photographers and writers, who wanted to get the first words from the odd pair—one wearing a modified hunting cap and the other sporting a mustache. One newspaperman characterized Gertrude as "a hearty, irreverent old lady." "Little Gerty" from San Francisco, the "matron saint of Paris art," was now front-page news.

Learning that Gertrude was coming to Baltimore to visit relatives, Etta offered Gertrude and Alice the use of her apartment for the stay. Gertrude had never seen the Cone collection, and would have recognized many of the pieces from her own home or Sally's and Mike's. It would have been a perfect setting for the grande dame of the Parisian art world to hold court when she visited Baltimore, because it was a setting not unlike the rue de Fleurus.

But Gertrude, perhaps remembering Etta's snub the previous year, declined the offer. Her letter was cold and dismissive. "My dear Etta, Thanks so much for your invitation, but I am not accepting any invitations. There is so much more happening than in our wildest dreams—I am simply seeing no one except a few very dear friends . . . ."

Gertrude and Alice eventually arrived in Baltimore. Gertrude did spend time with relatives, and shared Christmas Eve with Scott and Zelda Fitzgerald.

But by that time, Etta, hurt and humiliated, had left town for Greensboro. For a woman who adhered to a ritualistic schedule, it was unheard of to travel south in the winter, but she did so that December, after giving away tickets to a lecture Gertrude was to give at the very Baltimore Museum of Art whose director was doing everything possible to win Etta Cone's trust and, ultimately, her entire collection. The Cone family generally assumed she left Baltimore because she wanted to avoid Gertrude.

The trip south nearly killed Etta. The train's sleeping car between Baltimore and Greensboro was drafty, and Etta caught a cold that turned into pneumonia.

Etta's brilliant year ended with the reopening of an old wound. Once again, in retreat to North Carolina, she quietly suffered a physical ailment, though her more severe problem most likely was emotional.

Gertrude and Etta never saw each other again, even when Etta returned to Paris. Gertrude's dagger had struck too deep for Etta to forgive her, and the successful writer no longer needed the financial support of Miss Etta Cone. The old friends, who had no doubt once loved each other, were completely and forever estranged.

# Paris, 1938

*Meanwhile the trees were just as green as before; the birds sang, and*
*the sun shone as clearly now as ever. The familiar surroundings had*
*not darkened because of her mistake, nor sickened because of her*
*regret. Time went on, and she dressed herself up picturesquely, as she*
*had formerly done . . .*

— Thomas Hardy, *Tess of the d'Urbervilles*, 1891

*E*tta's great sorrow passed like all the others. For her age
and various ailments, she was a resilient woman who would
not let an emotional thrashing by Gertrude Stein cripple her
for long. Matisse had said that his paintings had a healing
effect, and perhaps for Etta they did.

Since 1922, the Cone collection—that massive grouping
of objects and art—had threatened to overtake the sisters'
apartments. Behind the glass-paneled door covered in
Japanese brocade, a visitor entered another world. The sisters' textile collection alone comprised more than 1,000
items, including more than 100 Turkish towels used in
harems, and arguably the finest collection of lace in America.
An expert from the Detroit Institute of the Arts called the
Cone textile collection second in the world only to Vienna's.

Years of study had produced an extraordinary art library.

More than a thousand volumes overflowed into an unused kitchen.

The walls were so covered in art that it was difficult to walk down the narrow halls. In some cases, it was impossible to step back far enough to admire the works. In Etta's bedroom hung her latest acquisitions, which she examined in bed—a vantage point, she felt, where she could study them best. Her bedroom was also the sanctuary where she would review favorite older pieces. Though her collection possessed a sampling of works by the recognized masters of French painting, her bedroom was almost exclusively the domain of Henri Matisse.

Etta no doubt cherished the time she could spend quietly among her things, but those quiet times had become less frequent. The Cone Collection attracted hordes of art pilgrims because, as one expert said, "there was no comparable gathering of the work of Matisse accessible anywhere in America."

Increasingly Etta also received requests from museums and galleries in the United States and Europe interested in including her pieces in their shows—if they could not have all the collection's pieces permanently. When the requests were from the Baltimore Museum of Art, Etta most often agreed. If the requests were from Matisse himself, she always consented, and sent her precious works overseas to exhibitions he designated as worthy.

With all these later year transactions, Etta had the advice and counsel of Adelyn Breeskin, now the director of the Baltimore Museum of Art, and the indispensable help of BMA staff members. Breeskin herself patiently acquiesced to Etta's demands, however odd they might be.

Etta, for example, insisted that, when carrying art from her apartment, everyone, even burly moving men, must wear white gloves, despite the fact that Etta's own staff took less care with the work. One visitor remembered seeing, with horror, a Van Gogh in Claribel's room hung upside down after being dusted. Breeskin was earning Etta's trust, so that when the time came, the Baltimore Museum of Art continued to stand first in line for her hugely valuable collection—a collection she knew would forever draw art fans from around the world.

As Etta's fame as a collector grew, she increasingly became the target of aspriring artists, who hoped to win her financial support, and were not afraid to beg for it. Letters arrived frequently at her home from numerous young painters who lavished her with gushy praise, to which she, in her loneliness, often succumbed.

If she liked the artists well enough, she bought their work. Leon Kroll, whose paintings Etta bought, wrote her numerous letters saying how much her friendship meant to him. On several envelopes containing Kroll's letters, Etta noted in her own hand that the enclosed missive was "lovely."

The artist Ben Silbert flooded her with letters of his travels, and described in intricate detail his works in progress. Etta was obviously flattered by the attention, and may not have suspected that the correspondents were at least partly motivated by their own financial considerations.

But, in a new round of letters from Leo, she recognized that old cry for cash. Leo Stein was once again trying to make his living as a painter and proposed that she join a group of collectors who would buy a painting of his a year for $100. This, he said, would help tide him over until "I can get to exhibiting and perhaps get somewhere." It was the same scheme Matisse proposed at the beginning of his career, but it hadn't worked for Matisse, and it wouldn't work for Leo either.

Leo later wrote to Etta from Florence, "The prospects that I had formed for this winter in America came to nothing. After I wrote to you Nina continued ill and for worse and I had to give up all projects whatever. I didn't write again as I heard nothing from you ... But anyway, Nina wants me to write to you ... well, it's a beautiful world and everyone must be happy to be in it. Leo." On the envelope, Etta wrote "hard up."

A Baltimore artist, Aaron Sopher, was luckier. He ultimately sold Etta 142 works, and later recalled, "I would come in there a poor artist and she a grand lady." Sopher visited Etta often at her apartment, but to him she was more an institution than a person. Etta, said Sopher, appeared to him like "Queen Victoria," with her black dress sweeping the floor. And though she was small in height, he said, she appeared tall because she was so imposing.

She was also a remote figure who studied the art he brought her, saying little by way of small talk. In fact, in all his visits, Sopher said Etta never smiled. The artist's seven-year-old daughter once asked Etta, who appeared to have so much in the way of material things, what else she could possibly want. The much-pursued Miss Cone replied, "I'd like to have one true friend."

In the spring, Etta was back on the *Statendam*, heading to Europe, where at least one special friend, Monsieur Matisse, awaited her each year. On her voyage, she always had the same stateroom going east, and a corresponding room on the opposite side of the ship on her return trip westward.

Her life, in fact, had become a ritual of coming and going. In the summer, she bought, and in the winter, she displayed. Her pursuits were as regular as a salaried job, and she had not yet reached the age of retirement. But the Europe she returned to in 1935 was very much changing, and the changes would force her to rethink her routine.

France's years of economic depression after World War I

produced political and social turmoil. In February 1934, the public's general frustration, along with protests over political corruption, triggered Parisian riots that left seventeen people dead and 2,000 injured.

While the country was being torn apart from within, a breeze blowing from Germany once again carried the scent of war. Hitler, named chancellor of Germany in 1933, had begun his aggressive program to restore that country to its pre-World War I strength. He denounced the Versailles Treaty that had cost his country much in reparations.

Michael and Sally Stein decided it was time to leave Paris. For the past ten years, they had lived in a house outside the city called Les Terraces. It had a beautiful view of St. Cloud and the roofs of Paris. Inside, its walls were covered in paintings. But in 1935 they left that home to return to California with their grandson, Danny. After 30 years abroad, they quit Europe and settled in Palo Alto, as far from the brewing conflict as possible.

Etta's summer abroad in 1935 was unusually quiet. She bought only one painting, Matisse's *Les yeux bleus* (The Blue Eyes), which she purchased from Margot in Paris. The painting was of a young Russian woman named Lydia Delectorskaya, who had worked as Matisse's assistant on the Barnes mural and been a companion and nurse for Madame Matisse in 1934. But beginning in 1935, Lydia played an increasingly important role in the artist's life—first as his model, then as secretary, household manager, and hostess and, for the rest of his life, companion.

Madame Matisse, confined to her bed since the early 1930s, was acutely depressed, replaced by a young woman who was giving the sixty-five-year-old artist a new life. The Matisse family was distressed by the affair. By no means was it his first, but it was the most significant, and it threatened to split the family apart.

When Amelie Matisse had finally had enough of the situation, she asked her husband to choose between her and Lydia. Lydia won. Madame Matisse shrieked what she might have been suffering silently for years, "You may be a great artist, but you're a filthy bastard." The couple, however, did not divorce, and, to the outside world, seemed to continue much as they always had.

Etta knew nothing of the Matisses' split until years later, when she received word from Margot that her mother was very badly off. "My God, so many terrible things have arrived at our home," wrote Margot with considerable bitterness. "I am at this moment close to my mother who you should know has lived alone since March. My father lives someplace else. The news could not surprise you. The drama was expected. My mother alone, with the blindness that is general among wives as it concerns their home, did not see it coming.

"A separation after 41 years of living together, and you know what that life was. If I say that my father used the reason that my mother impeded his work and that only his work and the protection of that work is what he is guarding in separating their lives, you will think like me that the reason is false and that he is looking for life elsewhere. I only see my father rarely ... I will never talk to you again of his work."

But that official notice from Margot concerning the state of the Matisse household came in 1939. Etta had apparently been spared the drama during its early years. In fact, Etta bought the fruits of the artist's liaison with his young lover. In 1936, she purchased the *Grand nu couché* (Large Reclining Nude), better known as the *The Pink Nude*, a major piece depicting a fully nude Lydia lounging on a print background. The artist gave Etta twenty-two photographs documenting the development of the large painting from its first stage in

May 1935 through its completion in October of that year.

During that 1936 summer abroad, Etta made up for a lack of purchases the year before by buying with a frenzy. She purchased twenty-three pieces of art, including works by Braque, Manet, Matisse, Renoir, Rousseau, Toulouse-Lautrec, Van Gogh, de Chirico, and Picasso.

Etta bought the Picassos even though her interest in the artist had sharply diminished. She had no time for Cubism, though she was said to be the subject of Picasso's shattered portrait, *Femme a l'eventail* (Woman with a Fan). She was not intrigued by his post-Cubist works, either.

But her duty to develop a collection representative of modern French painting required her to buy works by the artist, who, along with Matisse, had been central to its development. She had not seen Picasso for years, in part because it would have embarrassed her to see an artist whose work she bought but no longer actively supported.

Etta's unusual number of purchases in 1936 may also have been an indication that she knew her time in Europe was running out, and she felt she had to collect as much as she could while she was still able to visit. It was not that Etta was physically unable to make the trip, but that the political situation in Europe grew increasingly tense each year.

Italy, now led by the fascist dictator Mussolini, had invaded Ethiopia. Germany had sent a force of 22,000 troops into the demilitarized Rhineland. And civil war had erupted in Spain. All around, France was surrounded by war and hatred. Fear was everywhere, and France was reluctantly beginning to re-arm.

During the next two years, 1937 and 1938, Etta returned to Europe, spending thousands of dollars on art as she went. In Luçerne, she purchased a Degas for $1,080, a Gauguin for $15,000, a Picasso on paper for $1,800, as well as a Modigliani and an Ingres. In Paris, she bought Matisses, a Cézanne, a Toulouse-Lautrec, and a Rouault. She squirreled away her prizes, as if fortifying for a long winter, while France and the world conserved provisions in case of war.

By 1938, Germany had invaded Austria, Mussolini had proclaimed Libya part of Italy, and domestic violence had erupted in France. Even the United States geared up its war machine. After much hand-wringing by politicians and continual and blatant provocation, France declared war on Germany in 1939. The majority of Americans believed the United States would eventually be drawn into the conflict.

# Blowing Rock, 1949

*Once we had a country and we thought it fair,*
*Look in the atlas and you'll find it there:*
*We cannot go there now, my dear, we cannot go there now.*
> —W.H. Auden, *Ten Songs*, March 1939

*E*tta returned to Baltimore to wait out the war. There was no reason for her to think it would not end soon, and that she would not soon resume her travels. Her collection was full, but not complete, and she no doubt felt the agitation of a job left partly done.

But 1939 would be a dreary year for her. Not only was she to stay in the United States for the entire year—the first time since 1922—but the situation in Europe grew darker by the day. In the fall of 1938, reports trickled back to the United States of a German pogrom called *Kristallnacht*, which resulted in the disappearance of 20,000 Jews in Germany alone.

As Etta read and listened to dispatches from abroad, she found herself saddened by her own personal tragedies. Two of her brothers, Sydney and Sol, died in 1939. With their deaths, just four of the original thirteen Cone siblings survived.

Etta bought a sentimental Picasso painting that year, *Mere et enfant* (Mother and Child). Its soft pastel tones and comforting subject—a mother's clear but unspoken love for her daughter—were tinged with melancholy. It must have spoken to her mood. She was surrounded by her ever-growing family and her nieces and nephews, but the original Cones were dying off, she had never married nor had children, and the Europe she loved was denied her, its symbols of civilization perhaps in the process of being irreparably damaged.

Etta also began to feel her own mortality. She received a letter from Sally Stein, who was similarly alone with her grandson now that Mike had died: "My dear, I am living in the past a great part of the time ... living on here in the home that Mike chose and arranged with every contrivance for convenience—surrounded by the things that meant beauty and experience to us ...."

Etta must have felt the same way. She was living among her things and the memories they evoked, but increasingly the people who were part of those memories were departing.

〜

Etta split her time between Baltimore, New York, and Blowing Rock, North Carolina. She bought what art she collected through New York dealers, including Pierre Matisse, who had a gallery in the city.

At her best socially when people came to see her collection, she guided them through the paintings and sculpture, watching their reactions as they looked at the works and heard the stories behind them. Otherwise, she was shy in company—some people thought her mean and haughty. She was neither. Increasingly, she simply chose to let her art speak for her.

If Etta was quiet with her memories, so was Matisse. The artist spent the summer of 1939 in Paris at the Lutetia, but when France declared war, he headed south. He even secured a Brazilian visa and passage to Rio, but decided not to leave.

"When I saw everything in such a mess," said Matisse, "I had them reimburse my ticket. It seemed to me as if I would be deserting. If everyone who has any value leaves France, what remains of France?" Instead, he returned to Nice, where he lived in a huge, pink Victorian hotel outside the city.

Matisse was nostalgic for the old days and wrote Etta in October 1939: "We did not see you this summer and we supposed that the rumblings of war made you put off your usual trip to Paris—you were only too justified, alas, in doing so. All the same we would like to hear your news—to know if all is going well with you, if your health is satisfactory—a word from you about this would indeed give us pleasure.

"The whole family is well, but Pierre who had not yet gone back to New York was mobilized in Paris—his wife is managing his gallery and Jean has also been mobilized in Paris. I do not want to talk to you about the sadness of the moment which everyone knows about.

"As for me, I am always working happily. When it becomes easier to ship books I will send you an album of drawings ... and another one of color reproductions of paintings from the same publishers ... Wishing you good health and also that this terrible war may not be as dreadful as one might expect it to be, I send you our very best, affectionately and devotedly, Henri Matisse."

But by November, his mood was less optimistic. He wrote, "You would say that I work always, more than ever— at this moment, what better way to forget?"

In 1940, another of Etta's brothers, Julius, died, just as the world appeared to be imploding. Europe was at war. Hitler was marching virtually unimpeded through Denmark, Norway, Holland, Belgium, and Luxembourg. He began aerial bombardments of England, and entered Paris unopposed.

To Etta, it must have seemed inconceivable that her other home was now occupied by an anti-Semitic army, and it must have made her feel even more isolated. Paris had been synonymous with happiness for her since 1905, when she first fell in love with its spirit. Now Europe's great lady was being trampled on by a beast and his minions, who had no appreciation or regard for her splendor.

There was one bright spot for her amidst the growing darkness, and that was the discovery of "one true friend." Etta had met a German refugee named Lily Schwartz, hiring her to play four-handed piano with her in Baltimore.

The two became intimate. Miss Schwartz was a widow in her forties with no family or ties in America, and thus could devote all her time to the seventy-year-old Etta. The association enlivened Etta's life in the same way the relationship with Lydia had energized Matisse's.

～

Etta's years in Baltimore during the war were marked by a steady stream of visitors from around the world. In fact, she was visited by a who's who of art world figures hoping to see—and perhaps win—the now-renowned collection.

Margot Matisse's husband, Georges Duthuit, visited in 1941. He wrote Etta: "I had for many years cherished the desire to know your collection more intimately but in reality, I had not imagined that it was so unusual and important. You and your sister have erected a monument of the art of your time that seems to me to be without comparison anywhere."

Daniel-Henry Kahnweiler, Picasso's old Paris dealer, visited her and wrote, "I still remember the wonderful hours spent at your home."

The art historian Herbert Read saw Etta's collection and

remarked, "It was one of the most memorable experiences of this visit of mine to America."

And Alfred Barr, Jr., the reigning authority on Matisse, said the Cone Matisses, taken as a whole, far surpassed those of any museum in the world.

While Etta surely enjoyed the praise, she became in the next several years less inclined to show her collection or to have people in to visit it. She had received all the accolades she desired, and wanted time to be alone with her art. A lifetime of collecting required contemplation. She had, after all, purchased the pieces for her own pleasure, and in the 1940s —now stranded in America—she would take the time to enjoy them.

Her correspondence with Matisse continued despite the war. Each year he would send Christmas greetings, and keep her up-to-date on his situation through letters. They were two elderly people exchanging stories and reminiscing in a world dominated by young people bent on killing.

They had known each other for more than thirty years and had gone through much. The physical distance would continue to divide them, but their thoughts likely drifted back to happier times, when they themselves were young, and the world revolved around their bohemian Paris.

In 1941, surgery left Matisse physically drained. He wrote Etta, "For three months I have had to remain in bed and I think often of you, also of my other old and dear friends, and I wanted to tell you, that is the object of this letter."

Etta responded, "Dear Monsieur Matisse, Nothing in the world could give me the pleasure of your charming letter written on May 20. It is real evidence that your health is returning and I am very happy. The good news of Mme. Matisse and Marguerite and Jean is also welcome." But Etta admitted to him, "My life without my annual visit to France is empty."

Etta also corresponded regularly with the artist's son Pierre, now back in New York. It was through him that she learned the terrifying news that both Madame Matisse and Margot Matisse, while working for the French underground, had been arrested by the Gestapo. Margot was captured by the Germans in Brittany, tortured, and sent to Germany in a train, then to the Ravensbruck concentration camp. Madame Matisse, arrested the following day, was sentenced to six months in jail for helping her daughter.

Because of an Allied air raid, Margot managed to escape before she arrived at the concentration camp, but the seventy-three-year-old Madame Matisse remained in prison for some time before being released. Pierre's friend wrote, "I have never seen such supreme courage and heroism in my life. In spite of her terrible experience, Mme. Matisse carries her head high."

Jean Matisse was also involved in the resistance—he hid dynamite in his sculptures. But Henri Matisse was not able to aid the resistance. Enfeebled by duodenal cancer, he convalesced in Nice while his family fought against Germany.

At the end of the war, after the Germans agreed to surrender, the aging artist was honored. In 1945, the Salon d'Automne was dedicated to Matisse. It was the only one-man show featuring a living artist ever mounted at the salon. The painter with the bold vision symbolized the freedom France had fought to preserve. And while it was a great moment for Matisse—and perhaps his greatest moment—Etta did not travel to see it. She was, she decided, too old and too unwell to make the trip.

Etta's heart was weak, she suffered from persistent stomach troubles, and her younger brother Fred had died. That left just Etta and her brother Bernard as the only living members of the original Cones.

All around her, Etta's contemporaries were quickly passing away, too. On July 27, 1946, Gertrude died of cancer. Leo Stein read of it in *Newsweek* magazine. He wrote to his cousin Howard Gans, "I can't say it touches me. I had lost not only all regard but all respect for her."

But Leo did not last much longer. He died the next year, almost to the day of Gertrude's death, on July 29, 1947.

That year, Leo's book *Appreciation: Painting, Prose and Poetry* was published. It might have brought him some money had he lived long enough to learn of the book's favorable reception. He had sent Etta a copy of the book's manuscript, apparently as a thank-you for something she had sent him. She thought the book brilliant.

George Boas wrote to Etta of Leo soon after his passing. "I had a letter from him a week or so before his death, which I knew nothing of until a friend of mine mentioned it. It was a great shock, as his letter didn't even speak of an illness, but on the contrary mentioned a trip to America as in the cards. One by one they seem to go, and I confess I don't see who is going to take their places. For a man like Leo had such depth of learning and experience, in spite of all his funny little ways, that he was really unique."

Even though Etta had not been entirely responsive to Leo's financial straits in his later life, she always remembered, and cherished, their friendship. As the years passed and Gertrude's fame grew, Gertrude was often mentioned as the discoverer of the great generation of European artists at the turn of the century. And she was invariably mentioned as having introduced the Cone sisters to the new art.

But Etta knew better. It was Leo's lessons in Florence in 1901 and Paris in 1905 that formed the foundation for her career. His lessons still guided her purchases forty years later. No matter how much she had taught herself, or by whom she had been influenced, it was Leo, she always said, who taught her what she knew about art.

With Leo and Gertrude dead, Alice was left to guard the Stein reputation in France. She eventually converted to Catholicism, but the conversion brought with it a new worry. Alice was afraid that, under Catholic doctrine, because she was baptized and Gertrude had not been, she wouldn't see Gertrude again after death. But Alice found a sympathetic priest who assured her that "heaven can be fixed," and that he would work on getting Gertrude out of limbo.

Sally Stein, widow of Michael, Gertrude and Leo's brother, was living in California with her grandson Danny, to whom she was blindly devoted. But her financial situation was difficult. Danny had a taste for race horses. Sally sold off her art collection—piece by piece—to pay for his hobby, and losses. She lived a long life, until 1953, but it was not a happy one.

Etta was perhaps the luckiest of her old friends. She had the serenity of a close family and a beautiful home filled with the things that might as well have been her children.

On May 18, 1949, she drew up her Last Will and Testament, bequeathing her 3,000-piece collection to the Baltimore Museum of Art, whose staff, in the twenty years since Claribel's death, had proved to Etta that the spirit of art appreciation in Baltimore had indeed improved. In her will, Etta also set aside $400,000 for the museum to build a wing to house the works.

↫

Etta began her collection of French paintings in 1905 with a Picasso drawing that cost her only a few dollars. In 1949, she was offered another Picasso from that era. Allan Stein was ill and needed money, so he telephoned Etta at Blowing Rock, North Carolina, and offered to sell her a gouache Picasso had done of him in 1906.

Agreeing to a price of $15,000, she awaited the piece she was sure she had seen hanging at Sally and Mike's in the early days on the rue Madame. For Etta, the thought of the drawing must have conjured up a thousand other images, making for full and happy days as she waited.

But Etta never saw the drawing in her home. She died of heart failure on August 30, 1949, before the Picasso arrived.

⤳

A Pinkerton guard stood outside Etta and Claribel's Baltimore apartments, guarding their collection while assessors examined its many pieces. Before Baltimore Museum of Art staff members arrived to begin moving the collection to their facility, it was as if a time capsule had been opened.

Claribel's long dresses were still hanging neatly in her closet, two decades after her death. Fresh flowers were in a vase in her room, as she would have wanted them.

A half century of collecting, estimated at the time to be worth $3 million, was neatly in its place.

The only missing pieces were the two sisters.

# Epilogue

⌒〜

$\mathcal{B}$efore Etta died, she selected a committee to sort through her vast holdings and to choose works that would eventually become part of the official Cone Collection at the Baltimore Museum of Art.

The committee included the president of the BMA Board of Trustees, museum director Adelyn Breeskin; Etta's sister-in-law, Laura Cone; Walters Art Gallery technical adviser David Rosen; and BMA Board member and U.S. Solicitor General Philip B. Perlman, who also had served as Etta Cone's personal attorney and was named the estate's executor.

Those items not deemed appropriate for the BMA collection, or duplicates, were donated to the Women's College of the University of North Carolina, for use in its art department and at the nearby Weatherspoon Art Gallery.

The remainder of the collection, including some paintings, textiles, and mementos, were divided among Cone family members and friends. Everything else was auctioned off—though the auction house was expressly not permitted to identify the items as being from the Cone family.

Etta's and Claribel's large collection easily satisfied two art institutions, a sprawling family, and an auction house. At the time of Etta's death, the art collection alone consisted of more than 300 items — 149 paintings, 97 drawings, 54 sculptures, 114 prints, and three illustrated books by Henri Matisse, including his much-prized Mallarmé set.

Of a total of 3,000 items ultimately decided on for the collection, one-sixth, or about 500, were by Matisse, and ranged from paintings and sculpture, to prints and illustrated books. Not only did no other museum have nearly as many Matisse items, but the Matisse items in the collection were comprehensive rather than episodic, representing virtually every phase of the artist's long and remarkably diverse career. He died five years after Etta, in 1954. Despite cancer that struck him at the start of the second world war, Matisse had lived to the grand old age of 85, and was still working as an innovative artist almost to the end.

The collection also included a world-renowned textile and lace collection.

Etta set strict conditions on her bequest to the BMA. The collection was not to be modified in any way. Nothing could be sold or traded. And nothing could be added to the collection. If she had not completed her mission to provide a comprehensive view of modern French art and painting, so be it. The collection ended with her.

In October 1949, shortly after Etta's death, the Baltimore Museum of Art allowed the general public to see the new collection. One thousand people attended the official opening.

The Baltimore *Sun* noted, "Last night, although some persons expressed dislike of some of the pictures, the general reaction left no doubt that Baltimore felt it had been greatly enriched."

Even the city fathers were convinced of the collection's value, and offered to add $175,000 in governmental funds to Etta's $400,000 bequest to construct a special wing to house the Cone works.

The three-story Cone Wing opened to the public nearly eight years later, in February 1957. But even with 470,000 cubic feet of exhibition space, only about 4 percent of the collection has been on view at any given time.

Since its opening, perhaps as many as 20 million visitors to the BMA have been introduced to the Cone sisters through the art they bought. The collection has also traveled to the Wildenstien Gallery and the Guggenheim Museum in New York, the Los Angeles County Museum, the Kimbell Art Museum in Fort Worth, the Museum of Fine Arts Boston, the Museum of Fine Arts Houston, the Cleveland Museum of Art, the Seattle Art Museum, and museums as far away as Tokyo and Osaka, Japan, among others.

In 2001, the Baltimore Museum of Art opened a renovated Cone Wing. Still not large enough to display more than about 120 out of the collection's 3,000 items at any one time, the renovated wing offers visitors several fascinating additions. Before the renovation, visitors could only see a tiny, glass-encased sample of the sisters' Marlborough Appartments, to sense how much they collected, and how they displayed it. Now, because of the renovation, an entire room has been set up to simulate one of the apartment rooms, complete with furniture and books.

Even more remarkable is a computer simulation, done through BMA cooperation with the University of Maryland at Baltimore County (UMBC), that takes the viewer through many of the apartments' rooms, for a much more complete sense of the cozy museum the sisters had made for themselves.

Because of both these innovations, any visitor to the collection can not only imagine the world of Claribel and Etta Cone, but step into the sisters' home and live with them, during a brief but enriching afternoon, among their much-treasured art.

〜

But while their collection is justly celebrated in its new and glorious environs, and the collection's value in 2002 thought to be nearly $1 billion, the two sisters themselves are a bit neglected—the money set aside for their perpetual graveyard care apparently ran out in the year 2001.

Not more than two hundred yards from the main office of Baltimore's Druid Ridge Cemetery, up a slight hill in a secluded, park-like area called Hickory Knoll, sits, inconspicuously, the family mausoleum. Only the word "Cone"—appearing above the portico in all-capitalized letters—marks the site. James O. Olney, a famous New York City architect of the 1930s and 1940s, designed the stately but modest building (approximately ten feet by ten feet).

Through two heavy, age-darkened, and ill-maintained bronze doors, flanked by two traditional, Roman-looking columns of Vermont granite, one enters the small chamber, which is made of solid Tennessee marble.

On the left side, stretching the building's length, are the final resting quarters of Etta, on top; brother Fred, in the middle; and Claribel, on the bottom.

Imprinted on each vault are simply their names and their respective dates of birth and death: Etta Cone, November 30, 1870—August 31, 1949; Frederick Cone, August 29, 1878—May, 20, 1944; and Claribel Cone, November 14, 1864—September 20, 1929. On the tomb's right side are three distinct but unused burial spaces.

Neither here, nor on the mausoleum's exterior, appears even the briefest commemoration of what these two "maiden ladies" accomplished during their lifetimes. In death as in life, Etta and Claribel Cone thought it undignified to call much attention to themselves as people.

A visitor would have no idea that buried here are two of the world's greatest, most philanthropic, yet least recognized, art collectors of the twentieth century. .

# Bibliography

## PUBLIC AND PRIVATE COLLECTIONS

The Archives of American Art, Smithsonian Institutions, Washington, DC

The Baltimore Museum of Art, Baltimore, MD

The Enoch Pratt Free Library, Baltimore, MD

The Jewish Historical Society of Maryland, Baltimore, MD

The Johns Hopkins University Eisenhower Library, Baltimore, MD

The Johns Hopkins University Welch Medical Library, Baltimore, MD

The Library of Congress, Washington, DC

The Maryland Historical Society, Baltimore, MD

The Yale University Beinecke Rare Book and Manuscript Library, New Haven, CT

The University of Maryland Medical School Library, Baltimore, MD


## NEWSPAPER AND MAGAZINE ARTICLES

Azrael, Louis. *Jewish Historical Society of Maryland Archives, Baltimore American* (1962): NP

Bowman, H.G. "A Million In Modern Masters." *Baltimore Sun* (Oct. 9, 1949): 12-13, 20-21.

Breeskin, Adelyn. "Some Notes On The Cone Collection." *Baltimore Sun* (June 10, 1934): Section 2, 2.

— "Three Generations of Buying French in Baltimore." *Art News* (December 1951): 36.

Burke, Carolyn. "Gertrude Stein, The Cone Sisters and the Puzzle of Female Friendship." *Critical Inquiry* (Spring 1982): 543-564.

"Carnegie Show." *Time Magazine* (Oct. 20, 1930): 48-49

Catling, Patrick Skene. "Critics Acclaim Cone Exhibition In Formal Opening at Museum." *Baltimore Sun* (Jan. 14, 1950): 20.

— "Critic Finds 'The Finest'." *Baltimore Sun* (Jan. 13, 1950): 12.

— "Etta Cone, Friend of Great Artists Lived Quietly Among Their Works." *Baltimore Sun* (Sept. 14, 1949): 32.

"Cone Art Collection Returns From New York Display." *The Evening Sun, Baltimore* (March 1, 1955): 23.

"Cone Art Unit May Pass To City Museum." *Baltimore Sun* (Nov. 22, 1929): 30.

"Cone Collection Index To Modern Art Field." Baltimore Sun (June 22, 1941): Section 1, 9.

"Cone Collection Textiles Are Termed Outstanding." The Evening Sun, Baltimore (Dec. 2, 1949): 64.

Cone, Edward T. "Aunt Claribel's Blue Nude Wasn't Easy To Like." Art News (Sept. 1980): 162-163.

— "The Miss Etta Cones, The Steins, and M'sieu Matisse, A Memoir." The American Scholar Vol 42 #3 (Summer 1973): 441-460.

"Cone Family Gems Will Go On View." The Evening Sun, Baltimore (Jan. 11, 1950): 36.

"Cone Textile Collection Finest In Country, Authority Declares." Baltimore Sun (Dec. 4, 1949): NP

Dickman, Sharon. "Sopher Recalls Patron, Etta Cone." The Evening Sun, Baltimore (April 5, 1971): Section C, 1.

"Dr. Claribel and Miss Etta, Collectors." Art News (January-February, 1950): 38-41.

"Dr. Claribel Cone A Remarkable Woman." The Evening Sun, Baltimore (April 8, 1911): 4.

"Dr. S.M. Cone, Orthopedic Surgeon, Dies." Baltimore Sun (Dec. 20, 1939): 26.

"Eccentric Esthetes." Maryland Medical News Magazine 4:2 (February 1960): 94-99.

Emmart, A.D. "The Cone Art Collection." Baltimore Sun (Nov. 22, 1929): 13.

— "Matisse Disclaims Prophetic Knowledge of Future of Art." Baltimore Sun (Dec. 18, 1930): 5, 22

Emmart, A.D. and Fleming, H. Kingston. "Baltimore City of Average Men." New Republic (Nov. 9, 1927): 309.

Gold, Barbara. "Cone's Collection of Love." Baltimore Sun (Aug. 21, 1966): Section D, 15.

Harriss, R.P. "Matisse: The Baltimore Art Museum's Incomparable Cone Collection." News American, Maryland Living Magazine (Sept. 27, 1964): 8-9.

"Matisse Paintings." Baltimore Sun (Jan. 24, 1937): Section 2, 6.

"Miss Etta Cone." The Evening Sun, Baltimore (Sept. 1, 1949): 29.

"The New Cone Wing At the Museum of Art." Baltimore Sun (Feb. 24, 1957) 26, 40.

"New Season Marks Historic Events." Baltimore Sun (Sept. 25, 1969): Section B, 1.

"NY Art Gallery To Show Cone Collection." The Evening Sun, Baltimore (Jan. 20, 1955): NP

Rackemann, Francis. "Permanent Home Ready for Cone Collection." The Evening Sun, Baltimore (Jan. 29, 1957): 17.

BIBLIOGRAPHY

Rogers, Charles Ross. "The Cone
Collection of Modern Art." Baltimore
Sun (June 3, 1934): 11.

"The Romance of Fine Old Lace."
Baltimore Sun ( Sept. 14, 1949): NP

Rosen, Israel. Helicon Nine, The Journal
of Women's Arts and Letters, Number
Nine (1983): 78-85

——In Generations (December 1982):
3-14.

Sawyer, Kenneth B. "Cone Collection
Stirs the 'Street'." Baltimore Sun
(Feb. 6, 1955): Section 2, 14.

Scarborough, Katherine. "Baltimore
Collection Widely Known."
Baltimore Sun (April 15, 1928): 13.

"Selections From the Cone Collection."
Baltimore Museum of Art News
(October 1949).

Shamer, Bertha Tapman, "Claribel Cone,
M.D." Journal American Medical
Women's Association 7:11
( Nov. 1952): 431-32.

Skinner, B.F. "Has Gertrude Stein a
Secret?" Atlantic Monthly 153
(January 1935): 50-57.

Spaeth, Joseph. "Medical Studies And
Women." Wiener Medizinishe
Presse 13 (1872): 1109-1118.

Stimpson, Catharine R. "The Mind, The
Body and Gertrude Stein." Critical
Inquiry (Spring 1977): 489-506.

Sutherland, Donald. "Alice and Gertrude
and Others." Prairie Schooner 45
(1971): 284-299.

"Up From Baltimore." Enoch Pratt
Library, Maryland Room Archives,
Herald Tribune (January 1955): NP

Wagner, J.A. "Nineteenth Century
Pathologists and the Development of
Pathology in Maryland." Maryland
State Medical Journal 9 (1969):
58-59.

Wallace, Weldon. "Cone Art Exhibit
Opens at Museum." Baltimore Sun
(Oct. 8, 1949): 24.

Wharton, Carol. "A Fabulous Heritage."
Baltimore Sun (Jan. 15, 1950):
Section A, 3.

BOOKS AND PAMPHLETS

Abrahams, Harold J. Extinct Medical
Schools of Baltimore, Maryland.
Baltimore: Maryland Historical
Society, 1969.

Adamthwaite, Anthony. France And
The Coming of the Second World
War. London: Frank Cass and Co.
Ltd., 1977.

Anderson, Bonnie S., and Zinsser, Judith
P. A History of Their Own, Women
In Europe From Prehistory to the
Present, Vol. II. New York: Harper
& Row, 1988.

Andrews, Matthew P. Tercentenary
History of Maryland II. Chicago,
Baltimore: S.J. Clarke Publishing
Co., 1925.

Apollinaire, Guillaume. Henri Matisse,
1907-1918. Paris: L'Echoppe, 1993.

Auden, W.H. Collected Poems. New York: Vintage International Edition, 1976

Austen, Jane. Emma. New York: Franklin Watts Ltd. Edition, 1971.

Banner, Lois. American Beauty. New York: Alfred A. Knopf, 1983.

Barr Jr., Alfred H. Matisse: His Art and His Public. New York: The Museum of Modern Art, 1951.

Benstock, Shari. Women of the Left Bank Paris, 1900-1940. Austin: University of Texas Press, 1986.

Beirne, Francis F. Baltimore: A Picture History, 1858-1958. New York: Hastings House, 1957.

Brugger, Robert J. Maryland A Middle Temperament, 1634-1980. Baltimore: Johns Hopkins University Press and the Maryland Historical Society, 1988.

Chesney, Alan M. The Johns Hopkins Hospital and the Johns Hopkins University School of Medicine, Vols. I, II, III. Baltimore: Johns Hopkins Press, 1943.

Clinton, Catherine. The Other Civil War: American Women in the Nineteenth Century. New York: Hill and Wang, 1984.

Cone, Claribel. Alice Derain. Woodside, California: Occasional Works, 1984.

— Aunt Etta and the Personalities. Phoenix, Arizona: Imaginative Idea-Realistic Editions, Ink., 1986.

Cone, Etta. The Cone Collection of Baltimore, Maryland, Catalogue of Paintings, Drawings, Sculpture of the Nineteenth and Twentieth Centuries. Baltimore: E.Cone. 1934.

Cone Jr., Sydney. The Cones From Bavaria. Baltimore: Maryland Historical Society, 1965.

Cordell, Eugene Fauntleroy. Medical Annals of Maryland 1799-1899. Baltimore: Medical and Chirurgical Society of Marylan,. 1903.

Daix, Pierre. Picasso: Life and Art. Translated by Olivia Emmet. New York: HarperCollins, 1993.

Dictionary of American Biography, Supplement Four. New York: Scribner, 1974.

Donnelly, Mabel Collins. The American Victorian Woman: The Myth and the Reality. New York: Greenwood Press, 1986.

Drabek, Alexander. Die Dr. Senckenbergische Anatomie von 1914 bis 1945, Vol. 7. Frankfurt, Germany, 1988.

Eliot, George. Daniel Deronda. London: Penguin Classics Edition, 1986.

— Middlemarch. New York: The New American Library of World Literature, Signet, 1964.

Faderman, Lillian. Odd Girls and Twilight Lovers, A History of Lesbian Life in Twentieth-Century America. New York: Penguin Books, 1991.

— Surpassing the Love of Men,
Romantic Friendship and Love
Between Women From the
Renaissance to the Present. New
York: William Morrow and
Company, Inc., 1981.

Fecher, Charles A. ed. The Diary of H.L.
Mencken. New York: Vintage Books,
1991.

Fein, Isaac M. The Making of an
American Jewish Community: The
History of Baltimore Jewry from
1773 to 1920. Philadelphia: The
Jewish Publication Society of
America, 1971.

Fitzgerald, F. Scott. The Crack Up. New
York: New Directions Edition, 1945.

Flam, Jack, ed. Matisse: A Retrospective.
New York, Avenel, N.J.: Wings
Books, 1988.

Flanner, Janet. Men & Monuments:
Profiles of Picasso, Matisse, Braque
& Malraux. New York: Harper &
Row, 1957.

Flexner, Simon, and Flexner, James
Thomas. William Henry Welch
& The Heroic Age of American
Medicine. New York: The Viking
Press, 1941.

Gallup, Donald, ed. The Flowers of
Friendship: Letters Written to
Gertrude Stein. New York: Alfred A.
Knopf, 1953.

Gilbert, Martin. The Second World War:
A Complete History. New York:
Henry Holt and Company, 1989.

Gillet, Louis. L'Allonge, Une Visite A
Henri Matisse. Paris: L'Echoppe,
1993.

Glassco, John. Memoirs of
Montparnasse. Toronto, New York:
Oxford University Press, 1970.

Gordon, Lois, and Gordon, Alan. The
American Chronicle, Six Decades in
American Life 1920-1980. New
York: Atheneum, 1987.

Green, Harvey. The Light of the Home:
An Intimate View of the Lives of
Women in the Victorian Era.
New York: Pantheon Books, 1983.

Hanser, Richard. Putsch! How Hitler
Made Revolution. New York:
Peter H. Wyden, Inc., 1970.

Hardy, Thomas. Tess of the D'Ubervilles.
London: Penguin Classics Edition,
1985.

Hemingway, Ernest. A Moveable Feast.
New York: Charles Scribners and
Sons, 1964.

Henderson, Gavin, ed. Augustus Hare In
Italy. New York: The Ecco Press, 1988.

Herrera, Hayden. Matisse: A Portrait.
New York: Harcourt Brace and
Company, 1993.

Himmelfarb, Gertrude. Marriage and
Morals Among the Victorians and
Other Essays. New York: Vintage
Books, 1975.

Hirschland, Ellen. The Cone Sisters and
the Stein Family, in Four Americans
In Paris, The Collections of Gertrude

Stein and Her Family. New York:
The Museum of Modern Art,
New York, 1970.

Hobhouse, Janet. Everybody Who Was
Anybod:, A Biography of Gertrude
Stein. New York: Anchor Books
Doubleday, 1975.

Huddleston, Sisley. Paris Salons, Cafes,
Studios. Philadelphia and London:
J.B. Lippincott Company, 1928.

James, Edward T., ed. Notable American
Women. Cambridge, Mass.: Belknap
Press of Harvard University, 1971.

James, Henry. The Portrait of a Lady.
London: Penguin 1986.

Janvier, Meredith. Baltimore In the '80s
and '90s. Baltimore: H.G. Roebuck &
Son, 1933.

The Johns Hopkins University Register.
Baltimore: Johns Hopkins University
Press, 1897-98.

Ketchum, Richard M. The Borrowed
Years, 1938-1941: America On
The Way To War. New York:
Anchor Book, Doubleday, 1989.

Lovejoy, Esther Pohl. Women Doctors of
the World. New York: MacMillan,
1957.

Mellow, James R. Charmed Circle:
Gertrude Stein & Company. Boston:
Houghton Mifflin Company, 1974.

Mencken, H..L. A Mencken
Chrestomath:, His Own Selection of
His Choicest Writings. New York:
Vintage, 1982.

Marcus, Jacob Rader. This I Believe,
Documents of Jewish Life. CITY:
Jason Aronson, Inc., 1990.

Naujoks, Horst, and Preiser, Gert, eds.
225 Years of the Senckenberg
Foundation, Frankfurt, Germany,
1988.

Nevinson, C.R.W. Paint and Prejudice.
London: AAA, 1937.

Nyburg, Sidney. The Buried Rose:
Legends of Old Baltimore. New York:
Alfred A. Knopf, 1942.

Olivier, Fernande. Picasso and His
Friends. New York: Appleton-
Century, 1933.

Olson, Sherry M. Baltimore: The
Building of an American City.
Baltimore: Johns Hopkins University
Press, 1980.

Packard, Francis. Some Accounts of
the Pennsylvania Hospital of
Philadelphia, 1751-1938. New York:
Eagle Press, 1938.

Paintings, Sculpture and Drawings in
the Cone Collection. Baltimore: The
Baltimore Museum of Art, 1955.

Pollack, Barbara. The Collectors:
Dr Claribel and Miss Etta Cone.
Indianapolis: Bobbs Merrill Co.,
1962.

Reitlinger, Gerald. The Final Solution.
South Brunswick and New York:
Thomas Yoseloff Publisher, 1953.

Richardson, Brenda. Dr. Claribel & Miss
Etta, The Cone Collection of the
Baltimore Museum of Art. Baltimore:
The Baltimore Museum of Art, 1985.

Richardson, John. *A Life of Picasso,*
*Vol I,* 1881-1906. *New York:*
*Random House,* 1991.

Richler, Mordecai, ed. *Writers On World*
*War II: An Anthology. New York:*
*Alfred A. Knopf,* 1991.

Rogers, W.G. *Ladies Bountiful. New*
*York: Harcourt, Brace & World,*
*Inc.* 1968.

—— *When This You See Remember*
*Me: Gertrude Stein In Person.*
*New York: Charter Books,* 1948.

Saarinen, Aline B. *The Proud Possessors.*
*New York: Random House,* 1958.

Schlereth, Thomas J. *Victorian America:*
*Transformations in Everyday Life,*
1876-1915. *New York: Harper*
*Collins,* 1991.

Schneider, Pierre. *Matisse. New York:*
*Rizzoli,* 1984.

Shannon, David A. *Between the Wars:*
*America,* 1919-1941. *Boston:*
*Houghton Mifflin Co.,* 1979.

Shattuck, Roger. *The Banquet Years:*
*The Arts in France,* 1885-1918.
*New York: Harcourt Brace,* 1955.

Sprigge, Elizabeth. *Gertrude Stein: Her*
*Life and Work. New York: Harper*
*& Brothers Publishers,* 1957.

Spurling, Hilary. *The Unknown Matisse,*
*A Life of Henri Matisse: The Early*
*Years,* 1969-1908. *New York: Alfred*
*A. Knopf,* 1998.

Stein, Gertrude. *The Autobiography of*
*Alice B. Toklas. New York: Vintage*
*Books,* 1990.

—— *Everybody's Autobiography. New*
*York: Exact Change Edition,*
1993.

—— *Fernhurst, Q.E.D., and Other*
*Early Writings. New York and*
*London: Liveright Edition,* 1971.

—— *Three Lives. New York: Vintage*
*Books,* 1936.

—— *Two: Gertrude Stein and Her*
*Brother and Other Early*
*Portraits,* 1908-12. *New Haven,*
*Conn.: Yale University Press,*
1951.

Stein, Leo. *The ABC of Aesthetics. New*
*York: Boni & Liveright,* 1927.

—— *Appreciation: Painting, Poetry*
*and Prose. New York: Crown*
*Publishers,* 1947.

—— *Journey Into the Self. New York:*
*Crown Publishers,* 1950.

Sullivan, Mark. *Our Times, IV, The*
*War Begins,* 1909-1914. *New York:*
*Charles Scribner & Sons,* 1932.

—— *Our Times, V, Over Here* 1914-
1918. *New York: Charles*
*Scribner & Sons,* 1933.

Toklas, Alice B. *What Is Remembered.*
*New York: Holt, Rinehart and*
*Winston,* 1963.

Tuchman, Barbara. *The Guns of August.*
*New York: Macmillan,* 1962.

Vicinus, Martha. *Suffer and Be Still:*
*Women in the Victorian Age.*
*Bloomington, Ind.: Indiana*
*University Press,* 1972.

Wagner-Martin, Linda. *Favored Strangers: Gertrude Stein and her Family.* New Brunswick, N.J.: Rutgers University Press, 1995.

Walsh, Mary. *Doctors Wanted: No Women Need Apply, Sexual Barriers in the Medical Profession, 1835-1975.* New Haven: Yale University Press, 1977.

Warnod, Jeanine. *Washboat Days.* Translated by Carol Green. New York: Grossman Publishers, 1972.

Welsh, Lillian. *Reminiscences of 30 Years In Baltimore.* Baltimore: Norman Remington Co., 1920.

Wertenbaker, Lael. *The World of Picasso, 1881-1973.* Alexandria: Time-Life Books, 1967

Wiebe, Robert H. *The Search for Order, 1877-1920.* New York: Hill and Wang, 1967.

Wineapple, Brenda. *Sister Brother: Gertrude and Leo Stein.* New York: G.P. Putnam & Sons, 1996.

Wiser, William. *The Crazy Years: Paris in the Twenties.* New York: Thames and Hudson Inc., 1983.

# Chapter Notes

## ABBREVIATIONS

ABT    Alice B. Toklas

BMA    Baltimore Museum of Art

CC    Claribel Cone

CCol    Cone Collection, BMA

EC    Etta Cone

EPFL    Enoch Pratt Free Library

GS    Gertrude Stein

HM    Henri Matisse

JHU    Johns Hopkins University

JHS    Jewish Historical Society MD

LS    Leo Stein

MDHS    Maryland Historical Society

MS    Michael Stein

SteinCol    Stein Collection, Yale


## *Baltimore, 1930*

1. "I'm still on my portraits"... Schneider, Matisse, 416.

2. In those days... Rogers, Ladies Bountiful, 3.

3. The once penniless... Herrera, Matisse: A Portrait, 150.

4. "Yes, but sometimes the...", Pollack, The Collectors, 200-201.

5. Nearly every surface... Baltimore Sun, Sept. 14, 1949, np.

6. Later, in an interview, ... Baltimore Sun, Jan. 15, 1950, Sec. A, 3.

7. The bespectacled artist... Baltimore Sun, Dec. 18, 1930, 5, 22.

8. The artist spent the night... Pollack, The Collectors, 217.

9. And for many, his... Gutman interview.


## *Baltimore, 1872*

1. "I have none of the usual..." Austen, Emma, 103.

2. The established Jewish community ... MDHS, Cone, Sydney Jr., The Cones of Bavaria, 10.

3. Cone and his partner... ibid, 31.

4. That, coupled with the... Fein, The Making of an American Jewish Community, 95.

5. In 1870, only about... Brugger, Maryland: A Middle Temperament, 391.

6. Southwest Baltimore, not far... ibid, 401.

7. In the center of town... Olson, The Building of an American City, 206.

8. In addition, horse-drawn carriages... ibid, 161.

9. But the family resided... Brugger, Maryland: A Middle Temperament, 347.

10. "Today, for the first time,"... Pollack, The Collectors, 19.

11. The nineteenth century woman was... Faderman, Surpassing the Love of Men, 204-205.

12. She was supposed to strive... Banner, American Beauty, 49.

13. In 1874, Dr. Edward Clark... Clinton, The Other Civil War, 130-131.

14. In a speech to the Maryland... Cordell, Medical Annals of Maryland, 173.

15. *The formulaic books had... Spaeth, "Medical Studies and Women," 1109; Walsh, Reminiscences of 30 Years, 180.*

16. *One reason offered... Clinton, The Other Civil War, 130.*

17. *Its goal was to provide... Abrahams, Extinct Medical Schools, 71.*

18. *Women doctors at the... Clinton, The Other Civil War, 144.*

## Baltimore, 1892

1. *"Then we went to Baltimore..." Stein, Gertrude, Everybody's Autobiography, 157*

2. *The two youngest Stein... Sprigge, Gertrude Stein Her Life, 16.*

3. *From the proceeds... ibid, 20-21.*

4. *Her cousin Helen... ibid, 22-23.*

5. *The Baltimore Sun said... Pollack, The Collectors, 38.*

6. *In fact, Dr. Claribel... Benstock, Women of the Left Bank, 146.*

7. *During their separation... Stein, Gertrude, Autobiography of Alice B. Toklas, 77.*

8. *Moses was a large... MDHS, Cone, Sydney Jr., The Cones of Bavaria, 59.*

9. *She was the epitome of... Vicinus, Suffer and Be Still, 57.*

10. *Popular magazines featured... Banner, American Beauty, 162.*

11. *Interest in artists grew... Green, The Light of the Home, 93.*

12. *... and the trend became... Donnelly, The American Victorian Woman, 103.*

13. *Her money purchased... Richardson, Brenda, Dr. Claribel and Miss Etta, 167.*

14. *When the purchases arrived... Pollock, The Collectors, 34.*

15. *Louis Prang and Company... Green, The Light of the Home, 107.*

16. *Claribel at the time was one of... Chesney, The Johns Hopkins Hospital, 22.*

17. *Leo, declaring he could... Mellow, The Charmed Circle, 42-43.*

18. *Claribel and Gertrude would ride ... Pollack, The Collectors, 37.*

19. *Anyone who knew Gertrude... Sprigge, Gertrude Stein Her Life, 38-39.*

20. *Gertrude's thesis was... BMA CCol, Stein, Gertrude, "Value of a College Education for Women".*

21. *The "new woman" or "bachelor... Banner, American Beauty, 151; Vicinus, Suffer and Be Still, 165.*

## Florence, 1901

1. *"There was an open door..." Nyburg, The Buried Rose, 154.*

2. *... as a "holiday from Victorianism..." Banner, American Beauty, 180.*

3. *"Awoke at 4:30 am..." BMA CCol, EC Diary, May 23, 1901.*

4. *"... as a general rule..." Pollack, The Collectors, 41.*

5. *"Isn't it odd that..." ibid, 234.*

6. *"It was glorious..." BMA CCol, EC Diary, May 29, 1901.*

7. *"Saw women ploughing..." BMA CCol, EC Diary, May 27, 1901.*

8. *Mary, Berenson's companion, ... Mellow, Charmed Circle, 44.*

9. *"Keep your eye on..." Stein, Leo, Appreciation, Painting, Poetry and Prose, 143.*

10. *"...too much covered..." BMA CCol, EC Diary, May 28, 1901.*

11. *"Made our third visit..." BMA CCol, EC Diary, June 5, 1901.*

12. She wrote of being "keenly"... BMA CCol, EC Diary, June 3, 1901.

13. "Finally reached Uffizi by..." BMA CCol, EC Diary, June 13, 1901.

14. Etta described their "lonely march"... BMA CCol, EC Diary, June 18, 1901.

15. "hospitality touching but..." BMA CCol, EC Diary, July 21, 1901.

16. During a visit to... BMA CCol, EC Diary, July 27, 1901.

17. "I was not in the mood..." BMA CCol, EC Diary, Aug. 29, 1901.

18. "Went to the Louvre..." BMA CCol, EC Diary, Aug. 31, 1901.

19. In fact, the decision to stay ... she had flunked four... Mellow, Charmed Circle, 44-45.

20. "detested women doctors..." Mencken, H.L., The Diary of H.L. Mencken, 115.

21. The air of experimentation... Hobhouse, Everybody Who Was Anybody, 25.

22. In it, she described... Mellow, Charmed Circle, 59.

23. As early as the 18th century... Faderman, Surpassing, 298.

24. The unions were not believed... ibid, 152.

25. Women who were attracted... ibid, 239.

26. In 1897, Havelock Ellis... ibid. 241.

27. A sensational 1892 case... Clinton, The Other Civil War, 164.

28. "Arose late & Gertrude..." BMA CCol, EC Diary, Sept. 10, 1901.

29. "...Got up at 1 p.m...." BMA CCol, EC Diary, Sept. 4, 1901.

30. "...talked with Gertrude..." BMA CCol, EC Diary, Sept. 15, 1901.

31. Gertrude left her at 2 a.m.... BMA CCol, EC Diary, Sept. 23, 1901.

32. Etta retired for the evening... BMA CCol, EC Diary, Sept. 22, 1901.

33. In her diary..."I've got the fever..." BMA CCol, EC Diary, Sept. 17, 1901.

34. The only diary entry... BMA CCol, EC Diary, Sept. 13, 1901.

35. While Etta and her group... Herrera, Matisse, A Portrait, 43.

36. "Uneventful in every..." BMA CCol, EC Diary, Oct. 3, 1901.

37. On October 7 ..."I fear I am not..." BMA CCol, EC Diary, Oct. 7, 1901.

38. But on October 8..."Clear beautiful day..." BMA CCol, EC Diary, Oct. 8, 1901.

39. The underlined phrase... Richardson, B., Dr. Claribel and Miss Etta, 63.

40. The request indicated that... Burke, "Gertrude Stein," 548.

41. "We went to the Uffizi..." BMA CCol, EC Diary, June 16, 1903.

42. The next day, Etta wrote..."enormous difference in..." BMA CCol, EC Diary, June 17, 1903.

43. And she began "working out the influence..." BMA CCol, EC Diary, June 21, 1903.

44. "Went to the Academy..." BMA CCol, EC Diary, June 22, 1903.

45. "Started off after..." BMA CCol, EC Diary, June 23, 1903.

46. "Walked to the Fiesole..." BMA CCol, EC Diary, June 26, 1903.

47. But within four days ..."Gertrude and I had..." BMA CCol, EC Diary, June 30, 1903.

48. On July 2, ..."The woods were gorgeous..." BMA CCol, EC Diary, July 2, 1901.

49. It was by the post-Impressionists .. Saarinen, The Proud Possessors, 180.

50. *Gertrude said she would live...* Mellow, *Charmed Circle*, 53.

51. *In February 1904... Olson, The Building of an American City*, 246.

## Paris, 1905

1. *"The art of the time is paradoxically...* Stein, Leo, *Appreciation...*, 85.

2. *"I told him not to have it..." Pollack, The Collectors*, 62.

3. *Their European itinerary was...* Richardson, B., Dr. *Claribel and Miss Etta*, 82.

4. *In 1903, Bernard Berenson... Stein, Leo, Appreciation...*, 153-154.

5. *What he found in Cezanne ... ibid*, 146.

6. *There was nothing to even indicate... ibid*, 154-155.

7. *Vollard, said Leo, liked... ibid,*. 194.

8. *Leo stretched out... Saarinen, The Proud Possessors*, 183.

9. *During his frequent musings on...* Mellow, *Charmed Circle*, 63.

10. *Years later, Leo wrote, "What you don't know..." Stein, Leo, Appreciation...*, 100-101.

11. *From 1905 to 1907, wrote Matisse... Barr, Matisse His Art*, 57.

12. *To the public he sold art... Warnod, Washboat Days*, 80-81.

13. *The ex-clown, said Leo, "twinkled..."... Stein, Leo, Appreciation...*, 168-169.

14. *When Picasso looked at a drawing... ibid*, 170.

15. *But he reserved that bit... Olivier, Picasso and his Friends*, 22.

16. *Picasso's mistress, Fernande Olivier, described ..."There weren't many..." ibid*, 30.

17. *One ramshackle building... ibid*, 26.

18. *Opposite the building... Warnod, Washboat Days*, 3.

19. *The Picasso gang would... Olivier, Picasso and his Friends*, 36.

20. *The Bateau Lavoir... Warnod, Washboat Days*, 15-17.

21. *Shortly after purchasing... Stein, Leo, Appreciation...*, 169.

22. *Fernande Olivier wrote, "I remember how surprised..." Olivier, Picasso and his Friends*, 82.

23. *Leo described Picasso... Stein, Leo, Appreciation...*, 170.

24. *On that first visit, the Steins purchased... Mellow, Charmed Circle*, 99.

25. *The sisters entered at ... Warnod, Washboat Days*, 109.

26. *The art critic Louis Vauxcelles... Flam, Matisse, A Retrospective*, 47.

27. *Claribel wrote: "The Walls were covered with..." Mellow, Charmed Circle*, 79.

28. *Leo found "La Femme..." Stein, Leo, Appreciation...*, 158.

29. *In the Journel de Rouen... Barr, Matisse His Art*, 55.

30. *But to Leo, it was "art with a capital A..." Stein, Leo, Appreciation....*, 159.

31. *He told Matisse... Hobhouse, Everybody Who Was Anybody*, 41.

32. *The woman with whom.... Herrera, Matisse A Portrait*, 19.

33. *The child, however, could... ibid*, 29.

34. *By 1900, Matisse and Amelie had two... Barr, Matisse His Art*, 40.

35. *Matisse took a job painting... ibid*, 40-41.

36. *In the spring of 1901... Herrera, Matisse A Portrait*, 43-44.

37. *They didn't follow through... ibid*, 43-44.

38. In August 1904, Matisse wrote ..."I think painting will..." ibid, 48.

39. Early in his struggles... Stein, Leo, Appreciation..., 159-160.

40. Leo found him intelligent...ibid, 158.

41. Sally considered herself an artist... Barr, Matisse His Art, 58.

42. On November 2, 1905, Etta... Richardson, B., Dr. Claribel and Miss Etta, 90.

43. A smiling though harried concierge... Warnod, Washboat Days, 12.

44. The doors were scarred... ibid, 5.

45. Cinder was piled beside... Olivier, Picasso and his Friends, 47.

46. The curtainless windows... ibid, 48.

47. In the winter, a bitter... Warnod, Washboat Days, 17.

48. Picasso painted standing up... Olivier, Picasso and his Friends, 53-54.

49. His palette was dirty... Stein, Leo, Appreciation..., 170.

50. At the time, Fernande said ... Olivier, Picasso and his Friends, 21.

51. Later, Gertrude teased... Stein, Gertrude, The Autobiography..., 52.

52. The Michael Steins were known... Toklas, What is Remembered, 22.

53. "They all had a sense..." Saarinen, The Proud Possessors, 187.

54. "From 1905 to the beginning..." ibid, 197.

## Paris, 1906

1. "What can be said about..." Flam, Matisse A Retrospective, 68-69.

2. To the artist who needed her... Rogers, Ladies Bountiful, 3.

3. He had even ordered his wife..."The dirtiness of some of... " BMA CCol, CC Notes on Nevinson.

4. Two weeks after she purchased... Richardson, B., Dr. Claribel and Miss Etta, 168.

5. Gertrude needed someone to... Sprigge, Gertrude Stein Her Life, 54.

6. She began writing under... ibid, 56-58.

7. Three Lives marked... Benstock, Women of the Left Bank, 166-167.

8. Leo would not say he liked... Sprigge, Gertrude Stein Her Life, 58.

9. Etta, she wrote, was... Stein, Gertrude, Autobiography..., 52-53.

10. He said it remained "unequivocal"... Sutherland, "Alice and Gertrude and Others," 297.

11. Gertrude once wrote, "It is one of the peculiarities..." Stein, Gertrude, Q.E.D., 55.

12. There was Max Jacob... Olivier, Picasso and his Friends, 56; Warnod, Washboat Days, 99.

13. Picasso took the money... Olivier, Picasso and his friends, 118.

14. Even Signac, who had previously... Barr, Matisse His Art, 81-82.

15. There is some question, too, ... Richardson, B., Dr. Claribel and Miss Etta, 158.

16. It would have been a very expensive... Barr, Matisse His Art, 82.

17. Etta left Paris reluctantly... Pollack, The Collectors, 79-80.

18. John Stuart Mill wrote, "All the moralities tell..." Vicinus, Suffer and Be Still, 161.

19. Ironically, Etta received a marriage proposal that winter... Mellow, Charmed Circle, 101.

20. Years later, she explained that... Edward T. Cone interview.

21. Nursing what she called her "bum gut"... Pollack, The Collectors, 85.

22. Etta said she would probably ..."Goodness knows how long..." ibid, 86.

23. Etta responded: "Poor little Picasso!..." Yale, SteinCol., EC to GS, Oct. 6, 1906.

24. Sunday newspaper supplements at the... Banner, American Beauty, 238.

25. "It may seem very strange..." Sprigge, Gertrude Stein Her Life, 66.

26. Matisse, now 37, appeared... Olivier, Picasso and his Friends, 88.

27. ... old man of art compared with Picasso... Saarinen, Proud Possessors, 186.

28. Fernande called Matisse... Barr, Matisse His Art, 84-85.

29. The twenty-five-year-old Picasso,... Stein, Leo, Appreciation..., 170-172.

30. And when he didn't... Olivier, Picasso and his Friends, 151.

31. The younger artist... Barr, Matisse His Art, 85.

32. Within a year of each other... ibid, 86.

33. For Picasso, it was his... ibid, 86; Wertenbaker, The World of Picasso, 53.

## Blowing Rock, 1908

1. "Make up your mind to..." Eliot, Daniel Deronda, 107.

2. In December 1907, Etta and her... Pollack, The Collectors, 90.

3. Both were used to having their... ibid, 92.

4. In the years after Moses... EPFL, Cone, Bertha Lindau, notes.

5. And, fully in charge... Edward T. Cone interview, Nov. 21, 1992.

6. Solomon, four years younger than... MDHS, Cone, Sydney Jr., Cones of Bavaria, 127-128.

7. If Moses felt it necessary... Edward T. Cone interview, Nov. 21, 1992.

8. She utterly exasperated Moses... Pollack, The Collectors, 92.

9. During a journey down the Nile... ibid, 92.

10. Moses purchased stone Buddhas... ibid, 92-93.

11. On February 6, 1907, from Cairo, she wrote..."Every whit of my oriental..." ibid, 91.

12. When she did, she stepped... Sprigge, Gertrude Stein Her Life, 81.

13. From Cairo, she wrote Gertrude, "I am most jealous that..." Yale SteinCol, EC to GS, Feb. 6, 1907.

14. In Darjeeling..."I am hating the idea..." Yale SteinCol, EC to GS, March 30, 1907.

15. In a Rosh Hashanah greeting..."Happy New Year to you..." Yale SteinCol, EC to GS, Sept. 9, 1907.

16. From China, she wrote Gertrude..."Now do be amiable and send..." Yale SteinCol, EC to GS, May 11, 1907.

17. And though Etta..."I hate, I despise Baltimore..." Yale SteinCol, EC to GS, Jan. 7, 1908.

18. Claribel did not invite Etta... Yale SteinCol, EC to GS, Sept. 9, 1907.

19. Etta's Paris fever was heightened... Richardson, B., Dr. Claribel and Miss Etta, 168.

20. Etta commented: "I love Picasso and..." Yale SteinCol, EC to GS, Feb. 24, 1908.

21. Shortly after, Etta wrote Gertrude, "I shall sail sure as fate on ..." Pollack, The Collectors, 97.

22. Ida, a prominent woman, ... Arthur J. Gutman interview.

23. Etta described her... Yale SteinCol, EC to GS, Dec. 4, 1907.

24. Etta described her..."heart still beats hot..." Yale SteinCol, EC to GS, Jan. 7, 1908.

25. "The poor thing," she lamented, "is so walled..." Yale SteinCol, EC to GS, April 14, 1908.

26. Gertrude's new companion was... Mellow, Charmed Circle, 105.

27. "Gertrude took me in Florence..." Toklas, What Is Remembered, 48.

28. With his death in 1906... "the man of the moment."... Stein, Leo, Appreciation..., 174.

29. But as early as 1907... Barr, Matisse His Art, 83.

30. Matisse called Picasso "unsympathetic as a man..." Toklas, What Is Remembered, 38-39.

31. The Parisian art world ..."served to increase..." Barr, Matisse His Art, 94-95.

32. Just as Picasso and Matisse... Stein, Leo, Appreciation..., 174.

33. Now, a sufficient number of younger... Flam, Matisse A Retrospective, 103.

34. The prospering artist also... Herrera, Matisse A Portrait, 72.

35. "On the strength of these..." Barr, Matisse His Art, 113.

36. In June 1908... "Like nearly all the other..." ibid, 113-114.

37. James Gibbons Huneker... ibid, 114.

38. In August, they returned... Pollack, The Collectors, 99.

39. In June, Etta wrote..."It is the dream of my life..." Yale SteinCol, EC to MS, June 15, 1908.

40. In April, Etta wrote... "I have meant to write..." Yale SteinCol, EC to GS, April 11, 1909.

41. July 25: "My silence only means that..." Yale SteinCol, EC to GS, July 25, 1909.

42. August 22: "...honestly Gertrude, you cannot..." Yale SteinCol, EC to GS, Aug. 22, 1909.

43. September 26: "There is no need to deny..." Yale SteinCol, EC to GS, Sept. 26, 1909.

44. And finally, in December she wrote ... "My brother's death almost..." Yale SteinCol, EC to GS, Dec. 12, 1909.

45. And, "I wish, oh I do wish..." Yale SteinCol, EC to GS, Jan. 10, 1910.

## Frankfurt, 1910

1. "You want to see life—...." James, The Portrait of a Lady, 203.

2. She wrote Etta that... "most terribly flattered..." BMA CCol, CC to EC, Dec. 2, 1906.

3. And, in another letter, she confided ... "I cannot hear from too..." BMA CCol, CC to EC, July 7, 1910.

4. Albrecht no doubt... BMA CCol, CC to EC, May 30, 1904.

5. Even at the height ... "usually too late to..." "Eccentric Esthetes," 95-96.

6. She told an interviewer... "I never get my work..." The Evening Sun, April 8, 1911, 4..

7. To describe the last group... "Idleness has as a good..." Pollack, The Collectors, 88.

8. Claribel, the woman with ... "credit to both their..." Abrahams, Extinct Medical Schools, 72.

9. "There is a sort of intolerable..." BMA CCol, CC to EC, June 22, 1910.

10. "Do you know as to..." BMA CCol, CC to EC, June 30, 1910.

11. "You do not know what..." BMA CCol, CC to EC, Sept. 2, 1910.

12. As the middle Cone sister ... "Dr. Cone has often been..." The Evening Sun, April 8, 1911, 4.

13. She was described by... "the only lady who combines..." BMA CCol, MS to CC, Dec. 26, 1910.

14. And, in fact, at some point ... Cone, Claribel, Aunt Etta, 2.

15. "Do you know every now..." BMA CCol, CC to EC, Aug. 7, 1910.

16. From FRankfurt, Claribel traveled ... "music-music-music..." BMA CCol, CC to EC, July 8, 1910.

17. "Oh how I love this..." BMA CCol, Aug. 25, 1910.

18. "How awesome it was..." BMA CCol, Aug. 25, 1910.

19. Drastic changes had come ... "salon des refuses"... Toklas, What is Remembered, 62.

20. Leo and Gertrude quarreled... Saarinen, The Proud Possessors, 192-193.

21. He thought her writing ... she disapproved of his romance... Sprigge, Gertrude Stein Her Life, 83.

22. In the past, Leo... Saarinen, The Proud Possessors, 186.

23. But increasingly, Leo sat... ibid, 192.

24. Leo explained the change simply... "When my interest..." Stein, Leo, Appreciation..., 201.

25. The Cubists' leading influence ... Warnod, Washboat Days, 173.

26. Maurice Princet, said Leo ... Stein, Leo, Appreciation..., 175-176.

27. Gertrude, unlike Leo, admired Picasso's... Saarinen, The Proud Possessors, 176.

28. He said of Picasso, "It is not the lack..." Stein, Leo, Appreciation..., 181.

29. In 1909, he had moved from... Warnod, Washboat Days, 195-196.

30. Matisse, said Leo, was "too intelligent and ..." Stein, Leo, Appreciation..., 191-192.

31. Matisse was robust... Flam, Matisse A Retrospective, 132-133.

32. For some time, he had been... Herrera, Matisse A Portrait, 84.

33. Urinals in Montmartre ... "Matisse has done more..." Flam, Matisse A Retrospective, 124.

34. Arthur Hoeber ... "like the work of a..." Barr, Matisse His Art, 149.

35. Gertrude Vanderbilt Whitney considered... ibid, 148.

36. And Isabella Stewart Gardner... Flam, Matisse A Retrospective, 119.

37. By 1912, Gertrude... Stein, Leo, Appreciation..., 186.

38. During a visit that fall... Pollack, The Collectors, 105-106.

39. Claribel wrote: "There were two of them..." Richardson, B., Dr. Claribel and Miss Etta, 27.

40. She occasionally spoke... Pollack, The Collectors, 107-108.

41. A flu epidemic hit ... ibid, 109.

42. One American critic labeled the Cubist grouping... Mellow, Charmed Circle, 171.

43. A New York Times critic wrote, "We may as well say..." Barr, Matisse His Art, 150.

44. In Chicago, students... ibid, 150.

45. But the controversy... Saarinen, The Proud Possessors, 217.

46. He told the collector... "I can't stand Gertrude..." ibid, 192-193.

47. He said the success of Cubism... Herrera, Matisse A Portrait, 112-113.

48. *For his part, Picasso's... Sprigge,*
*Gertrude Stein Her Life, 97.*

## Munich, 1914

1. *"We had seen three days..." Sullivan,*
*Our Times, Vol V, 1914-18, 26.*

2. *Munich in 1914... Hanser, Putsch,*
*38-48.*

3. *Adolf Hitler, still... ibid, 57.*

4. *The year Claribel took up residence ...*
*was bursting with... ibid, 76.*

5. *"This city is feverish..." Sullivan,*
*"Our Times, Vol V," 5.*

6. *One American writer... "gave an*
*impression..." ibid, 2-3.*

7. *"Suddenly," one reporter, "the paraly-*
*sis..." ibid, 405.*

8. *The correspondent for the ... "In their*
*eagerness to get..." ibid, 13.*

9. *In fact, during the first year of...*
*Hanser, Putsch, 117.*

10. *Search lights, mounted atop...*
*Sullivan, Our Times, Vol. V, 18.*

11. *"Paris is dark at three..." Herrera,*
*Matisse A Portrait, 121.*

12. *Picasso remained in Paris... Sprigge,*
*Gertrude Stein Her Life, 107.*

13. *Braque, Derain, Apollinaire... Barr,*
*Matisse His Art, 178.*

14. *Gertrude and Alice had... Sprigge,*
*Gertrude Stein Her Life, 109.*

15. *In America, the New York Stock*
*Exchange... Sullivan, Our Times, Vol*
*V, 48-49.*

16. *President Woodrow Wilson ..."Peace*
*Sunday,"... ibid, 44.*

17. *As one of its first acts of war, Britain*
*had cut the only... ibid, 68.*

18. *Correspondents traveled with... ibid,*
*70-71.*

19. *"Her Day's Work" ...1. get red but-*
*tons. 2...." Pollack, The Collectors,*
*113.*

20. *"My dearest sister: I think..." ibid,*
*114.*

21. *In one letter to Etta, she wrote..., ibid,*
*115.*

22. *And she said, "over here they put*
*me..." ibid, 114.*

23. *In apparent response..."I am strictly*
*neutral..." ibid, 115.*

24. *By October of 1916... BMA CCol,*
*CC to EC, Oct. 1-6, 1916.*

25. *Claribel's suite included three... BMA*
*CCol, CC to EC, Nov. 17, 1916.*

26. *Her daily routine included... BMA*
*CCol, CC to EC, Nov. 17, 1916.*

27. *Among them was a soldier... BMA*
*CCol, CC to EC, Nov. 8, 1916.*

28. *"Along with the rest..." Pollack, The*
*Collectors, 116.*

29. *In 1917, Claribel's family... MDHS,*
*Cone, Sydney Jr., The Cones of*
*Bavaria, 102.*

30. *Claribel wrote to her brother Sydney,*
*"I thank you for..." BMA CCol, CC*
*to Sydney Cone, Jan. 1, 1917.*

31. *In February 1917, Claribel...*
*Pollack, The Collectors, 116-117.*

32. *Even after the Lusitania.... Sullivan,*
*Our Times, Vol V, 126.*

33. *But repeated German attacks... ibid,*
*299-300.*

34. *The great German gun... ibid,*
*84-85.*

35. *Thirteen percent of the... ibid, 288.*

36. *As the war continued... ibid, 476.*

37. *In 1918, U.S. Food... ibid, 420.*

38. *In fact, just several blocks... " Olson,*
*The Building of an American City,*
*293.*

39. *The war in Baltimore... ibid, 300-301.*

41. *What is known is that the... Alfred J. Gutman interview.*

42. *In 1912, in a published book..."Jews who had not..." Hanser, Putsch, 73.*

43. *Alfred Schuler called... ibid, 57.*

## Munich, 1918

1. *"We're turning everything..." Hanser, Putsch, 145.*

2. *In November 1918, Munich's streets were filled... ibid, 119-121.*

3. *The demonstration was... ibid, 122-123.*

4. *In addition to local... Sullivan, Our Times, Vol V, 654.*

5. *In a letter written several years earlier... BMA CCol, CC to EC, Nov. 17, 1916.*

6. *In the first weeks of November... Hanser, Putsch, 129-132.*

7. *Throughout the country, posters... ibid, 134.*

8. *The press dismissed Eisner... ibid, 145.*

9. *The Thule Society was.. ibid, 153.*

10. *On February 21, 1919... ibid, 161-162.*

11. *A state of siege was... ibid, 164.*

12. *A group of revolutionaries... ibid, 166.*

13. *She told them she had nothing... Pollack, The Collectors, 117-118.*

14. *Using cooking equipment ... Edward T. Cone interview, Nov. 21, 1992.*

15. *The putsch ushered in a new... Hanser, Putsch, 173-176.*

16. *According to one historian, "A state of hysterical..." ibid, 176.*

17. *In the "war after the war"... ibid, 180-184.*

18. *The nationalists, who had been... ibid, 186-191.*

19. *Claribel told an interviewer... The Baltimore Sun, Oct. 9, 1949, 12-13, 20-21.*

20. *Claribel wrote to Etta, "The close of the war and..." BMA CCol, CC to EC, Sept. 17, 1919.*

21. *The value of the mark plunged... Hanser, Putsch, 304-305.*

22. *"This will probably..." BMA CCol, CC to EC, Sept. 2, 1919.*

23. *In September 1919, he wrote his... Hanser, Putsch, 196.*

24. *In October, she contacted... BMA CCol, CC to EC, Oct. 2, 1919.*

25. *"...you were so kind..." BMA CCol, CC to EC, Oct. 29, 1919.*

26. *In response to a letter..."You are right—do not..." BMA CCol, CC to EC, March 16, 1920.*

27. *The same month... "I am ready to take myself..." Pollack, The Collectors, 119-20.*

28. *In February 1920, Hitler's... Hanser, Putsch, 213.*

29. *Announcements concerning the... ibid, 245.*

30. *The ultra-nationalist meetings... ibid, 252.*

31. *For Hitler, Munich was... ibid, 5.*

32. *Lion Feuchtwanger... ibid, 6.*

33. *Warnings were issued in.... ibid, 257.*

34. *Before leaving Munich ... "I shall be so glad to see you..." Pollack, The Collectors, 120.*

## Paris, 1922, Part One

1. *"There is never any ending to Paris..." Hemingway, A Moveable Feast, 211*

2. *The Claribel who returned... Pollack, The Collectors, 124*

3. *She began filling it with the things...* MDHS, Cone, Sydney Jr., *The Cones of Bavaria, 125*

4. *The two sisters and their brother...* Pollack, *The Collectors, 125*

5. *How to pay, however, was still...* BMA CCol, CC to EC, Oct. 29, 1919

6. *During the war, firms that.... Sullivan, Our Times, Vol. V, 484*

7. *The Cone Export and... Pollack, The Collectors, 124*

8. *One relative estimated... Edward T. Cone interview*

9. *During the war, a million... Wiser, The Crazy Years, 13*

10. *German bombs had fallen... ibid, 15*

11. *Gertrude, it was said, ... Sprigge, Gertrude Stein Her Life, 112*

12. *Gertrude said she and Alice... Pollack, The Collectors, 127*

13. *In a characteristic... Sprigge, Gertrude Stein Her Life, 123*

14. *She worked at night and left... ibid, 93*

15. *Gertrude would talk to the... ibid., 127*

16. *Leo Stein had spent the war... Mellow, Charmed Circle, 244*

17. *Leo Stein had ...or as one writer put it... Saarinen, The Proud Possessors, 194*

18. *Nina, the artist's model... Mellow, Charmed Circle, 244*

19. *Upon his return to Europe... Saarinen, The Proud Possessors, 194*

20. *But, despite his warm tone... Mellow, Charmed Circle, 244-246*

21. *Apollinaire was dead... Sprigge, Gertrude Stein Her Life, 121*

22. *Picasso's great love, Eva,... Mellow, Charmed Circle, 234*

23. *As Picasso's professional fortunes... Sprigge, Gertrude Stein Her Life, 119; Daix, Picasso, 166*

24. *Matisse spent the first year... Barr, Matisse His Art, 178*

25. *A Matisse retrospective had... ibid, 178*

26. *By 1916, Matisse was painting... ibid, 181*

27. *Claribel explained the change... BMA CCol, CC notes*

28. *In 1916, Matisse wrote to Hans... Barr, Matisse His Art, 181*

29. *And, as if in retreat... ibid, 195*

30. *Matisse took up residence... ibid, 195*

31. *He rose early ... then paint from... Herrera, Matisse A Portrait, 136*

32. *His gallery, Bernheim-Jeune... Barr, Matisse His Art, 183*

33. *In the year 1917, a... Herrera, Matisse A Portrait, 126-128*

34. *In the spring of 1919... Barr, Matisse His Art, 196*

35. *In 1920, three books on Matisse... ibid, 197*

## *Paris, 1922, Part Two*

1. *"Some are coming to know..." Stein, Gertrude, Two: Gertrude Stein and Her Brother and Other Early Portraits, 1908-12, 353-355.*

2. *Consumerism on a mass scale ... Sullivan, Our Times, IV, 95.*

3. *Encouraged by newly advertising companies ... ibid, 88.*

4. *...became, with an almost religious fervor... ibid, 121.*

5. *From their inheritance, the sisters had an annual... Hirschland, The Cone Sisters, 80.*

6. *But on July 11, 1922... Richardson, B., Dr. Claribel and Miss Etta, 170.*

7. *The sisters paid a visit ...considerably more than... ibid, 168.*

8. *She "became like a voiceless..." Cone, Claribel, Aunt Etta, 2.*

9. *The Jazz Age now gripped... Wiser, The Crazy Years, 73.*

10. *The cosmetic industry... Banner, American Beauty, 271-272.*

11. *Hemlines went up, necklines... ibid., 279.*

12. *They were described as... Rogers, Ladies Bountiful, 18.*

13. *On July 24, Claribel marched... Richardson, B., Dr. Claribel and Miss Etta, 170.*

14. *On July 14, Claribel posed for a... Richardson, B., Dr. Claribel and Miss Etta, 170; Pollack, The Collectors, 128.*

15. *Picasso wanted 1,000 francs... Pollack, The Collectors, 128.*

16. *Matisse had much good news... Barr, Matisse His Art, 198.*

17. *Now Matisse, and by reflection... Herrera, Matisse A Portrait, 144.*

18. *Years later... "If it is true, as has been..." EPFL, Herald Tribune, January or February 1955.*

19. *The Cones stayed in only the best... Edward T. Cone interview.*

20. *In fact, at some point during... Richardson, B., Dr. Claribel and Miss Etta, 173.*

21. *Claribel wrote to Etta, then in Brest... BMA CCol, CC to EC, July 29, 1922.*

22. *Etta complained to Gertrude... Yale SteinCol, EC to GS, Sept. 25, 1922.*

23. *Claribel later said, "As a matter of fact..." Baltimore Sun, April 15, 1928, 13.*

24. *Leo was living in... Gertrude's social life was... Sprigge, Gertrude Stein Her Life, 132.*

25. *Vanity Fair magazine ran... Hemingway, A Moveable Feast, 15.*

26. *In the 1920s, a new relationship... Hirschland, The Cone Sisters, 80-82.*

27. *"My dear Etta," Michael Stein wrote, "there are..." BMA CCol, MS to EC, Nov. 19, 1922.*

28. *A few blocks to the west... Olson, Building of an American City, 277-78.*

29. *Nearby Pennsylvania Avenue... ibid, 274.*

## *Paris, 1923-1924*

1. *"What shall we call our 'self'?..." James, The Portrait of a Lady, 253.*

2. *In June 1923, back at Bernheim... Richardson, B., Dr. Claribel and Miss Etta, 173.*

3. *Etta's purchases tended toward... ibid, 173.*

4. *In 1922, the Detroit Institute of Arts... Barr, Matisse His Art, 198.*

5. *Matisse, now fifty-four, called... Herrera, Matisse A Portrait, 147.*

6. *In 1920, a local movie agency ... ibid, 148.*

7. *"When I paint or draw," said Matisse, "I feel..." ibid, 147.*

8. *Baltimore's nationally known ... "the truth is, as everyone..." Mencken, A Mencken Chrestomathy, 61.*

9. *In July, they purchased... Richardson, B., Dr. Claribel and Miss Etta, 173.*

10. *The average American ... Shannon, Between the Wars, 97.*

11. *In fact, the sisters, on a sped up course... MDHS, Cone, Sydney Jr., The Cones of Bavaria, 125.*

12. *In the afternoon of July 23... BMA CCol, CC to EC, July 23, 1923.*

13. *On July 24th, she had lunch... BMA CCol, CC to EC, July 24, 1923.*

14. *"Went to Ararat's... Ararat is away..." BMA CCol, CC to EC, July 25, 1923.*

15. *She ordered silk stockings and... Pollack, The Collectors, 135.*

16. *Claribel ordered multiples... MDHS, Cone, Sydney Jr., The Cones of Bavaria, 126.*

17. *"I find my chief objection..." BMA CCol, CC to EC, Aug. 27, 1924.*

18. *During a drive together, Gertrude... Pollack, The Collectors, 141.*

19. *A.D. Emmart, then a literary... Emmart and Fleming, "Baltimore City of Average Men," 309.*

20. *Their fellow Baltimoreans saw... JHS, Azrael, Louis, Baltimore American, 1962.*

21. *A Maryland doctor wrote ..."The very few Baltimoreans..." Rosen, "The Cones," Helicon Nine, 78-85.*

22. *Miss Kaufman relayed to the sisters... Pollack, The Collectors, 154.*

23. *Claribel began to drape her body... Hirschland, The Cone Sisters, 78.*

24. *At private dinner parties, she wore... Pollack, The Collectors, 190.*

25. *In public, she and Etta... Sydney Cone Jr. interview.*

26. *As recreational pursuits, Etta lavished... Pollack, The Collectors, 131.*

27. *She even wrote in a note to herself... BMA CCol, CC notes.*

28. *"Please do not get the book sticky..." BMA CCol, CC notes, Dec. 6, 1924.*

29. *"I want to tell you something..." Yale SteinCol, GS to EC, June 22, 1924.*

30. *Etta, who referred to the manuscript... Yale SteinCol, EC to GS, Jan. 14, 1911.*

31. *To be sure, Gertrude was now a "famous..." Sprigge, Gertrude Stein Her Life, 129.*

32. *She was territorial when... Sutherland, Alice and Gertrude and Others, 297-298.*

33. *"I do indeed appreciate your..." Yale SteinCol, EC to GS, June 23, 1924.*

34. *Shortly after Etta refused... Yale SteinCol, MS to GS, Aug. 26, 1924.*

35. *In another case, he wrote... Yale SteinCol, MS to ABT, June 6, 1925.*

36. *"You train people to take..." BMA CCol, CC to EC, Sept. 14, 1924.*

37. *"I am not quite sure..." BMA CCol, CC to EC, Sept. 10, 1924.*

## *Lausanne, 1926-1929*

1. *"I'm beginning the buying..." BMA CCol, CC to EC, Sept. 2, 1924.*

2. *A Marie Laurencin oil from 1908... Richardson, B., Dr. Claribel and Miss Etta, 175.*

3. *Meanwhile, Claribel did not share... ibid, 110.*

4. *It was Cezanne's "La Montagne..." ibid, 109-110.*

5. *At one point, Claribel cabled ...."Bought pictures. Cable me... " Pollack, The Collectors, 182.*

6. *After 1922, Etta, in her art purchases, ... Richardson, B., Dr. Claribel and Miss Etta, 173.*

7. *In 1925, she continued to... Barr, Matisse His Art, 212.*

8. *At almost four feet by ... Richardson, B., Dr. Claribel and Miss Etta, 112.*

9. *Pierre Matisee, the artist's son..."very freely followed their own..." The Baltimore Sun*, Oct. 9, 1949, 12-13, 20-21.

10. *They were so large they...* Cone, Claribel, Alice Derain, 8.

11. *"He is really devoted to us..."* BMA CCol, CC to EC, Aug. 20, 1927.

12. *"My Dear Folks..."* Yale SteinCol, MS to GS, 1926.

13. *Claribel purchased the painting...* Richardson, B., Dr. Claribel and Miss Etta, 176.

14. *But in October, at the auction, Pierre found...* Pollack, The Collectors, 187-189.

15. *Claribel alertly noticed that Matisse had not...* Richardson, B., Dr. Claribel and Miss Etta, 117.

16. *Claribel considered two points when...* ibid, 119.

17. *There were Renaissance and Queen Anne...* Edward T. Cone interview, Nov. 21, 1992.

18. *...Oriental rugs, bronze sculptures...* "Eccentric Esthetes," 94-99.

19. *"She would complain that..."* MDHS, Cone, Sydney Jr., The Cones of Bavaria, 123.

20. *Claribel, for her part, knew she was a...* Sydney Cone Jr. interview.

21. *Claribel replied, "If I were considering putting..."* BMA CCol, CC to EC, Jan. 12, 1927.

22. *When he first arrived in Baltimore, said Boas...* "Paintings, Sculpture and Drawings in The Cone Collection," 9-10.

23. *"Though both Etta Cone and her..."* JHU, George Boas notes.

24. *"They never used their pictures..."* ibid.

25. *The 1927 American Chamber...* Wiser, The Crazy Years, 182-183.

26. *The new American was not...* ibid, 183-185.

27. *Claribel spoke of Americans as ... "a good natured crude..."* BMA CCol, CC to EC, Sept. 2, 1924.

28. *In June, they stopped in Paris ...* Richardson, B., Dr. Claribel and Miss Etta, 176-177.

29. *"If Matisse has something..."* BMA CCol, CC to EC, Aug. 18, 1927.

30. *"It is a question how many..."* BMA CCol, CC notes.

31. *By the end of the summer...* Richardson, B., Dr. Claribel and Miss Etta, 179.

32. *She bequeathed her entire ..."It is my desire in respect..."* ibid, 15-16.

33. *She wrote what she thought ... "My dear Sister Etta:..."* Pollack, The Collectors, 193-194.

34. *In the next quiet month together...* ibid, 194.

35. *Not until September 20, ...* Richardson, B., Dr. Claribel and Miss Etta, 182.

## *Baltimore, 1929*

11. *"She did not plan..."* Fitzgerald, The Crack Up, 149.

2. *Brother Fred had arrived ...* Pollack, The Collectors, 195.

3. *Matisse wrote Etta, "My Dear Mademoiselle..."* BMA CCol, HM to EC, Oct. 16, 1929.

4. *Etta replied, "My Dear Monsieur Matisse..."* BMA CCol, EC to HM, Oct. 16, 1929.

5. *Getrude wrote from the south of France, "My very dear Etta..."* Pollack, The Collectors, 197.

6. *"I do appreciate your understanding..."* ibid, 198.

7. *She bought four Matisse... Richardson, B., Dr. Claribel and Miss Etta, 182.*

8. *By October 28, the tremor... Wiser, The Crazy Years, 229.*

9. *In Paris, what Parisians were calling "Le Krach"... ibid, 227.*

10. *The Cone brothers had taken steps... Sydney Cone Jr. interview.*

11. *When Fred, Etta and... Pollack, The Collectors, 198.*

12. *Her clothes were to be hung... Richardson, B., Dr. Claribel and Miss Etta, 121.*

13. *The editor of the Sunday Sun... BMA CCol, Mark S. Watson to Jacob Moses, Nov. 1929.*

14. *The Sun's November 22, 1929 headline read, "Cone Art Unit May Pass..." The Baltimore Sun, Nov. 22, 1929, 30.*

15. *Etta spent a long winter... Pollack, The Collectors, 205.*

16. *She decided to fill in the gaps... Edward T. Cone interview, Nov. 21, 1992.*

17. *Michael wrote to Gertrude ... "I am practically sure..." Yale SteinCol, MS to GS, 1930.*

18. *Etta purchased fourteen... Richardson, B., Dr. Claribel and Miss Etta, 186.*

19. *The sculpture was a stylistic... Barr, Matisse His Art, 213.*

20. *Every morning at eleven Etta... Pollack, The Collectors, 206-207.*

21. *As if to mark her place... Richardson, B., Dr. Claribel and Miss Etta, 183.*

22. *"My father," wrote Margot Matisse... BMA CCol, Margot Duthuit to EC, Nov. 16, 1930.*

## Nice, 1933

1. *"Art has often been..." Stein, Leo, Appreciation..., 9.*

2. *A Sun reporter... Baltimore Sun, Sept. 14, 1949, 32.*

3. *It was not at all like that of... Saarinen, The Proud Possessors, 222.*

4. *Siegried Rosengart said Matisse... Pollack, The Collectors, 209.*

5. *When Etta was in Paris... BMA CCol, HM to EC, June or July 1934.*

6. *Her nephew Harold, who... Cone, Claribel, Aunt Etta, 8.*

7. *Matisse would dine... ibid., 10.*

8. *She once complained... Rosen, "The Cones," 85.*

9. *"The visit of your father..." BMA CCol, EC to Margot Duthuit, Jan. or Feb. 1931.*

10. *"My father was very touched..." BMA CCol, Margot Duthuit to EC, Feb. 1931.*

11. *When Matisse returned to France... Barr, Matisse His Art, 220.*

12. *He did not visit Baltimore... BMA CCol, HM to EC, March 25, 1933.*

13. *She herself...wrote daughter Margot... BMA CCol, EC to Margot Duthuit, Feb. 21, 1933.*

14. *By 1933 a quarter... Gordon, The American Chronicle, 127.*

15. *Squatter camps called... ibid, 108.*

16. *Outside Etta's windows... Brugger, Maryland A Middle Temperament, 502.*

17. *In fact, she purchased... Barr, Matisse His Art, 224.*

18. *The artist wanted to keep all... Richardson, B., Dr. Claribel and Miss Etta, 127.*

19. She wrote to Margot, "It is the most beautiful..." BMA CCol, EC to Margot Duthuit, Feb. 21, 1933.

20. Even through the 1920s... Faderman, Surpassing, 360-361.

21. She once told a great niece... Cone, Edward T., "The Miss Etta Cones," 458.

22. She was known to use... Sutherland, "Alice and Gertrude and Others," 297.

23. Etta always stayed at the... Cone, Edward T., "The Miss Etta Cones,". 458.

24. She traveled with a raft of purses... Cone, Claribel, Aunt Etta, 4.

25. Her nephew, Harold Cone was... Cone, Claribel, Alice Derain, 1-2.

26. That summer would take the group... Herrera, Matisse A Portrait, 165.

27. He was living in an apartment... Flam, Matisse A Retrospective, 291.

28. "My visit was a joy..." BMA CCol, EC to Fred Cone, July 22, 1933.

29. When Etta returned to her family... Edward T. Cone interview, Nov. 21, 1992.

30. "Raymond took us to the studio..." BMA CCol, EC to Fred Cone, July 22, 1933.

31. During their visit Matisse made it... Cone, Edward T., "The Miss Etta Cones," 455.

32. A little dejectedly... BMA CCol, GS to EC, July 24, 1933.

33. In 1926, Alice clipped Gertrude's... Sprigge, Gertrude Stein Her Life, 150-152.

34. But while her reputation as a... ibid, 168.

35. All that changed, however... ibid, 174.

36. Leo, who had been working... Yale SteinCol, LS to George Boas, Feb. 20, 1928.

37. ...called Gertrude's book... Stein, Leo, Appreciation..., 152.

38. ...and a "stupid brag and general..." Saarinen, The Proud Possessors, 200.

39. Hemingway never forgave her... Sprigge, Gertrude Stein Her Life, 199.

40. Georges Braque, Andre Salmon, Tristan... ibid, 196-197.

41. Etta showed no concern for Gertrude's... Edward T. Cone interview, Nov. 21, 1992.

42. "Dear Gertrude," she wrote in reply, "your very kind..." Yale SteinCol, EC to GS, Aug. 9, 1933.

43. Explaining to her family members... Cone, Edward T., "The Miss Etta Cones," 456.

## Baltimore, 1934

1. "Lent by...that was their identity...." JHU, George Boas notes.

2. In 1934, a movie ticker... Gordon, The American Chronicle, 136.

3. That same year, Etta bought... Richardson, B., Dr. Claribel and Miss Etta, 188.

4. Her brothers, again concerned... Edward T. Cone interview.

5. Etta's annual income, according to tax... BMA CCol materials, tax records.

6. "Etta bought because she..." Pollack, The Collectors, 208-209.

7. When talking...from which he often came... Angela Rosengart interview, June 1993.

8. In fact,...The Baltimore Museum for ... ibid, 14-15.

9. *Alfred H. Barr Jr.,...New York's
Museum of Modern Art... Richardson,
B., Dr. Claribel and Miss Etta, 15.*

10. *George Boaz..."There was never in the
minds of..." Cone, Etta, Cone
Collection*

11. *Alfred Barr Jr. ...declared the catalog... Barr, Matisse His Art, 224.*

12. *A Van Gogh nephew said... BMA
CCol, Johan Franco to EC, Sept. 11,
1937.*

13. *The book had been printed... Pollack,
The Collectors, 213-214.*

14. *In February, 1934, Etta wrote
Harcourt Brace... Yale SteinCol, EC
to Harcourt Brace, Feb. 28, 1934.*

15. *"Many museum directors..." Yale
SteinCol, EC to GS, April 17, 1934.*

16. *In New York, Times Square pulsed...
Mellow, Charmed Circle, 382.*

17. *One newspaperman characterized...
Rogers, When This You See, 2.*

18. *"Little Gerty"...the "matron saint of
Paris..." ibid, 380-381.*

20. *"My dear Etta, Thanks..." BMA
CCol, GS to EC, Oct. 30, 1934.*

21. *Gertrude and Alice eventually...
Sprigge, Gertrude Stein Her Life, 192.*

22. *Gertrude and Alice... and share
Christmas Eve... Toklas, What Is
Remembered, 149.*

23. *For a women who adhered... Edward
T. Cone interview, Nov. 21, 1992.*

## Paris, 1938

1. *"Meanwhile the trees were just..."
Hardy, Tess of the d'Ubervilles, 504.*

2. *The sisters' textile collection.. The
Evening Sun, Dec. 2, 1949, 64.*

3. *An expert from the Detroit... EPFL,
The Baltimore Sun, Nov. 12, 1935.*

4. *An expert from... EPFL, The Baltimore
Sun, Dec. 4, 1949.*

5. *Years of study had produced... JHS,
Alice Berney Hoffberger and Robert
Berney oral history, Dec. 22, 1982.*

6. *In Etta's bedroom hung... The
Baltimore Sun, Sept. 14, 1949, 32.*

7. *The Cone Collection..."There was
no..." Richardson, B., Dr. Claribel
and Miss Etta, 14.*

8. *The Cone collection... Pollack, The
Collectors, 237.*

9. *One visitor remembered... JHS, Alice
Berney Hoffberger, Oral History.*

10. *This, he said..."I can get to exhibiting
and..." BMA CCol, LS to EC, Nov.
19, 1938.*

11. *He ultimately..."I would come in
there..." The Evening Sun, April 5,
1971, Sec. C, 1.*

12. *On her voyage, she always... Cone,
Edward T.,"The Miss Etta Cones," 450.*

13. *In February 1934, the public's general... Adamthwaite, France and the
Coming, 12.*

14. *Michael and Sally Stein decided...
Saarinen, The Proud Possessors, 196.*

15. *It had a beautiful view... Rogers,
When This You See, 115.*

16. *But in 1935 they left... Mellow,
Charmed Circle, 426.*

17. *The painting was of a young... Barr,
Matisse His Art,. 251.*

18. *But beginning in 1935, Lydia...
Herrera, Matisse A Portrait, 170.*

19. *Madame Matisse shrieked... ibid, 176.*

20. *"My God, so many terrible..." BMA
CCol, Margot Duthuit to EC, Sept..
20, 1939.*

21. *During that 1936 summer...
Richardson, B., Dr. Claribel and
Miss Etta, 134.*

22. *She purchased 23 pieces of art... ibid,* 189-190.

23. *She was not intrigued... Daix,* Picasso, 94.

24. *She had not seen Picasso for... Edward T. Cone interview, Nov. 21, 1992.*

25. *Fear was everywhere and... Adamthwaite, France and the Coming, 26.*

26. *In Lucerne, she purchased... Richardson, B., Dr. Claribel and Miss Etta, 191-193.*

27. *By 1938 Germany had invaded... Adamthwaite, France and the Coming, 57.*

28. *Even the United States geared... ibid, XI.*

29. *...the majority of Americans... Gordon, The American Chronicle, p. 189.*

22. *She purchased 23 pieces of art... ibid,* 189-190.

23. *...even though she was... Daix,* Picasso, 94.

24. *She had not seen Picasso in... Edward T. Cone interview, Nov. 21, 1992.*

25. *Fear was everywhere and... Adamthwaite, France and the Coming, 26.*

26. *In Lucerne, she purchased... Richardson, B., Dr. Claribel and Miss Etta, 191-193.*

27. *By 1938 Germany had invaded... Adamthwaite, France and the Coming, 57.*

28. *Even the United States was... ibid, XI.*

29. *...and the majority of Americans... Gordon, The American Chronicle, p. 189.*

## *Blowing Rock, 1949*

1. *"Once we had a country and..."* Auden, Collected Poems, 265.

2. *In the fall of 1938 reports... Ketchum, The Borrowed Years, 110-111.*

3. *She recieved..."My dear, I am living..."* BMA CCol, Sarah Stein to EC, Jan. 20, 1939.

4. *Otherwise, she was shy in company...* Alfred J. Gutman interview.

5. *The artist spent the summer... Barr, Matisse His Art, 241.*

6. *"When I saw everything in such..."* ibid, 256.

7. *Matisse was..."We did not see you this summer..."* BMA CCol, HM to EC, Oct. 10, 1939.

8. *But by November,..."You would say that I work..."* BMA CCol, HM to EC, Nov. 21, 1939.

9. *Etta had met a German refugee... Edward T. Cone interview, Nov. 21, 1992.*

10. *He wrote Etta: "I had for many..."* BMA CCol, George Duthuit to EC, June 11, 1941.

11. *Daniel-Henry Kahnweiler... "I still remember the..."* BMA CCol, Daniel-Henry Kahnweiler to EC, May 6, 1949.

12. *The art historian... "It was one of the most..."* BMA CCol, Herbert Read to EC, April 29, 1948.

13. *And Alfred Barr Jr.,... Barr, Matisse His Art, 262.*

14. *While Etta...she became in the next several years... JHU, George Boas notes.*

15. *In 1941,..."For three months I..."* BMA CCol, HM to EC, May 20, 1941.

16. Etta responded, "Dear Monsieur Matisse..." BMA CCol, EC to HM, ND 1941.

17. It was through him that she... Barr, Matisse His Art, 258-259.

18. Pierre's friend wrote, "I have never seen..." BMA CCol, Pierre Matisse to EC, Sept. 25, 1944.

19. Jean Matisse was also involved... Herrera, Matisse A Portrait, 187.

20. In 1945, the Salon d'Automne... Barr, Matisse His Art, 259.

21. He wrote..."I can't say it touches me.." Mellow, Charmed Circle, 470.

22. But Leo did not... ibid, 470.

23. "I had a letter from him..." BMA CCol, George Boas to EC, Sept.. 10, 1947.

24. But Alice found a sympathetic... Sutherland, "Alice and Gertrude and Others," 292.

25. Sally Stein...was living in California... Saarinen, The Proud Possessors, 202.

26. She died of heart failure on... Pollack, The Collectors, 246-247.

27. A Pinkerton guard... ibid, 251.

## Epilogue

1. Before Etta died she... Pollack, The Collectors, 252-253.

2. Those items not deemed... Richardson, B., Dr. Claribel and Miss Etta, 165.

3. At the time of Etta's death... ibid, 167-194.

4. Etta set strict conditions... ibid, 165.

5. in October 1949, shortly after Etta's death... The Baltimore Sun, Oct. 8, 1949, 24.

6. Even the city's fathers... The Baltimore Sun, Feb. 24, 1957, 26, 40.

# Index

# INDEX

# INDEX

Robinson, Theodore, 15, 18, 191
Roché, Pierre, 44-45, 54
Rodin, Auguste, 160, 191
Rosenberg, Paul, 125
Rosengart, Siegfried, 174, 175, 178, 180, 189-190, 191, 192
Rouart, Louis, 55
Rouault, Georges, 204
Rousseau, Henri, 203
rue de Fleurus, xvi, 34, 54
rue Lafitte, 40-41
rue Ravignan, 51-52, 75

Sagot, Clovis, 42-43
Salmon, André, 187
Salon d'Automne
    1905, 45-46
    1945, 210
Salon des Indépendants, 48
    1906, 61-62
    Nu Bleu (Blue Nude) as exhibited at, 76
San Francisco Museum of Art, 190
Sargent, John Singer, 92
Schuler, Alfred, 106
Schwartz, Lily, 208
Scrip, 77
Senckenberg Institute, 31, 33, 83
Shaw, George Bernard, 149
Shelly, Percy Bysshe, 88
Signac, Paul, 160, 191
    Matisse and, 62
Silbert, Ben, 199
Sisley, Alfred, 191
Sopher, Aaron, 200
Statendum, 200
Steer, William, 34
Stein, Allan, 147, 212-213

STEIN, GERTRUDE, 12, 17-18, 26, 39, 41, 66, 174, 211
    Alice B. Toklas and, 71-72, 123
    Claribel Cone and, 13, 17, 18, 123, 144, 152, 169
    Cone sisters and, vii, 57-58
    description of, 12-13, 41
    death of, 211
    education of, 14, 16, 25
    Etta Cone and, 25, 26, 28, 29-30, 31, 32-33, 57, 58, 64-65, 71, 73-74, 78-79, 147-148, 194-195

family history of, 12
Leo and, 58, 59, 89
Matisse and, 75
Picasso and, 51, 60, 92, 170
as writer, vi, 34, 41, 57, 123-124, 135, 186, 192-193
    The Autobiography of Alice B. Toklas, vii
    Everybody's Autobiography, 11
    The Making of Americans, 64
    Q.E.D., 26, 30
    Three Lives, 41, 57

STEIN, LEO, 12, 13, 14, 16, 17, 34, 41
    Appreciation: Painting, Poetry and Prose, 39, 177, 211
    art according to, 22
    Cézanne and, 40, 75
    as art collector, 34, 40, 41, 42, 47, 49, 62, 76, 94, 141
    Cone sisters and, xiv, 135
    death of, 211
    description of, 22, 41
    description of Matisse, 49
    Etta Cone and, 14, 21, 42, 199-200, 211-212
    family history of, 12
    account of, Matisse and Picasso initial meeting, 66
    Gertrude Stein and, 58, 124, 211
    Matisse and Picasso
        discovery of, vi
        loss of interest in, 76
    rue de Fleurus and, 34, 95
    Sagot, Picasso, and, 42-43
    World War I and, 124

Stein, Michael
    Cone sisters and, 135-136, 155-156, 174
    death of, 206
    Etta Cone and, 77
    family history, 12
Stein, Sally, 50, 91, 206, 212
    Etta Cone, Matisse, and, 55
Steins (Leo and Gertrude), 28, 47
    Cone sisters and, 63, 145, 147, 148-149
    Matisse and, 49
    Picasso and, 44-45
    rue de Fleurus and, 34

253

# Acknowledgements

~

$\mathcal{T}$his book would have been much the poorer but for the splendid cooperation of various staff members of the Baltimore Museum of Art. Appreciation in abundance goes to them for their patience during my many years of research on this book. I particularly want to acknowledge BMA's current director, Doreen Bolger; Nancy Press in rights and reproductions; and the library staff, who generously gave me their time while I poured over Etta's diaries and Claribel's notes.

Many thanks also to the Jewish Historical Society of Maryland for access to their invaluable oral histories recorded by Arthur J. Gutman, Amalie Sonneborn Katz, M. Shakman Katz, Alice Berney Hoffberger, Robert Berney, and Louis Cahn.

I would also like to thank the following individuals for telling me their stories about the Cone sisters and their times: Edward T. Cone, Sydney Cone Jr., Claribel Cone II, Angela Rosengart, Arthur J. and Mary Louise Gutman, and Rueben Kramer.

I thank David Lawsky for his technical help and Anthony Krupp for help with German translations.

Words cannot adequately express my gratefulness to Hillary Spurling. A longtime writer of unassailable brilliance (witness her soon-to-be two volume biography of Henri Matisse), Ms.

Spurling graciously placed into words her kind comments about my book, *The Art of Acquiring*, before publication.

As if that weren't kindness enough, she then pointed out the upcoming existence and virtues of the book to the BBC, who then interviewed me for its documentary, "Michael Palin on the Cone Sisters." My chief objective in writing this biography was to help see to it that Etta and Claribel received, in perpetuity, the credit they richly deserved for their selfless contributions to art. With the BBC and Michael Palin now lending that goal their inestimable weight, I simply could not be happier—though a popular full-length movie on the Cone sisters might, I imagine, someday do them one better.

Bruce Bortz and Mary Yang at Bancroft Press get special thanks for their hard work, diligence, and perseverance on the many and complicated editorial aspects of this project. Bruce Bortz, as publisher, has shown an unwavering desire to publish the very best book possible. Who could ask for more? Sarah Azizi and Jaina Hirai, formerly of Bancroft Press, likewise deserve more than a mention for their early interest and editorial assistance and suggestions.

Theresa Williams designed this book's interior. I thank her for her classicly elegant layout and her painstaking care in executing it. Giving this book not only the right look, but one that matched the subject matter, was not easy, but she achieved it, I believe, in award-winning fashion.

Steve Parke, who always does world class work, put in more than his usual extra effort with the jacket design, photo and art insert, and my author photo. Sensing the significance of this book, this art-loving genius of a designer threw his heart and soul into this entire project, and I believe it shows. Thank you, Steve.

And finally my sincere thanks, as always, to Ron Goldfarb for his guidance.

# About the Author

⟿

Mary Gabriel, currently based in London, works as a reporter and editor for the world desk of *Reuters News Service*. Previously, she was executive editor of *Museum & Arts Washington*, and reported for United Press International.

Her first book, *Notorious Victoria: The Life of Victoria Woodhull, Uncensored*, was a *New York Times* "Notable Book" in 1998.

She holds a Diplome from the University of Paris at the Sorbonne, a Bachelor's of Fine Arts from the Maryland Institute College of Art, and a Master's Degree in Journalism from American University.